DK EYEWITNESS

B

JÜRGEN SCHEUNEMANN

DK PUBLISHING, INC.

Left **Berlin Reichstag** Right **A café in the Hackesche Höfe**

LONDON, NEW YORK, MUNICH
MELBOURNE, DELHI

Produced by Dorling Kindersley Verlag, Munich

Reproduced by Connecting People,
Starnberg & Colourscan, Singapore
Printed and bound in Italy by Graphicom

First American Edition, 2002
02 03 04 05 10 9 8 7 6 5 4 3 2 1

Published in the United States by
DK Publishing, Inc., 375 Hudson Street,
New York, New York 10014

**Copyright 2002 © Dorling
Kindersley Limited, London**

US ISBN 0-7894-8433-1

Within each Top 10 list in this book, no hier-
archy of quality or popularity is implied. All
10 are, in the editor's opinion, of roughly
equal merit.

Floors are referred to throughout in
accordance with German usage; ie the
"first floor" is the floor above ground level.

See our complete product line at
www.dk.com

Contents

Berlin's Top 10

**The information in this
DK Eyewitness Top 10 Travel Guide is checked frequently.**
Every effort has been made to ensure that this book is as up-to-date as possible at the time
of going to press. Some details, however, such as telephone numbers, opening hours,
prices, gallery hanging arrangements and travel information are liable to change. The
publishers cannot accept responsibility for any consequences arising from the use of this
book, nor for any material on third party websites, and cannot guarantee that any website
address in this book will be a suitable source of travel information. We value the views and
suggestions of our readers very highly. Please write to:
Publisher, DK Eyewitness Travel Guides,
Dorling Kindersley, 80 Strand, London WC2R 0RL, Great Britain.

Left **"East Side Gallery"** on the Berlin Wall Right **Façade of a house in Prenzlauer Berg**

Left **The *Berlin* memorial on Tauentzienstraße** Right **The park of Schloss Sanssouci**

BERLIN'S
TOP 10

BERLIN'S TOP 10

TOP10 Berlin Highlights

Berlin is Germany's liveliest city and one of the most fascinating capitals in the world. You'll find no other place where art and culture, museums and theatres, entertainment and nightlife are more diverse and exciting than on the banks of the Spree River. Once reunited, Berlin quickly developed into a cosmopolitan city, and today there is an air of energy and vibrancy about it.

1 Brandenburger Tor and Pariser Platz

The Brandenburger Tor, Berlin's most famous sight, is located in Pariser Platz, where the famous Hotel Adlon and the embassies breathe a modern, stylish elegance *(see pp8–9)*.

2 Reichstag

No other building is a more potent symbol of Germany's history than the Reichstag *(below)*. Since its redesign by Sir Norman Foster in 1997–9, the structure has become one of the most popular sights in Berlin. Visitors are attracted by its vast egg-shaped dome, affording fantastic views across the city *(see pp10–11)*.

3 Unter den Linden

The magnificent, tree-lined boulevard *(below)* in the eastern part of the city has always been a central axis. Berlin's most important historic buildings are assembled here *(see pp12–15)*.

4 Potsdamer Platz

The new heart of the old metropolis beats on Potsdamer Platz, where exciting new structures, such as the Sony Center, have been erected. With its restaurants, film museum, cinemas, shops and musical theatre it is a unique world of entertainment *(see pp16–9)*.

5 Pergamon-museum

Berlin's most impressive museum, a mecca for those interested in culture, houses the famous Pergamon Altar from ancient Greece *(see pp20–3).*

6 Kurfürstendamm

Berlin's much visited strolling and shopping avenue is the main thoroughfare in the heart of the western city. New restaurants and stylish boutiques have increased the hustle and bustle along this grand boulevard *(see pp24–5).*

7 Kaiser-Wilhelm Gedächtniskirche

The tower ruins of the memorial church, built to commemorate Kaiser Wilhelm I, still stand today as a silent reminder of the horrors of war *(see pp26–7).*

8 Schloss Charlottenburg

The historic rooms of the former Hohenzollern summer residence invite visitors to experience a slice of Prussian history, while the Baroque-style gardens, among the most beautiful in Germany, are perfect for strolling and sunbathing *(see pp28–31).*

9 Kulturforum

This complex of museums, which includes the famous Gemäldegalerie (gallery of paintings), the Kunstgewerbomuseum (museum of arts and crafts) and the Neue Nationalgalerie, as well as concert halls such as the Philharmonie, guarantees a unique cultural experience for visitors to Berlin *(see pp32–5).*

10 Zoologischer Garten

Germany's oldest zoo and aquarium, in the centre of the city, is the largest animal park in the world, boasting some 14,000 animals and over 1,800 different species *(see pp36–7).*

Multi-lingual tourist information: **www.berlin.de** or: **http://btm.de**

🔟 Brandenburger Tor & Pariser Platz

The best known of Berlin's symbols, the Brandenburg Gate stands proudly in the middle of Pariser Platz, asserting itself against the hyper-modern embassy buildings that now surround it. Crowned by its triumphant Quadriga sculpture, the famous Gate has long been a focal point in Berlin's history: rulers and statesmen, military parades and demonstrations – all have felt compelled to march through the Brandenburger Tor.

The Brandenburg Gate seen from the east

🔵 One of the best spots for a coffee break in Pariser Platz is Café Meyerbeer, in the Palais am Pariser Platz. Don't miss its great cake display.

🟢 A small exhibition, housed in the northern side wing of the Brandenburger Tor, tells the history of the Gate.

• Pariser Platz
• Map F3, K3

• Tourist information, Brandenburger Tor
• Map F3, K3
• 9:30am–6pm daily
• (0190) 01 63 16

Top 10 Sights

1. Brandenburger Tor
2. Quadriga
3. Hotel Adlon Berlin
4. DG Bank
5. Akademie der Künste
6. French Embassy
7. Palais am Pariser Platz
8. Eugen-Gutmann-Haus
9. Haus Liebermann
10. American Embassy

1 Brandenburger Tor

Since its restoration in 2002, Berlin's symbol is now lit up more brightly than ever before. Built by Carl G. Langhans in 1789–91 and modelled on the temple porticos of ancient Athens, the Gate has, since the 19th century, been the backdrop for many events in the city's turbulent history.

2 Quadriga

The sculpture, 6 m (20 ft) high above the Gate, was created in 1794 by Johann Gottfried Schadow as a symbol of peace. As a model for the laurel-crowned goddess of peace in the chariot, Schadow used his niece, who subsequently became famous throughout Berlin.

3 Hotel Adlon Berlin

Completed in 1997 and now favoured by visiting dignitaries, Berlin's most elegant hotel is a reconstruction of the original Hotel Adlon. This legendary hotel, destroyed in World War II, was host to the rich and famous, including Greta Garbo, Thomas Mann and Charlie Chaplin *(see p72)*.

4 DG Bank

This modern building, designed by the American architect Frank Owen Gehry, combines the clean lines of Prussian architecture with some daring elements.

360° view of Brandenburg Gate: www.berlinonline.de/ reisen/panorama/html/brandenburger_tor.html

5 Akademie der Künste

The new building, erected between 2000 and 2002 by Günter Behnich and Manfred Sabatke, incorporates behind a vast expanse of windows the ruins of the old art academy, which had been destroyed in World War II. Today it is the home of the Academy of the Arts of the Province of Berlin-Brandenburg.

6 French Embassy

In 1999–2001, an elegant new building was constructed by Christian de Portzamparc, on the site of the old embassy, which was destroyed in World War II. Its colonnades and tall windows, a homage to the former French Embassy palace, are particularly remarkable and worth seeing.

7 Palais am Pariser Platz

This complex by Bernhard Winking, a successful modern interpretation of Neo-Classical architecture, is slightly hidden to the north of the Brandenburger Tor. It is worth venturing inside where you will find a café, a restaurant and a souvenir shop, and a pleasantly shaded courtyard.

8 Eugen-Gutmann-Haus

With its clean lines, the Dresdner Bank, built in the round by the Hamburg architects' team gmp in 1996–7, recalls the style of the New Sobriety movement of the 1920s. In front of the building, which serves as the Berlin headquarters of the Dresdner Bank, stands the famous original street sign for the Pariser Platz.

9 Haus Liebermann

Josef Paul Kleihues erected this building at the north end of the Brandenburger Tor in 1996–8, faithfully recreating an earlier building on the same site. The house is named after the artist Max Liebermann *(right)*, who lived here. In 1933, watching Nazi SA troops march through the Gate, he famously said: "I cannot possibly eat as much as I would want to puke out."

10 American Embassy

The last gap in the line of buildings around Pariser Platz will by closed by 2003. A dispute between the embassy and the Berlin Senate delayed building for several years: an entire street was to be moved to satisfy the USA's security requirements. But in the end, the historical street stayed where it was.

For more on historical architecture in Berlin **see pp38–9**

TOP 10 Reichstag

Of all the buildings in Berlin, the Parliamentary Building is probably one of the most symbolic. The mighty structure, erected in 1884–94 by Paul Wallot as the proud manifestation of the power of the German Reich, was destroyed by arson in 1933 and bombed during World War II. In 1996, the artist Christo wrapped up the Reichstag and, in 1997–9, the British architect Sir Norman Foster transformed it into one of the most modern parliamentary buildings in the world. Today it is the official seat of the Bundestag, the German parliament.

Main entrance of the Reichstag

🔴 If a meal at the Käfer restaurant exceeds your budget, many stalls in the vicinity of the Reichstag sell hot dogs.

🔵 Large numbers of visitors come to see the Reichstag cupola. It is best to avoid weekends or to start queuing half an hour the opening time. Tuesday is the quietest day.

- Platz der Republik 1
- Map F3, K2
- Open 8am–midnight
- (030) 22 73 21 52
- www.bundestag.de

Top 10 Sights

1. The Cupola
2. Plenary Hall
3. Portico "Dem deutschen Volke"
4. Restored Façade
5. Restaurant Käfer
6. Installation "Der Bevölkerung"
7. Memorial for Delegates to the Reichstag
8. German Flag
9. Platz der Republik
10. Memorial for Victims of the Wall

2 Plenary Hall

The newly designed plenary hall is the seat of the Deutscher Bundestag, the German parliament, which has convened here again since 20 April 1999. Technologically, the hall is one of the most advanced in the world. The federal eagle caused a row: considered too "fat", it had to be slimmed down.

1 The Cupola

The new Reichstag cupola by Sir Norman Foster affords breathtaking views of Berlin. It is open at the top to air the building and – a touch of irony here – to allow for the dissemination of debates throughout the country. A ramp winds its way up to the top.

3 Portico "Dem deutschen Volke"

The dedication "To the German People" was designed in 1916, against the will of Wilhelm II.

4 Restored Façade
Despite extensive renovations, small bullet holes from World War II are still visible in the building's façade.

6 Installation "Der Bevölkerung"
Hans Haacke's work of art "To the People" is a counterpoint to the portico inscription opposite.

5 Restaurant Käfer
This luxury restaurant next to the cupola on the Reichstag's roof offers an excellent view of the historical centre of Unter den Linden. It is very popular and you may well have to wait for a seat *(see p101)*.

8 The German Flag
The giant German flag was first raised on the occasion of the official national celebrations of German reunification on 3 October 1990.

7 Memorial by Dieter Appett
Unveiled in 1992, the memorial commemorates 97 Social Democratic and Communist Reichstag delegates who were murdered under the Third Reich.

9 Platz der Republik
Celebrations often take place on the lawn in front of the Reichstag, most recently in 1996, when the building was wrapped up by Christo.

The Reichstag Fire

When the Reichstag went up in flames on 27 February 1933, the Dutch Communist van der Lubbe was arrested and charged with arson. It is, however, much more likely that the Nazis had started the fire themselves. Adolf Hitler used the Reichstag fire as a pretext to get the "Enabling Act" passed by parliament. This allowed him to dispose of all his opponents, marking the beginning of a 12-year reign of terror.

Memorial for Victims of the Wall 10
Opposite the southern side of the Reichstag, a memorial recalls the Berlin Wall, which ran only a few steps away from this spot. One of the crosses commemorates Chris Gueffroy: shot in February 1989 when trying to escape, he was one of more than 100 people who died at the Wall.

Berlin governmental buildings **see pp40–1**

🔟 Unter den Linden

"As long as the lime trees still blossom in Unter den Linden, Berlin will always be Berlin," Marlene Dietrich once sang about this magnificent avenue. Today the lime trees blossom more beautifully than ever in the historical centre of Berlin, because the old buildings along the street have been extensively restored and modern architecture has created new highlights. The "Linden" – originally a royal bridle-path linking the Stadtschloss (the king's town residence) and Tiergarten – became Berlin's most fashionable street in the 18th century, and was synonymous with the city that was then the capital of Prussia.

Deutsches Historisches Museum in the Zeughaus

🔵 The largest selection of cakes in Berlin tempts visitors in the Café im Opernpalais. In summer, you can enjoy them outside.

• Map F/G3, K3/4

• Deutsches Historisches Museum, Unter den Linden 2 • 10am–6pm Tue–Sun, until 10pm Thu • (030) 20 30 40 • www.dhm.de • Admission charge

• St Hedwigskathedrale, Bebelplatz • 10am–5pm Mon–Sat, 1–5pm Sun • (030) 203 48 10 • www.hedwigs-kathedrale.de

• Staatsoper, Unter den Linden 7 • Ticket office 11am–7pm Mon–Fri, 2–7pm Sun • (030) 20 35 45 55 • www.staatsoper-berlin.de • Admission charge

Top 10 Sights

1. Deutsches Historisches Museum in the Zeughaus
2. Staatsoper Unter den Linden
3. St Hedwigskathedrale
4. Humboldt-Universität
5. Neue Wache
6. Kronprinzenpalais
7. Bebelplatz
8. Opernpalais
9. Russian Embassy
10. Frederick the Great's Statue

St Hedwigs-kathedrale 3

Designed by Georg W. Knobelsdorff in 1740–2 and modelled on the Pantheon in Rome, this is the seat of the Catholic archdiocese in Berlin. Frederick the Great commissioned the cathedral to appease Catholics in Berlin after conquering Silesia *(see p44).*

1 Deutsches Historisches Museum

Germany's largest history museum, reopened in 2002, provides an overview of more than 1,000 years of German history. Housed in the Zeughaus – the royal arsenal built in 1706 – it is the oldest and, architecturally, the most interesting building in the avenue Unter den Linden *(see p14).*

2 Staatsoper Unter den Linden

The richly ornamented National Opera House is one of Germany's most attractive. Neo-Classical in style, it was built by Knobelsdorff in 1741–3 as Europe's first free-standing opera house, to plans devised by Frederick the Great himself *(see p56).*

Buses No 100 and No 200 run along the entire length of Unter den Linden, with bus stops at nearly all the famous sights.

4 Humboldt-Universität
Berlin's oldest and today its most highly regarded university was founded in 1890, on the initiative of Wilhelm von Humboldt. Twenty-nine Nobel Prize winners were educated here, including Albert Einstein.

5 Neue Wache
The central German memorial for all victims of war was created in the years 1816–8 and designed by Karl Friedrich Schinkel. An enlarged reproduction of the moving *Pietà* sculpture by Käthe Kollwitz stands in the centre of the room.

8 Opernpalais
The charming building next to the Staatsoper, built in 1733–7, served as a palace for the princesses.

6 Kronprinzenpalais
The Neoclassical Palais, built in 1732–3 by Philipp Gerlach, was originally a residence for the heirs to the Hohenzollern throne. An art museum after World War I, the East German government accommodated state visitors in the palace after 1948. Until 2002 it was used for exhibitions of the Deutsches Historisches Museum opposite.

7 Bebelplatz
Originally named Opernplatz, this wide, open space was designed by Georg W. Knobelsdorff as the focal point of his Forum Fridericianum. The elegant park was meant to introduce some of the splendour and glory of ancient Rome to the Prussian capital. In May 1933, it became the scene of the infamous Nazi book burning

9 Russische Botschaft
The gigantic Russian Embassy, built in Stalinist "wedding-cake style", was the first building to be constructed in Unter den Linden after World War II *(see also p118)*.

10 Frederick the Great's Statue
One of Christian Daniel Rauch's grandest sculptures, this statue shows the "Old Fritz" (13.5 m/ 45 ft high) on horseback, wearing a uniform and tricorn hat *(see also p113)*.

For more on Unter den Linden **see pp112–21**

13

Old print roll from 1821 with views of the avenue Unter den Linden

Deutsches Historisches Museum

1 The Dying Warriors
The 22 sculptures by Andreas Schlüter, displayed on the walls of the courtyard rather than in one of the museum's exhibitions, portray the horrors of war in an unusually immediate way.

2 Martin Luther
Luther's portrait, by Lucas Cranach the Elder, is the focal point of exhibition rooms devoted to Martin Luther and the Reformation.

3 Europe and Asia
This group of Meissen porcelain figures reflects the fascinating relationship between the two continents.

4 Steam Engine
A full-sized steam engine from the year 1847 marks the entrance to the exhibition on the Industrial Revolution.

5 Clothes from the Camps
Among the many exhibits illustrating the years under Nazi rule is the jacket of a concentration camp inmate – a chilling reminder of the Third Reich.

6 Gloria Victis
The moving allegorical figure of Gloria Victis, created by the French sculptor Antonin Mercié, bears witness to the death of a friend during the final days of the Franco-Prussian War of 1870–1.

Gloria Victis Statue

7 Soldiers Plundering a House
This painting by Sebastian Vrancx, dating from around 1600, depicts a scene from the wars of religion that tore the Netherlands apart during the 16th century.

8 Saddle
A valuable saddle, dating from the middle of the 15th century, is decorated with elaborately carved plaques made of ivory.

9 The Berlin Wall
An original section of the Wall, together with the banners of a peaceful pro-unification demonstration in 1989, commemorates the fall of the Berlin Wall.

10 SS 20 Rocket
In the foyer, an original SS 20 rocket of the former Soviet Union reminds visitors today of the perils of the Cold War years and the attempts to create a so-called "nuclear equilibrium".

Portrait of Martin Luther in the Zeughaus

For more on Berlin museums see pp46–7

Top 10 Events

Zeughaus Unter den Linden

Schlüter's "Dying Warrior"

Originally the royal arsenal, the Zeughaus was built in 1706 in the Baroque style according to plans by Johann Arnold Nering. It is an impressive structure, with its main and side wings surrounding an historical central courtyard that is protected by a modern glass cupola roof. Especially memorable are Andreas Schlüter's figures of 22 dying warriors, lined up along the arcades in the courtyard. They portray vividly the horrors of war.

A cone-shaped glass annex, erected by the Chinese-born architect Leoh Ming Pei in 2001 for special exhibitions and temporary shows, stands behind the museum.

The permanent exhibition in the main historical building includes a collection entitled "Images and Testimonials of German History". Highlighting the most important periods and events in the history of the country, the displays include a surprising variety of exhibits dating back to the days of the early Medieval German Empire through the period of the Reformation and the Thirty Years' War as well as the wars of Liberation and the failed Revolution of 1848, right up to the two World Wars and more recent events of the 20th century.

The opening of the Reichstag in the White Salon of Berlin Schloss on 25 June 1888

Deutsches Historisches Museum: www.dhm.de

⌖⏰ Potsdamer Platz

The heart of the new metropolis of Berlin beats on Potsdamer Platz. This square, where Berliners and tourists alike now flock to cinemas, restaurants and shops, was already a hub of urban life in the 1920s. After World War II, it became a desolate wasteland, but since the fall of the Berlin Wall, Potsdamer Platz – for a long time Europe's largest building site – has become a city within the city, surrounded by imposing buildings erected in the last ten years, and still being added to today.

Reconstruction of the first traffic lights in Europe

🅐 Apart from visiting the famous Café Josty, make sure you do not miss Diekmann in the Weinhaus Huth.

- Potsdamer Platz
- Map F4, L2/3

- Filmmuseum Berlin
- Potsdamer Str. 2
- 10am–6pm Tue, Wed, 10am–8pm Thu
- (030) 300 90 30
- Admission charge

- Stella-Musical-Theater
- Marlene-Dietrich-Platz 1
- 5:30 and 8pm daily
- Admission charge

- Spielbank Berlin
- Marlene-Dietrich-Platz 1
- noon–2am daily
- (030) 25 59 90
- Admission charge

- Cinemaxx
- Voxstr. 4
- 12:30pm–1:30am daily
- (030) 44 31 63 16
- Admission charge

Top 10 Sights

1. Sony Center
2. Filmmuseum Berlin
3. Café Josty
4. Weinhaus Huth
5. Marlene-Dietrich-Platz
6. Potsdamer Platz Arkaden
7. Spielbank Berlin
8. Cinemaxx
9. DaimerChrysler Quartier
10. Stella-Musical-Theater

Sony Center 1

The Sony Center is the most ambitious, the most successful and architecturally the most interesting building in the new Berlin. The cupola structure, designed by Helmut Jahn and opened in 2000, is the European headquarters of the Sony company, and with its cinemas and restaurants it is also a social magnet on Potsdamer Platz.

2 Filmmuseum Berlin

This museum takes you backstage in the Hollywood and Babelsberg film studios. Exhibits include Marlene Dietrich's costumes *(see p18)*.

3 Café Josty

Café Josty harkens back to its legendary predecessor, a regular haunt for artists and intellectuals in the 19th century. The new Café Josty is partially housed in the historic Kaisersaal (Emperor's Hall) of the former Grand Hotel Esplanade.

4 Weinhaus Huth

The only building on Potsdamer Platz to have survived World War II, the Weinhaus today accommodates restaurants and the fascinating art gallery of the DaimlerChrysler company.

➡ *The best time to visit the Sony Center is in the early evening, when the inside of the Plaza is lit up.*

5 Marlene-Dietrich-Platz

This square in front of the Stella-Musical-Theater is dedicated to the great actress. A brash *Flower Balloon (left)*, by the artist Jeff Koons, enlivens the centre of the square.

Locator Map

6 Potsdamer Platz Arkaden

The arcades draw visitors with over 130 shops, exclusive boutiques and popular restaurants on three storeys. The lower ground floor is a food court, serving dishes from around the world.

7 Spielbank Berlin

Berlin's new casino invites visitors to *faites vos jeux*. Apart from roulette, Black Jack is also played, and an entire floor is given over to gambling machines.

8 Cinemaxx

The Cinemaxx on Potsdamer Platz with its 17 screens is one of Berlin's largest cinemas. The bigger screens of the multiplex cinema show current Hollywood blockbusters, while the three smallest screens are for viewings of foreign-language films. There is also a small bar serving drinks.

9 DaimlerChrysler-Quartier

The Berlin headquarters of the famous car manufacturers was designed by Hans Kolhoff and Renzo Piano. The software company "debis", a former offshoot of Daimler, is also based here.

10 Stella-Musical-Theater

Berlin's largest musical stage, this venue has been showing the Broadway hit *The Hunchback of Notre Dame* since 2000. The 1,300-seat theatre is often sold out.

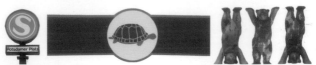

Left **S-Bahn sign** Centre **Café Josty sign** Right **Arty bears on Potsdamer Platz**

TOP 10 Exhibitions in the Filmmuseum

Film poster

1 Marlene Dietrich
This exhibition of the film star's estate includes costumes, touring luggage, photographs, letters and notes, posters and film clips.

2 Metropolis
This film, directed by Fritz Lang in 1927, has an alarming vision of a future world as its subject. Models and props from the film are on display.

3 Caligari
The best known German film of the 1920s, *The Cabinet of Dr. Caligari* (1920), was a masterpiece of Expressionist filmmaking by Walter Rührig.

4 Leni Riefenstahl
This exhibition reveals the technical tricks used in the Nazi propaganda film *Olympia,* made by Leni Riefenstahl in 1936–8.

5 Film and National Socialism
This exhibition features documents relating to the propaganda uses of film, everyday cinema and the industry's victims: some film stars allowed themselves to be used by the Nazis, others refused to cooperate. The life and work of the actor Kurt Gerron, who was persecuted and murdered, is documented as an exemplary case.

6 Post-War Cinema
The story of films and film-making in East and West Germany, with props and costumes of popular stars of post-war German cinema such as Hanna Schygulla, Romy Schneider, Heinz Rühmann and Mario Adorf.

7 Artificial Worlds
The tricks employed by special effects studios, ranging from the first effects of the 1930s to computer animation.

8 Transatlantic
This exhibition of documents, letters, keepsakes and souvenirs retraces the careers of German film stars in Hollywood.

9 Pioneers and Divas
The infant days of cinema are featured here – as well as stars of the silent era such as Henny Porten and Asta Nielsen.

10 Exile
Documents relate the difficulties encountered by German filmmakers when making a new start in the USA in 1933–45.

Façade of the Filmmuseum

For more on Berlin museums see pp46–7

Top 10 Architects

Europe's largest building site

In the 1920s, Potsdamer Platz was Europe's busiest square, boasting the first automatic traffic lights in the world. During World War II this social hub was razed to the ground. Untouched for almost 50 years, the empty square shifted back into the centre of Berlin when the Wall came down. During the 1990s, Potsdamer Platz became Europe's largest building site – millions of curious onlookers from around the world came to watch progress from the famous red info box. Altogether, around 17 billion euros were invested to create the present square.

DaimlerChrysler House

Moving the Esplanade

The Council of Berlin stipulated that Sony should preserve the "Breakfast Room" and the "Emperors' Hall" of the Grand Hotel Esplanade, both protected following destruction in World War II. Accordingly, in 1996, the rooms were moved – 1300 tons were loaded onto wheels and shifted by 75 m (246 ft) during the course of a week.

The historic Emperors' Hall is today incorporated into the modern Sony Center

Pergamonmuseum

The Pergamonmuseum is one of the most important museums of ancient art and architecture in the world. The museum was built in 1909–30 by Alfred Messel and Ludwig Hoffmann to house Berlin's collection of antiquities as well as vast temples and palace rooms in their original size. These works of art, excavated by German archaeologists in the Near East at the end of the 19th century, were shown here for the first time.

Main entrance of the Pergamonmuseum

On the Museumsinsel itself there are no inviting cafés. However, the cafés under the S-Bahn arches opposite the museum entrance are worth a visit.

Visitors wishing to explore all the museums on Museumsinsel on the same day, should buy a day ticket for € 4. Admission is free every first Sunday in the month. However, Sundays are generally best avoided because of the long queues and large groups of visitors.

• Museumsinsel, Bodestr. 1–3 (entrance Am Kupfergraben)
• Map G3, J5
• (030) 20 90 55 55
• www.smpk.de
• 10am–6pm Tue–Sun, until 10pm Thu
• Admission charge

Top 10 Exhibits

1. Pergamon Altar
2. Market Gate of Miletus
3. Assyrian Palace
4. Ishtar Gate
5. Goddess Persephone
6. Goddess Athena
7. Aleppo Room
8. Roman Mosaic
9. Palace of Mshatta
10. Temple of Athena

1 Pergamon Altar
The colossal Pergamon Altar, dating from the year 160 BC, is the largest and most important treasure of the Berlin museums. The altar was part of a much larger temple complex in the Greek town of Pergamon (today the town of Bergama in Turkey), excavated in the 19th century by the German archaeologist Carl Humann *(see also pp22–3)*.

2 Market Gate of Miletus
This vast gate (AD 120) is over 16 m (52 ft) high. To the right of the entrance, a hairdresser has carved an advertisement for his shop into the stone.

3 Assyrian Palace
The interior of this palace from the days of the Assyrian kings (12th century BC) has been completely restored and boasts impressive statues of lions.

4 Ishtar Gate
The imposing Ishtar Gate and the Processional Way that led to it are fully preserved. The original avenue in ancient Babylon was 180 m (590 ft) long. The gate was built in the 6th-century BC, during the reign of Nebuchadnezar II. Original faïence wall tiles depict the sacred lions.

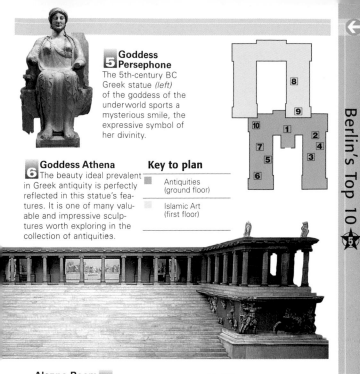

5 Goddess Persephone

The 5th-century BC Greek statue *(left)* of the goddess of the underworld sports a mysterious smile, the expressive symbol of her divinity.

6 Goddess Athena

The beauty ideal prevalent in Greek antiquity is perfectly reflected in this statue's features. It is one of many valuable and impressive sculptures worth exploring in the collection of antiquities.

Key to plan

■ Antiquities (ground floor)

■ Islamic Art (first floor)

7 Aleppo Room

Dating from the the year 1603, this small room features magnificent wooden cladding taken from the house of a Christian merchant's family in Syria. A beautiful example of Ottoman architecture, the room originally served as a reception hall.

8 Roman mosaic

This magnificently executed Roman floor mosaic dates back to the 2nd or 3rd century BC. It was excavated in Gerasa in Jordan.

9 Palace of Mshatta

A gift from Sultan Hamid II to Kaiser Wilhelm II, this desert palace, built in AD 744 in Jordan, has an elaborately decorated southern façade.

10 Temple of Athena

Dedicated to Athena of Nikephoros, this full-scale temple from the 2nd century BC has a simple yet elegant design.

A Roman sarcophagus from the 2nd century AD, showing scenes from the story of Medea

Top 10 Figures on the Pergamon Altar

1 Eastern Altar Frieze
The eastern side of the altar frieze – the side first lit up by the rising sun – depicts the battle between the gods and the giants.

2 The God Apollo on the Eastern Frieze
Like no other deity on the altar, the god Apollo is depicted as a noble man of ideal beauty, thus bearing witness to the artistic mastery of Classical sculpture in Greece.

3 The Titaness Phoebe
An impressive figure depicted on the southern frieze, Phoebe is shown, with her daughter Asteria, fighting an enormous giant with a torch, sword and lance.

4 Zeus in Battle
On the eastern frieze, the father of all the gods on Mount Olympus fights three giants at the same time. Zeus is armed for this battle with his most dangerous weapons – thunder and lightning.

5 The Goddess Athena
The goddess Athena is also shown on the eastern frieze, as a powerful figure of light who drags her opponents to their deaths by their hair.

Athena

6 The Gods of the Sea
Three pairs of sea gods are depicted on the staircase frieze (on the northern staircase): Doris and Nereus, Oceanus and Tethys as well as Triton and Amphitrite.

7 The Goddess Aphrodite
Victorious, the fighting goddess rises proudly above two dead giants.

8 Statues of Women
Larger-than-life figures of women, found near the altar in the excavations, are displayed in front of the Pergamon Altar.

9 The Beisser Group
The so-called Beisser Group on the northern frieze is a group of unknown deities. One god, almost defeated, desperately tries to fight off a giant who has clamped his teeth into his arm.

10 Telephos Frieze
The frieze in the upper altar courtyard depicts Telephos, son of Hercules. The kings of Pergamon thought themselves to be descended from Telephos and worshipped him accordingly.

The goddess Athena in the altar frieze

For more on Berlin museums see pp46–7

Saving the Museumsinsel

The "island of museums" is a treasury of antique architecture – yet it was slowly decaying. Since 1992 a total of 1.6 million euros has been spent on the renovation and modernization of Museumsinsel. A "master plan" was hatched by renowned

The Palace of Mshatta

architects, such as David Chipperfield and O. M. Ungers, which would transform the complex into a unique museum landscape – just as it had first been conceived in the 19th century by Friedrich Wilhelm IV, when he established the "free institution for art and the sciences". By 2008, all museums will be linked by an "architectural promenade", creating a conceptual as well as a structural link between the various parts (and providing disabled access). This promenade will consist of a variety of light rooms, courtyards and vaults as well as new exhibition halls. The core of the complex will be a new central entrance building. Once renovated, the museums will gradually reopen – the Alte Nationalgalerie opened in December 2001. In 1999, the Museumsinsel was declared a World Heritage Sight by UNESCO.

Pergamon and Asia Minor
From 241 until 133 BC, the antique city of Pergamon was the capital of the Hellenistic Pergamenian Empire, ruling the northwestern region of Asia Minor. Apart from many temples, the town, which is now known as Bergama, and is in Turkey, also boasted a famous library.

A 17th-century carpet with floral motifs from western Anatolia

TOP10 Kurfürstendamm

After years of decline, the Kurfürstendamm, or Ku'damm for short, has once again become a fashionable hot spot. Breathtaking architecture, elegant boutiques and a lively scene with street artists around Breitscheidplatz have made this shopping boulevard Berlin's most attractive and – at 3.8 km (2.5 miles) – also its longest avenue for strolling.

Corner of Kurfürstendamm and Joachimsthaler Straße

Only a few cafés in the Ku'damm have survived: the most charming is Café Wintergarten in the Literaturhaus at the southern end of Fasanenstraße.

It is best to avoid Ku'damm on Saturday mornings when the boulevard is teeming with locals and tourists out on shopping trips.

- Map B/C5, P3/4

- Tourist information
- Europa-Center, Budapester Str.
- 8:30am–8:30pm Mon–Sat, 10am–6:30pm Sun
- (030) 25 00 25

- Story of Berlin, Kurfürstendamm 207–8
- 10am–8pm daily
- (030) 88 72 01 00
- www.story-of-berlin.de

- Europa-Center, Tauentzienstr. 9
- 9am–midnight daily (shops: 10am–8pm)
- (030) 348 00 88
- www.24EC.de

Top 10 Sights

1. Breitscheidplatz
2. Kaiser-Wilhelm-Gedächtniskirche
3. Europa-Center
4. Neues Kranzler-Eck
5. Fasanenstraße
6. Ku'damm-Eck
7. Lehniner Platz
8. The Story of Berlin
9. Galerie Brusberg
10. Iduna-Haus

Breitscheidplatz 1
Here, in the heart of the city, artists, Berliners and visitors swarm around the globe fountain, known by locals as "Wasserklops" (water meatball).

Kaiser-Wilhelm-Gedächtniskirche 2
One of Berlin's most haunting symbols, the tower of the original church – destroyed during World War II – stands in the centre of Breitscheidplatz, serving as both memorial and reminder of the terrors of war *(see p26)*.

Europa-Center 3
The oldest shopping centre in West Berlin, originally opened in 1962, is still worth a visit. You will find shops and restaurants as well as the tourist information centre here *(see p163)*.

4 Neues Kranzler-Eck
One of Berlin's most ambitious new constructions, this glass and steel skyscraper was built in 2000 by the architect Helmut Jahn. The legendary Café Kranzler was retained as a bar in front of the office block *(see pp86–7)*.

5 Fasanenstraße
A small street off Ku'damm, Fasanenstraße with its galleries, expensive shops and restaurants is one of Charlottenburg's most elegant areas *(see pp80–1)*.

6 Ku'damm-Eck
This hotel and business complex (2001) has endowed the boulevard with new splendour.

7 Lehniner Platz
The square is home to the Schaubühne, built as Universum cinema in 1928 by Erich Mendelsohn, converted in 1978,

8 The Story of Berlin

This interesting multi media show takes visitors on a tour of 800 years of Berlin's history – from the Great Elector to the capital of Prussia, from Willy Brandt to the Fall of the Wall. Underneath the museum a nuclear bunker can be visited.

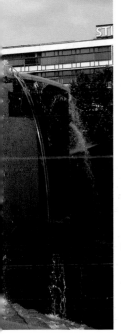

9 Galerie Brusberg
This Neoclassical building provides a glimpse of Ku'damm's erstwhile splendour.

10 Iduna-Haus
The remarkable turreted house at this street corner is one of few bourgeois houses preserved from the turn of the 20th century. The richly ornamented, gleaming white Art Nouveau façade has been lavishly restored.

When Ku'damm was no more than a log road

In 1542, today's magnificent boulevard was just a humble "Knüppeldamm", or log road. It served the Electors as a bridle path, linking the town residence (Stadtschloss) and their hunting lodge (Jagdschloss). It was not until 1871 that the area around the Ku'damm developed into a fashionable "new west end". Chancellor Otto von Bismarck had the boulevard modelled on the Champs Elysées in Paris, and requested that his statue be erected in the street as a thank you. So far, however, the Berliners have failed to oblige him.

For more on the Kurfürstendamm area see pp78–83

Kaiser-Wilhelm-Gedächtniskirche

One of the most haunting symbols of Berlin, the ruins of the memorial church in the heart of the city's West End, have been irreverently nick-named "the hollow tooth". The Neo-Romanesque church was given the name of Kaiser Wilhelm Memorial Church in 1895, to honour Wilhelm I. Following damage by severe bombing raids in 1943, the ruins of the tower were left standing as a memorial. Next to it, Egon Eiermann erected a new church in 1957–63. Religious services are now conducted here.

The "hollow tooth" – the Tower Ruins

○ There are fantastic views of the church from the Mövenpick Café in the Europa-Center opposite.

✔ If possible, visit the interior of the new church on a sunny day around lunch-time, when the blue glass window is at its most impressive.

• Breitscheidplatz
• Map D4, N4 • www.gedaechtniskirche.de
• (030) 218 50 23
• Church 9am–7pm, memorial hall 10am–4pm Mon–Sat
• Services 10am and 6pm Sun
• Admission free

Top 10 Sights

1. Tower Ruins
2. Kaiser's Mosaic
3. Mosaic of the Hohen-zollerns
4. Coventry Crucifix
5. New Bell Tower
6. Main Altar
7. Tower Clock
8. The Orthodox Cross
9. Original Mosaics
10. Figure of Christ

Kaiser's Mosaic

One of the mosaics that have been preserved depicts Emperor Heinrich I on his throne, with imperial orb and sceptre *(below)*. Originally decorated through-out with scenes from German imperial history, the church interior was meant to place the Hohenzollerns within this tradition.

Tower Ruins

Only the tower of the memorial church survived the destruction of World War II that razed much of the city to the ground. Today only 63 m (206 ft) high, it once rose to 113 m (370 ft). The hole in the tower's roof has a sharply ragged edge which is why the tower was nicknamed "hollow tooth" by the Berliners.

Mosaic of the Hohenzollerns

The surprisingly coloured mosaic of the Hohenzollerns adorns the vestibule of the church ruins. It depicts Emperor Wilhelm I together with Queen Luise of Prussia and her entourage.

4 Coventry Crucifix

This small crucifix was forged from old nails that were found in the ruins of Coventry Cathedral. It commemorates the bombing of Coventry, England, by the German Luftwaffe in 1940.

5 New Bell Tower

The new hexagonal bell tower rises 53 m (174 ft) high next to the tower ruins, on the site of the old church's main nave.

6 Main Altar

The golden figure of Christ created by Karl Hemmeter is suspended above the modern main altar in the new church. In the evening light, the windows behind the altar glow in an overwhelming dark blue.

7 Tower Clock

The tower bears a clock based on a Classical design, with Roman numerals. At night, it is lit in blue by modern light-emitting diodes to match the lighting inside the new church.

8 The Orthodox Cross

A gift from the Russian Orthodox bishops of Volokolomsk and Yuruyev, this cross was given in memory of the victims of Nazism.

A Church with Two Lives

The Kaiser-Wilhelm-Gedächtniskirche has the Berliners to thank for its preservation: originally, the Senate had planned to demolish the tower Ruins in 1947 for safety reasons. In a referendum only about ten years later, however, one in two Berliners voted for its preservation. And so the idea came about to build a new church next to the ruin and to preserve the vestibule of the old church as a memorial hall to the horrors of war.

9 Original Mosaics

Mosaics showing Prussian dukes are preserved on the walls and ceilings all along the stairways.

10 Figure of Christ

Miraculously, the vast, plain sculpture of Christ, which is suspended from the ceiling, survived the bombing of the church.

For more on Berlin churches see pp44–5

Schloss Charlottenburg

The construction of Schloss Charlottenburg, designed as a summer residence for Sophie Charlotte, wife of the Elector Friedrich III, began in 1695. Between 1701 and 1713 Eosander von Göthe added a cupola and the Orangerie was extended. Today, it has been extensively renovated.

Schloss Charlottenburg

🍽 The Orangery Café (left of the main entrance) has an attractive garden.

🌙 At weekends, the palace park is over-crowded, but a midweek early-evening stroll can be very romantic (open till 8pm).

- *Spandauer Damm*
- *Map A/B3 • Admission charge in all museums*
- *Two-day ticket for all museums: € 12*
- *Altes Schloss: 9am–5pm Tue–Fri, 10am–5pm Sat, Sun; Neuer Flügel: 10am–6pm Tue–Fri, 11am–6pm Sat, Sun*
- *(030) 32 09 11*

- *Belvedere • Apr–Oct: 10am–5pm Tue–Sun; Nov–Mar: noon–4pm Tue–Fri, noon–5pm Sat, Sun*

- *Neuer Pavillon*
- *10am–5pm Tue–Sun*
- *(030) 32 09 12 12*

- *Mausoleum •*
10am–noon and 1–5pm Tue–Fri, noon–5pm Sat, Sun, • (030) 32 09 12 80

- *Museum für Vor- und Frühgeschichte*
- *10am–6pm Tue–Fri, 11am–6pm Sat, Sun*
- *(030) 326 74 80*

Top 10 Sights

1. Altes Schloss
2. Porzellankabinett
3. Schlosskapelle
4. Monument to the Great Elector
5. New Wing
6. Palace Park
7. Belvedere
8. Neuer Pavillon
9. Mausoleum
10. Museum for Vor- und Frühgeschichte

1 Altes Schloss

The Baroque tower of the oldest part of the palace (1695) by Johann Arnold Nering is crowned by Richard Scheibe's golden statue of Fortuna.

2 Porzellankabinett

The small, exquisite mirrored gallery has been faithfully restored to its original glory. Valuable porcelain items from China and Japan are on display.

3 Schlosskapelle

The luxurious splendour of the palace chapel recalls the once magnificent interior design of the palace, before it was destroyed in World War II. But appearances can be deceptive: apart from the pulpit which is preserved in its original form, the entire chapel – including the king's box – is a costly reconstruction.

Monument to the Great Elector 4

The equestrian monument of Friedrich Wilhelm I is considered to be one of his most dignified portraits. Made in 1696–1703 by Andreas Schlüter, it originally stood in the destroyed Stadtschloss's courtyard.

Neuer Flügel 5

Built between 1740 and 1747 by Georg Wenzeslaus von Knobelsdorff, the new wing contains Frederick the Great's private quarters.

Palace Layout

Schlosspark 6

The palace park, originally Baroque in style, was redesigned by Peter Joseph Lenné between 1818 and 1828 as an English-style landscape garden.

Belvedere 7

Friedrich Wilhelm II liked to escape to the romantic Belvedere, a summer residence built in 1788 by Carl Gotthard Langhans, which served as a tea pavilion. Today it houses a collection of precious porcelain objects.

Neuer Pavillon 8

This Italianate villa behind the palace, designed by Schinkel for Friedrich Wilhelm III in 1825, was inspired by the Villa Reale del Chiatamone in Naples. The pavilion clearly shows the Hohenzollern's love of the Italian style.

Mausoleum 9

Slightly hidden in the palace park is this Neo-Classical building (above) by Schinkel, the final resting place for many of the Hohenzollerns.

Museum für Vor- und Frühgeschichte 10

The museum displays archaeological finds from prehistory right up to the Middle Ages, including tools, ceramics and textiles. Also on display is part of the famous Priamus treasure excavated by Heinrich Schliemann in Troy, which comprises precious golden jewellery from antiquity.

For more on Charlottenburg see pp78–83

Left **The new wing** Centre **Frederick the Great's Watteau painting** Right **Neuer Pavillon**

🔟 Palace Rooms

1 Goldene Galerie
The festival salon in the Neuer Flügel, 42 m (138 ft) long, was designed, in the Rococo style, by W. von Knobelsdorff for Frederick the Great. The richly ornamented room has a cheerful appearance.

2 Alte Galerie
The wooden panelling of the so-called oak gallery is carved with preciously gilded portraits of the Hohenzollern ancestors.

3 Gris-de-Lin-Kammer
This small chamber in Friedrich's second palace apartment is decorated with paintings, including some by his favourite artist, Antoine Watteau. The room was named after its violet-coloured damask (gris-de-lin in French) wall coverings.

4 Schlafzimmer Königin Luise
Queen Luise's bedchamber, designed in 1810 by Karl F. Schinkel, features the clear lines typical of the Neo-Classical style. The walls are clad in silk fabrics and wallpaper.

5 Winterkammern
Friedrich Wilhelm II's early Neo-Classical rooms contain fine paintings, wall carpets and superb furniture of the time.

Alte Galerie

6 Bibliothek
Frederick the Great's small library has outstanding elegant book cases and an unusual, light green colour scheme.

7 Konzertkammer
Furniture and gilded panelling in the concert hall have been faithfully recreated as during Frederick the Great's time. Here hangs *Gersaint's Shop Sign*, which the king bought directly from the artist Watteau.

8 Grünes Zimmer
The green room in Queen Elisabeth's quarters gives an excellent impression of royal chambers furnished in the 19th-century Biedermeier style. Also on display in this room are two models of the palace, made from mother-of-pearl and ivory.

9 Rote Kammer
The elegant chamber, decorated entirely in red and gold, is adorned by portraits of King Friedrich I and Sophie Charlotte.

10 Friedrich I's Audienzkammer
The ceiling paintings and Belgian tapestries in Friedrich I's reception chamber depict allegorical figures symbolizing the fine arts and the sciences. There are also magnificent lacquered cabinets, modelled on Asian originals.

Top 10 Hohenzollern rulers

1. Friedrich Wilhelm (the Great Elector, 1620–88)
2. Friedrich I (1657–1713)
3. Friedrich Wilhelm I (1688–1740)
4. Friedrich II (the Great) (1712–86)
5. Friedrich Wilhelm II (1744–97)
6. Friedrich Wilhelm III (1770–1840)
7. Friedrich Wilhelm I (1795–1861)
8. Wilhelm I (1797–1888)
9. Friedrich III (1831–88)
10. Wilhelm II (1859–1941)

Frederick the Great

The Hohenzollern and Berlin

In 1412, the Hohenzollern dynasty, not originally resident in the Berlin area, was asked by the Ascanian King Sigismund to liberate the province of Brandenburg from the menace of robber barons. Burggraf Friedrich of Hohenzollern from

Prussia's first king: Friedrich I

Nuremberg was so successful in this enterprise that he was made an Elector in 1414 – this is where the histories of the Hohenzollerns and Berlin first became entwined, a relationship that was to last for 500 years. Right from the start, the family attempted to limit the powers of the town. Culture flourished under its rulers, especially under the Great Elector, who brought 20,000 Huguenot craftsmen to Berlin, as well as founding an art gallery and several schools. Friedrich I, father of Frederick the Great, transformed Berlin into a military camp, with parade grounds and garrisons, and scoured the town for tall men to join his body guard. In the 19th century, however, relations between Berlin and the Hohenzollerns became decidedly less cordial.

Frederick the Great in Charlottenburg

Frederick II had two apartments furnished for himself in the palace, and he took a strong personal interest in the design of the Neuer Flügel in 1740–3. From 1745, after the end of the Second Silesian War, he stayed at the palace less and less often, preferring his palace at Sanssouci, although larger festivities in the presence of the King still took place at Charlottenburg.

The Altes Schloss, designed in 1695 by Johann Arnold Nering

For more on historical architecture in Berlin see pp38–9

Kulturforum

The Kulturforum is a unique complex of museums, concert halls and libraries, based at the southeastern end of the Tiergarten. Every year, some of the most outstanding European art museums, as well as the famous concert hall of the Berlin Philharmonic Orchestra, attract millions of visitors who are interested in culture and music. The Kulturforum, based in the former West Berlin in the divided city, has been growing since 1956, as a counterpoint to the Museumsinsel in the former East Berlin. Here visitors can admire some of the best examples of modern architecture in Berlin.

Neue Nationalgalerie in the Kulturforum

- Enjoy a break around the quiet back of the Nationalgalerie.

- A day ticket (€ 4) gives admission to all museums.

- Map E4, L1/2

- Gemäldegalerie, Matthäikirchplatz 8 • 10am–6pm Tue–Sun, till 10pm Thu • (030) 20 90 55 55
- Admission charge

- Neue Nationalgalerie, Potsdamer Str. 50 • 10am–6pm Tue, Wed, 10am–10pm Thu, 10am–8pm Fri, 11am–8pm Sat, Sun • (030) 266 26 62
- Admission charge

- Kunstgewerbemuseum, Matthäikirchplatz • 10am–6pm Tue–Fri, 11am–6pm Sat, Sun • (030) 266 29 02
- Admission charge

- Musikinstrumentenmuseum, Tiergartenstr. 1 • 9am–5pm Tue–fri, 10am–5pm Sat, Sun • (030) 25 48 10
- Admission charge

Top 10 Sights

1. Gemäldegalerie
2. Neue Nationalgalerie
3. Philharmonie
4. Kunstgewerbemuseum
5. Musikinstrumentenmuseum
6. Kammermusiksaal
7. Kupferstichkabinett
8. St. Matthäuskirche
9. Staatsbibliothek
10. Kunstbibliothek

1 Gemäldegalerie

Berlin's largest art museum boasts some of the finest masterpieces of European art. They are displayed in the modern Neubau, built in 1998 by the architects Heinz Hilmer and Christoph Sattler. The superb collection includes paintings by Holbein, Dürer, Gossaert, Bosch, Brueghel the Elder, Vermeer, Titian, Caravaggio, Rubens, Rembrandt and many others.

2 Neue Nationalgalerie

Based in a building by Mies van der Rohe, the gallery exhibits mainly 20th-century art, with an emphasis on German Expressionism, such as Karl Schmitt-Rottluff's *Farm in Daugart* (1910) *(see also p48).*

3 Philharmonie

This tent-like building, designed by Hans Scharoun in 1960–3, was the first new structure in the Kulturforum. Considered one of the best concert halls in the world, it is the seat of the Berlin Philharmonic Orchestra. It is also known, jokingly, as "Circus Karajani", after Herbert von Karajan (1908–89) who conducted the Philharmonic Orchestra for many years. From 2003 Sir Simon Rattle will be the conductor.

For more on Berlin museums see pp46–7

4 Kunstgewerbe-museum

Craft objects from the Middle Ages to the present day and from around Europe are on show here, including valuable items like this Baroque clock and the Guelphs' treasure *(see also p47)*.

5 Musikinstrumen-tenmuseum

Concealed behind the Philharmonie is this fascinating little museum of musical instruments. More then 750 exhibits, particularly of early instruments, such as harpsichords, are on show *(see also p47)*, as well as a 1929 Wurlitzer.

6 Kammer-musiksaal

The smaller relative of the larger Philharmonie, this concert hall is one of Germany's most highly regarded venues for chamber music. It was built in 1984–8, to a design by Hans Scharoun, carried through by his pupil Edgar Wisniewski.

7 Kupferstich-kabinett

The Gallery of Copper Engravings holds more than 520,000 prints and 80,000 drawings from all periods and countries, including this portrait of Dürer's mother *(see also p49)*.

8 St. Matthäuskirche

This church is the only historical building to have been preserved in the Kulturforum. Built by Stüler in 1844–6, it is also a venue for art installations as well as a hall for classical concerts.

9 Staatsbibliothek

Built in 1967–78 according to plans by Hans Scharoun, the National Library has a collection of five million books, manuscripts and journals, making it one of the largest German-language libraries in the world.

10 Kunstbibliothek

The unassuming Art Library holds, among other items, a vast collection of art and advertising posters. It also hosts temporary exhibitions on architecture and art as well as design shows.

Left **Merchant Georg Gisze** Centre **Venus and the Organ Player** Right **Portrait of Holzschuber**

Gemäldegalerie

1 Portrait of Hieronymus Holzschuber
Albrecht Dürer painted this portrait of the mayor of Nuremburg in 1529.

2 Portrait of the Merchant Georg Gisze
This painting by Hans Holbein (1532), showing the merchant counting his money, reflects the rise of the wealthy citizen during the Renaissance.

3 Madonna with Child and Singing Angels
A 1477 painting by Sandro Botticelli depicts the Madonna and Child, surrounded by angels carrying lilies.

4 The Birth of Christ
Martin Schongauer's altar painting (c1480) is one of only a few religious paintings by the artist that have been preserved.

Victorious Eros

5 Victorious Eros
Caravaggio's painting (1602), after Vergil's model, shows Eros, the god of love, trampling underfoot the symbols of culture, glory, science and power.

Key
■ Exhibition area

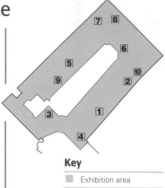
Botticelli's Madonna

6 Portrait of Hendrickje Stoffels
In a 1656–7 portrait of his lover Hendrickje Stoffels, Rembrandt's focus is entirely on the subject.

7 The French Comedy
This painting by Antoine Watteau belonged to Frederick the Great's collection.

8 The Glass of Wine
Skilfully composed by Vermeer (1658–61), this scene shows a couple drinking wine.

9 Venus and the Organ Player
This Titian (1550–2) reflects the playful sensuality typical of the Italian Renaissance.

10 Dutch Proverbs
More than 100 proverbs were incorporated into this painting by Pieter Brueghel (1559).

For more on Berlin's art galleries see pp48–9

Top 10 Architects

Architecture in the Kulturforum

The Kulturforum was planned to fill the large area between Potsdamer Straße and Leipziger Platz that had been destroyed during World War II. The original idea for a varied townscape of museums and parks is credited to the Berlin architect Hans

Sculpture by Henry Moore

Scharoun, who had designed plans for this in the years 1946 and 1957. It was also Scharoun who, with the construction of the Philharmonie in 1963, set the character of the Kulturforum: the tent-like, golden roofs of the music hall, the Kammermusiksaal and the Staatsbibliothek, all designed by Scharoun and – after his death – realized by his pupil Edgar Wisniewski, are today among Berlin's best-known landmarks. All the buildings are characterized by the generous proportions of their rooms. In their day, the Scharoun buildings were highly controversial but today they are considered to be classics of modern architecture.

Mies van der Rohe's Nationalgalerie
The Neue Nationalgalerie, built to plans by Mies van der Rohe in 1965–8, is the only museum in the world designed by this Bauhaus architect. Having emigrated to the USA in 1937, van der Rohe returned to Berlin for its construction.

The Philharmonie, designed by Hans Scharoun – famed for its superb acoustics

Gemäldegalerie: www.smpk.de/gg/s.html

35

Zoologischer Garten

Berlin's Zoological Garden is Germany's oldest zoo and, with over 1,400 different species, it is one of the best-stocked in the world. Animals have been kept and bred here, in the northwest of the Tiergarten district, since 1844. A total of about 14,000 animals live in the zoo, ranging from saucer jellyfish to the Indian elephant. Some enclosures are interesting buildings in their own right. In summer, a visit to the zoo is a favourite day out for Berliners, and many animals, such as the panda and a baby elephant, have become celebrities.

The Elephant Gate – the Zoo's main entrance

There is a café with terrace inside the zoo, to the left of the Elephant Gate.

A day at the zoo is not complete without a visit to the aquarium. The basins and terraria teem with life, as do the zoo enclosures. A combined ticket for € 13 entitles you to visit both zoo and aquarium.

Hardenbergplatz 8 and Budapester Str. 34 • (030) 25 40 10 • Map D4, N5 • www.zoo-berlin.de • Nov–Feb: 9am–5pm daily; Mar: 9am–5:30pm daily; Apr–Sep: 9am–6:30pm daily; Oct: 9am–6pm daily • Aquarium: 9am–6pm daily • Admission charge

Top 10 Zoo Sights

1. Panda Bears
2. Monkey House
3. Lions' Outdoor Enclosure
4. Giraffe House
5. Nocturnal Animal House
6. Elephant House
7. Aviaries
8. Crocodile Hall
9. Aquarium
10. Amphibians' Section

2 Monkey House
Monkeys and apes are at home in this house, and here you can watch gorillas, orang-utangs and chimpanzees swinging from tree to tree and playing in the straw. The venerable Eastern Lowland Gorillas, who raise several young in a group, are always a special hit with young and old alike. The big attraction, however, which draws the greatest crowds, is Sangha, a small baby gorilla, who is being raised by his carers.

1 Panda Bears
The Giant Panda Bao-Bao, a member of an endangered animal species, is the greatest star of the Berlin Zoo. He was presented to Germany by China as an official gift in 1980. Together with the female panda, Yan Yan, a baby was produced in 2001.

3 Lions' Outdoor Enclosure
The kings of the desert usually sit aloft the high rocks. The lions are fed at 2:30pm in summer and at 3:30pm in winter.

4 Giraffe House

The African-style Giraffe House is the oldest house (1871–2). Visitors enjoy watching the giraffes as they nibble the leaves of a tree or bend down, in slow motion, to take a drink.

5 Nocturnal Animal House

This house, in the cellar of the Predatory Animal House, houses the creatures of the night, including nocturnal reptiles and birds. Here you can admire striped bandicoots, fruit bats and slender loris. Asleep during the day, their hearing is outstanding and their eyes may light up uncannily in the dark.

6 Elephant House

These good-natured pachyderms have a healthy appetite: fully-grown male Indian elephants devour up to 50 kg (110 lb) of hay a day! Four elephants have been born in captivity.

7 Aviaries

Nowhere else in the city can you hear such singing, tweeting and whistling – cockatiels, birds-of-paradise, parrots, hornbills and humming-birds sound off in the Bird House aviaries.

8 Crocodile Hall

Not for the faint-hearted: in the crocodile hall visitors cross a small wooden footbridge, only 1 m (3 ft) above the dozing creatures. The reptiles are fed their meat every Monday at 3:30pm.

9 Aquarium

The greatest draw in the aquarium, where Caribbean and Amazonian habitats have been recreated, are the black reef and hammer-head sharks. The electric eel, able to generate up to 800 volts, and the sting-rays are also popular.

10 Amphibians' Section

Poisonous snakes, bird spiders and reptiles crawl and slither around behind glass on the second floor of the aquarium. A particularly spectacular event is the feeding of the spiders with live white mice.

Left **Statues at Altes Museum** Centre **Schloss Bellevue** Right **Portico of the Konzerthaus**

🔟 Historic Buildings

1 Brandenburger Tor
More than a mere symbol, the Brandenburg Gate is synonymous with Berlin *(see pp8–9)*.

2 Schloss Charlottenburg
This palace boasts Baroque and Rococo splendours and a beautiful park, making it one of the most attractive in Germany *(see pp28–31)*.

3 Schloss Bellevue
Built according to plans by Philipp Daniel Boumann in 1785–90, this palace was the residence of the Hohenzollerns until 1861. Since 1994 the stately building with its Neo-Classical façade has been the official residence of the President of the Federal Republic. The modern, egg-shaped Presidential Offices stand immediately next to the old palace. ⊗ *Spreeweg 1 • Map E4 • Not open to the public*

4 Reichstag
The seat of the Deutscher Bundestag, the German parliament, with its spectacular cupola, is a magnet for visitors *(see pp10–1)*.

5 Berliner Rathaus
Berlin's Town Hall, also known as "Red Town Hall" because of the red bricks from Brandenburg Province from which it is built, harks back to the proud days when Berlin became the capital of the new Empire. Built in 1861–9 according to designs by Hermann Friedrich Waesemann, the town hall was one of Germany's largest and most magnificent buildings, built to promote the splendour of Berlin. The structure was modelled on Italian Renaissance palaces, and the tower is reminiscent of Laon cathedral in France. The exterior was decorated with *Die steinerne Chronik* (the stone chronicle) in 1879, depicting scenes from the city's history *(see p131)*. ⊗ *Rathausstraße 15 • Map G3, K6 • 8am–6pm daily*

6 Konzerthaus
The Concert Hall, one of Karl Friedrich Schinkel's masterpieces, was until recently known as *Schauspielhaus* (theatre). The building has a portico with Ionic columns, and a large number of statues of allegorical and historical personages, some riding lions and panthers, as well as deities, muses and bacchants.
⊗ *Gendarmenmarkt 3–4 • Map L4*
• *10am–8pm daily*
• *(030) 203 09 21 01*

7 Hackesche Höfe
This complex of 19th-century warehouses consists of nine interlinked courtyards, some of

Southern façade of the Berliner Rathaus

which are decorated in Art-Nouveau style, originally by Berndt and August Endell. In the early 1990s the complex was completely renovated. The first courtyard is particularly attractive: coloured glazed tiles with geometric patterns decorate the house from the foundations up to the guttering. In the last courtyard, trees are grouped around an idyllic well. The Hackesche Höfe is one of Berlin's most popular hotspots; restaurants, cafés, a cinema and the Chamäleon variety show attract visitors from afar.
🅢 *Rosenthaler Str. 40–41* • *Map G3, J5* • *9am–2am daily*

Victoria, the goddess of victory, on the Siegessäule

Hackesche Höfe

Siegessäule
8 The Victory Column in Tiergarten, 62 m (203 ft) high, decorated with the statue of Victoria, offers great views *(see p97)*.

Altes Museum and Gardens
9 The façade of the Old Museum, possibly one of the most attractive Neo-Classical museums in Europe, is remarkable for the shiny red marble used in its construction, which is visible behind 18 Ionic columns. Built in 1830 according to plans by Karl Friedrich Schinkel, it was at the time one of the first buildings to be created specifically as a museum. Originally it was to house the royal collection of paintings and antique art treasures; today it is home to a collection of antiquities. In front of the museum, on Museumsinsel, are the gardens designed by Peter Joseph Lenné. Conceived as the king's herb garden, it is today decorated with a granite bowl by Gottlieb Christian Cantian, weighing 70 tons *(see p114)*.

Zeughaus
10 The former Royal Prussian Arsenal, redesigned by I. M. Pei, today houses the Deutsches Historisches Museum *(see pp12–5)*. Its façade is decorated with 22 haunting figures of dying warriors.

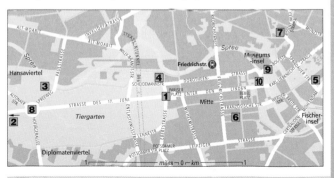

For more about historic buildings see Unter den Linden pp12–5

Left **Neue Nationalgalerie in the Kulturforum** Right **Nordic Embassies**

Modern Buildings

1 Sony Center
One of Berlin's largest new structures is the spectacular Sony Center *(see p16)*.

2 Neue Nationalgalerie
This impressive low building with its huge windows was built in 1965–8 according to plans by Mies van der Rohe. It was the first building to be designed by the pioneering Bauhaus architect after his emigration to the USA. He was able to make use of his earlier designs for the Havana headquarters of the Bacardi company, which had been abandoned following the Cuban Revolution *(see pp32, 48)*. ⊗ *Potsdamer Str. 50 • Map E4 • 10am–6pm Tue–Fri, until 10pm Thu, 11am–6pm Sat, Sun*

3 Bundeskanzleramt
Berliners are not too fond of the Chancellor's new offices, although this is the only new government building to have been designed by a Berlin architect. Axel Schultes developed a vast, elongated office complex, which extends north of the Reichstag, in a bend of the Spree, even stretching across the river. In the centre of the

The new Bundeskanzleramt

hyper-modern building stands a gleaming white cube with round windows, which Berliners quickly nicknamed "washing machine". Critics describe the design as pompous, while civil servants dislike their small offices. The interior of the building is decorated with valuable modern paintings. The Chancellor's office in on the 7th floor, with a view of the Reichstag. ⊗ *Willy-Brandt-Str. 1 • Map J/K2 • Not open to the public*

Ludwig-Erhard-Haus

4 Ludwig-Erhard-Haus
The seat of the Berlin Stock Exchange, Ludwig-Erhard-Haus was designed by the British architect Nicholas Grimshaw in 1994–8. Locals call it the "armadillo", because the 15 giant metal arches of the domed building recall the giant animal's armour. ⊗ *Fasanenstr. 83–84 • Map N4 • 8am–6pm Mon–Fri*

The Kant-Dreieck in Charlottenburg

7 Quartiere 205–207 Friedrichstraße

The Galeries Lafayettes and the Friedrichstadtpassagen are based within these three office blocks by architects Nouvel, Pei and Ungers *(see p119)*.

8 Nordische Botschaften

No other new embassy building has caused as much of a stir as the five embassies of the Scandinavian countries: the green shutters open and close depending on the amount of available light. ⊗ *Klingelhöferstr.* • *Map N6* • *Not open to the public*

5 Philharmonie and Kammermusiksaal

Two modern concert halls in the Kulturforum were designed by Hans Scharoun in 1961 and 1987 respectively – the Chamber Music Hall was completed according to Scharoun's plans by his pupil Edgar Wisniewski. Both buildings are renowned for their excellent acoustics as well as for their tent-like roof structures *(see also pp32–5 and 56–7)*.

9 DG Bank on Pariser Platz

This elegant building by Frank Owen Gehry combines Prussian and modern architecture. The giant dome inside is particularly remarkable *(see pp10–1)*. ⊗ *Pariser Platz 3* • *Map K3* • *10am–6pm Mon–Fri*

6 Philip-Johnson-Haus

This retail and office complex, built in 1994–7 by US star architect Philip Johnson, reflects in its design the clear lines of the Bauhaus style.
⊗ *Friedrichstr. 200* • *Map L4*

10 Kant-Dreieck

The aluminium sail on top the KapHag-Group's headquarters, built by Josef Paul Kleihues in 1992–5, has become a symbol of the new Berlin. Originally, the structure was to be built one-third higher than it is now, but the plans were vetoed by the Berlin Senate. ⊗ *Kantstr. 155* • *Map N4* • *9am–6pm Mon–Fri*

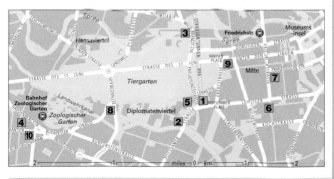

For more on architecture in Potsdamer Platz see **pp16–9**

Left **At Checkpoint Charlie** Centre **Grafitti on the Wall** Right **Marlene Dietrich in the "Blue Angel"**

🔟 Moments in History

1 1685: Edict of Potsdam

Berlin's history as a cultural capital began in 1685, when the far-sighted Great Elector announced in the Edict of Potsdam that around 20,000 Huguenots would be taken in by Berlin. Many were excellent craftsmen and scien-

Statue of the Great Elector

tists, who, having fled Catholic France because of their Protestant beliefs, brought a new age of cultural ascendancy to the provincial town.

2 1744: Frederick the Great

Although "Old Fritz", as Frederick the Great was nick-named, preferred the isolation of Sanssouci to the bustle of Berlin, in 1740 he began to transform the city into a new metropolis. In particular, the "Forum Frideri-cianum" in Unter den Linden brought new splendours to the town, and masterpieces such as the national opera house helped transform Berlin into one of the most important European cities.

Frederick playing the flute in Sanssouci

3 1928: Golden Twenties

Between 1919 and 1933, Berlin flour-ished culturally and became an important metropolis. Film, the-atre, cabaret shows and thousands of restaurants and bars transformed the town into an interna-tional centre of entertainment. In the realms of fine art and architecture, too, Berlin set new standards.

May 1945: Berlin in ruins

4 1945: Surrender

Signed in Berlin-Karlshorst on 8 May 1945, Germany's uncondi-tional surrender marked more than the end of World War II. The previous Jewish population of 161,000 had virtually disappeared and Berliners called their city "the empire's fields of rubble".

5 1953: Workers' Uprising in East Germany

On 17 June 1953, construction workers in Frankfurter Allee demonstrated against an increase in the average rate of

1953: workers on a frieze in Frankfurter Allee

production. Soviet tanks suppressed the rebellion while, in West Berlin, the uprising was interpreted as a demonstration for German unification.

6 1961: Building of the Wall

The building of the Berlin Wall, which commenced during the night of 12 August 1961, was, after the surrender of 1945, the second most traumatic event for many Berliners. Many families were torn apart by the concrete wall and more than 100 people were to be killed over the following 30 years at the border dividing East and West.

7 1963: "I am a Berliner"

No other politician was as enthusiastically received in Berlin as the US President John F. Kennedy. On 17 July 1963, in front of Rathaus Schöneberg, he declared to the cheering crowd: "I am a Berliner". Berliners had forgiven the US for staying silent when the Wall was built. Kennedy confirmed once more that the Western Allies would stand by Berlin and support the town, just as they had done during the blockade of 1948–9, when the US and Britain air-lifted food to the "island" of West Berlin.

8 1968: The late Sixties

During the late 1960s, West Berlin students transformed Germany. Rudi

1991: Berlin becomes the capital

Dutschke and others propounded political change, free love and a reappraisal of Germany's Nazi past. The movement came to an untimely end when Dutschke was assassinated in April 1968.

9 1989: Fall of the Wall

The fall of the Berlin Wall in November 1989 heralded a new dawn. For the first time in 30 years, Berliners from both halves of the divided city were able to visit each other. The town celebrated all along Ku'damm and in front of the Brandenburg Gate.

Celebrations after the Fall of the Berlin Wall

When the Wall was built, Willy Brandt, then governing mayor of West Berlin, had promised: "Berlin will survive!" He was right.

10 1991: Berlin becomes the capital of Germany

In 1991, Berlin was officially declared the capital of the reunified Federal Republic of Germany. Allied Forces left the town during 1994, but only when the Bundestag, the German parliament, moved from Bonn to Berlin on 19 April 1999, did the town become the "real" capital. Today, all the main ministries, the Bundesrat (upper house), and the Chancellor's and the President's offices are based in Berlin.

For famous Berliners **see pp50–1**

Left **St. Hedwigskathedrale** Centre **Berliner Dom interior** Right **Main altar in Marienkirche**

🔟 Churches & Synagogues

1 Berliner Dom

Berlin Cathedral, the largest and most lavish church in town, was reopened in 1993, after almost 40 years of restoration. Designed by Julius Raschdorf in 1894–1905, the building reflects the empire's aspirations to power. In particular, the imperial stairs, made from black marble, are a manifestation of the proximity of the Hohenzollern town residence opposite the cathedral. Members of this ruling dynasty are buried in the crypt. The main nave, topped by a 85-m (279-ft) high dome is remarkable. The church is dominated by a magnificent 20th-century Neo-Baroque pulpit and the giant Sauer organ. ⌕ *Am Lustgarten • Map K5 • 9am–7pm daily • (030) 202 69–0*

The interior of Nikolaikirche

(1437) and the fresco *Dance of the Dead* (1485) are among the church's oldest treasures. The richly ornamented Baroque pulpit was created by Andreas Schlüter in 1703. ⌕ *Karl-Liebknecht-Str. 8 • Map J6 • 10am–4pm Mon–Thu, noon–4pm Sat, Sun; Services 10:30am Sun • Admission charge*

2 St. Hedwigskathedrale

Berlin's largest Catholic church was commissioned by Frederick the Great in 1747–73 after his conquest of Silesia *(see pp 12–5)*. ⌕ *Bebelplatz • Map K4 • 9am–9pm Mon–Fri, 9am–5pm Sat*

Font in Marienkirche

3 Marienkirche

Work started in 1270 on the Church of St Mary, which nestles at the foot of the Fernsehturm. Mainly Gothic and Baroque in style, an impressive Neo-Gothic tower was added in 1790 by Carl Gotthard Langhans. The font

4 Nikolaikirche

Berlin's oldest sacred building, the Church of St Nicholas was built in 1230, in the Nikolaiviertel. The present church, with its red-brick twin towers, dates from around 1300. It is particularly famous for the portal on the west wall of the main nave, created by Andreas Schlüter. It is adorned with a gilded relief depicting a goldsmith and his wife. The church was rebuilt in 1987 and today houses parts of the municipal museum. ⌕ *Nikolaikirchplatz • Map K6 • 10am–6pm Tue–Sun • Admission charge*

5 Kaiser-Wilhelm-Gedächtniskirche

A landmark in West Berlin, the Kaiser Wilhelm Memorial Church successfully combines modern architecture with the ruins of the church tower *(see pp26–7)*.

6 Neue Synagoge

Berlin's largest synagogue, built originally in 1859–66, was demolished following World War II damage and completely reconstructed in 1988–95. Its magnificent dome is visible from afar *(see p123)*. ◈ *Oranienburger Str. 29–30 • Map G3, J4 • (030) 88 02 83 00 • Admission charge*

Dome of the Neue Synagoge

onion domes. Services are still held in Russian, following Orthodox rituals. ◈ *Hohenzollerndamm 166 • Map B6 • Only during service 10am & 6pm Sat, 10am Sun*

7 Friedrichswerdersche Kirche

This small brick church was built by Karl Friedrich Schinkel in 1824–30, in the Neo-Gothic style. Originally it was meant to serve the German and French communities of the Friedrichswerder district. Today, the Schinkel Museum is based here.
◈ *Werderscher Markt*

The nave of Friedrichswerdersche Kirche

10 Französischer Dom

At 66 m (216 ft) high, this Baroque tower, which dates back to 1701–05, is a magnificent ornamental structure for the church serving Berlin's Huguenot community.
◈ *Gendarmenmarkt 5 • Map L4 • (030) 20 16 68 83 • 10am–6pm daily*

8 Synagoge Rykestrasse

The small synagogue looks the same today as when it was originally built 100 years ago *(see p140)*.

9 Christi-Auferstehungs-Kirche

The only Russian-Orthodox church in Berlin, the Church of Christ's Ascension is known for its green

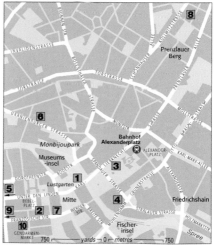

For more on Berlin's historic architecture **see pp38–9**

Left **Detail from the Pergamon Altar frieze** Right **Tapestry in the Kunstgewerbemuseum**

Museums

1 Pergamonmuseum
Berlin's most impressive museum is a vast treasure trove of antiquities *(see pp20–3).*

2 Ägyptisches Museum
Star exhibit in the Egyptian Museum is the mysteriously beautiful bust of Nefertiti, wife of Akhenaton. The long-necked limestone bust, discovered in 1912, probably served as a model. Also worth seeing is the "Berlin Green Head", a small bust from the 4th century BC. The museum also holds numerous mummies, sarcophagi, murals and sculptures.
- *Schlossstr. 70 • Map B3*
- *10am–6pm Tue–Sun • (030) 20 90 55 55*
- *Admission charge*

Bust of Nefertiti

3 Deutsches Historisches Museum
Germany's largest History Museum uses unique exhibits, documents and films to take the visitor on a journey through German history, from the Middle Ages to the present day. Special exhibitions are devoted to particular themes *(see pp12–5).*

4 Dahlem Museums
The five museums based in southern Berlin are a fantastic resource of exotic cultures. Four museums are devoted to Far Eastern, Indian, North American and African art, from prehistory to the present day. Among the star exhibits are bronzes from Benin and Japanese woodcuts. The Ethnologisches Museum (Museum of Ethnology), devoted to the cultures of the Pacific area, is equally impressive. Among its exhibits are gold treasures of the Inca *(see p89).*

5 Jüdisches Museum
The new Jewish Museum, housed in a spectacular building designed by Daniel Libeskind, documents the German–Jewish relationship through the centuries. There are special exhibitions on the influence of Berlin Jews on the town's cultural life, and on the life of the Enlightenment philosopher Moses Mendelssohn. An empty room commemorates the loss of Jewish culture. There is also an exciting programme of special events *(see p103).*

The Jewish Museum

Ägyptisches Museum: **www.smpk.de/amp/s.html**

6 Deutsches Technikmuseum

The fascinating Museum of Technology, on the site of a former station, has fascinating hands-on displays on the history of technology *(see p103)*.

7 Kunstgewerbemuseum

European crafts from over five centuries are on display at this museum. Its most valuable exhibits are the treasure of the Guelphs from Braunschweig and the silver treasure of the town council in Lüneburg. The museum also holds valuable Italian tin glazed earthenware, Renaissance faïence and German Baroque glass and ceramics. Popular displays show Neo-Classical porcelain and furniture, Jugendstil art and Tiffany vases, as well as 20th-century Art-Deco and modern designs. ◈ Matthäikirchplatz • Map L1/2
• 10am–6pm Tue–Fri, 11am–6pm Sat, Sun
• (030) 20 90 55 55
• Admission charge

8 Museum für Naturkunde

With over 60 million exhibits, the Natural History Museum is one of the largest of its kind. Star feature is the world's largest dinosaur skeleton, a brachiosaurus found in Tanzania in 1909. Six further dinosaur skeletons as well as many fossils of mussels, birds and mammals take the visitor back to prehistoric times. A visit to the glittering exhibition of meteorites and minerals is a special treat for fans of gems and precious stones.
◈ Invalidenstr. 43 • Map F2 • 9:30am–5pm Tue–Sun • Admission charge

Brachiosaurus in the Natural History Museum

9 Haus am Checkpoint Charlie

The museum at the former Allied checkpoint documents events at the Berlin Wall *(see p103)*.

10 Musikinstrumenten-Museum

Some 750 musical instruments can be heard in this museum, including such famous ones as Frederick the Great's harpsichord. Don't miss the silent-film organ which still works (First Sat in the month, noon).
◈ Tiergartenstr. 1
• Map L2 • 9am–5pm Tue–Fri, 10am–5pm Sat, Sun
• Admission charge

Amber cabinet in the Kunstgewerbemuseum

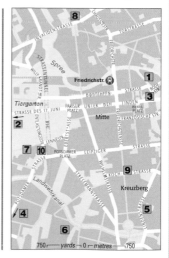

Left *The Adoration of the Shepherds* Centre *Cupid Victorious* Right **Hamburger Bahnhof**

🔟 Art Galleries

1 Gemäldegalerie

Berlin's best art museum, the Gemäldegalerie focuses on European art of the 13th to 19th centuries, such as Caravaggio's *Cupid Victorious (above)*, and works by Dürer, Rembrandt and Rubens *(see pp34–5)*.

2 Neue Nationalgalerie

The National Gallery's collection includes modern German art and classics of the 20th century. It often holds spectacular temporary exhibitions. ✇ *Potsdamer Str. 50 • Map E4 • 10am–6pm Tue–Fri, 11am–6pm Sat, Sun • Admission charge*

3 Alte Nationalgalerie

The Old National Gallery, built by Friedrich August Stüler in 1866–76 on the Museumsinsel, has been completely restored. Today it holds a collection of 19th-century (and mainly German) paintings, including works by Adolf von Menzel, Wilhelm Leibl, Max Liebermann and Arnold

Mao by Warhol, in the Hamburger Bahnhof

Böcklin. The gallery also has sculptures by Schadow, Rauch and Reinhold Begas. ✇ *Bodestr. 1-3 • Map J5 • 10am–6pm Tue–Fri, 11am–6pm Sat, Sun • (030) 20 90 55 55 • Admission charge*

4 Hamburger Bahnhof

A "museum of the present day", the historic Hamburg Station is home to modern paintings, installations and multimedia art. One of its highlights is the Erich Marx Collection, with works by Joseph Beuys. Apart from famous artists such as Andy Warhol, Jeff Koons and Robert Rauschenberg, it also owns more recent works by Anselm Kiefer, Sandro Chiao and others. ✇ *Invalidenstr. 50–51 • Map F2 • 10am–6pm Tue–Fri, till 10pm Thu, 11am–6pm Sat, Sun • Admission charge*

The Glass of Wine by Jan Vermeer, in Gemäldegalerie

Neue Nationalgalerie: www.smpk.de/nng/s.html

Head of a Faun by Picasso (Berggruen)

5 Sammlung Berggruen
Heinz Berggruen, born in Berlin in 1936, emigrated but later returned to Berlin. His collection, including works from Picasso's "blue period", is based in a historic building by Stüler. ⌖ *Schlossstr. 1 • Map B3 • 10am–6pm Tue–Fri, 11am–6pm Sat, Sun • Admission charge (free 1st Sun of the month)*

6 Bauhaus-Archiv
Few schools have exercised as much influence on 20th-century architecture and design as the Bauhaus, founded in 1919 by Walter Gropius. On show in the museum are furniture, sketches, everyday objects and paintings. ⌖ *Klingelhöferstr. 14 • Map N3 • 10am–5pm Wed–Mon • Admission charge*

7 Deutsches Guggenheim
Sponsored by the Deutsche Bank, the museum hosts temporary exhibitions, often showing modern art from the US *(see p113).* ⌖ *Unter den Linden 13–15 • Map K4 • 11am–8pm daily, till 20pm Thu • Admission charge*

8 Brücke-Museum
This museum is devoted exclusively to "Die Brücke" (the bridge), an artists' group founded in 1905. The core of the collection is 80 works of art by Schmidt-Rottluff. ⌖ *Bussardsteig 9 • 11am–5pm Wed–Mon*

9 Bröhan-Museum
A unique collection of Art-Nouveau and Art-Deco objects from around Europe is on display at this small museum. There is also an exhibition of paintings by Berlin artists. ⌖ *Schlossstr. 1a • Map B3 • 10am–6pm Tue–Sun • Admission charge*

10 Kupferstichkabinett
Five centuries of prints and calligraphies, including works by Botticelli, Dürer, Rembrandt, Goya, Daumier and the Dutch Old Masters, are on display in this gallery. ⌖ *Matthäikirchplatz 6 • Map L1 • 10am–6pm Tue–Fri, 11am–6pm Sat, Sun • Admission charge*

Art Deco vase in the Bröhan-Museum

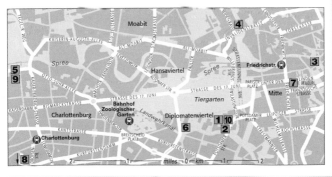

For more on art galleries in the Kulturforum see pp32–5

49

Left **Philosopher G.W. F. Hegel** Centre **The brothers Grimm** Right **Conductor von Karajan**

🔟 Famous Berliners

1 Marlene Dietrich
The famous filmstar (1901–92), born in Schöneberg, began her career in Berlin in the 1920s. Her breakthrough came with the film *The Blue Angel* (1931). Today she lies buried in the Friedenau cemetery in Steglitz. Her personal possessions are exhibited in the Filmmuseum Berlin in the Sony Center on Potsdamer Platz.

2 Albert Einstein
In 1914, the physicist Albert Einstein (1879–1955) became the director of the Kaiser Wilhelm-Institute for Physics. He was awarded the Nobel Prize for Physics in 1921 for his Theory of Relativity, first developed in 1905. Einstein mostly lived and worked in Potsdam, but stayed closely connected with Berlin through his lectures and teaching activity. In 1933 Einstein, who was Jewish, had to emigrate from Germany to the USA where he stayed until his death.

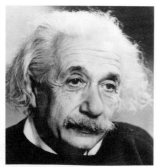

Albert Einstein taught in Berlin

3 Bertolt Brecht
Born in Augsburg, Bavaria, Bertolt Brecht (1898–1956) wrote some of his greatest works,

Brecht's study

such as the *Threepenny Opera*, in a small apartment in Charlottenburg. In the Third Reich, the playwright emigrated to the US, but he returned to Germany after World War II and founded the Berliner Ensemble in East Berlin in 1949. Until his death, Brecht lived in Chausseestraße in Berlin-Mitte, with his wife, Helene Weigel. His renovated apartment has been turned into a museum.

4 Herbert von Karajan
This famous Austrian conductor (1908–1989) was head of the Berlin Philharmonic Orchestra from 1954 until 1989. During this time he helped create the orchestra's unique sound, which remains legendary until this day. Herbert von Karajan was both revered and feared by his musicians because of his genius and his fiery temperament. Berliners still refer to the Philharmonie as "Circus Karajani".

Robert Koch *(caption)*

5 Robert Koch

Like few other physicians of his day, Robert Koch (1843–1910) laid the foundations and shaped the face of modern medicine with his pioneering discoveries. The Director of the Institute for Infectious Diseases, Koch also taught and researched at the Charité Hospital. In 1905 he received the Nobel Prize for Medicine for his discoveries in the field of microbiology.

6 Theodor Fontane

A Huguenot, Fontane (1819–98) was one of the most important 19th-century novelists in Germany. He also worked as a journalist for more than 20 years, penning many of his articles and essays in the Café Josty on Potsdamer Platz. Fontane is particularly well known for his *Walks in the Province of Brandenburg*, in which he describes the mentality of the people, historic places and the Brandenburg landscapes.

7 Käthe Kollwitz

The sculptor and painter Käthe Kollwitz (1867–1945) portrayed the social problems of the poor, and her work provides a powerful, haunting commentary on human suffering. Kollwitz spent a large part of her life in a modest abode in the square that is now named after her, in the Prenzlauer Berg district. A monument recalls how she captured the lives of poor Berlin families, burdened with large numbers of children, and of social outcasts. Her *Pieta* now adorns the Neue Wache *(see p13)*.

8 Jacob and Wilhelm Grimm

The brothers Jacob (1785–1863) and Wilhelm (1786–1859) Grimm are well known around the world, thanks to their collection of classic fairy tales including *Little Red Riding Hood* and *Hansel and Gretel*. Equally important, however, was their linguistic output, the *German Grammar* and *German Dictionary* which are standard reference works even today.

9 Georg Wilhelm Hegel

The influential philosopher Hegel (1770–1831) taught at Humboldt University from 1818 until his death.

Sculpture by Kollwitz *(caption)*

10 Felix Mendelssohn Bartholdy

The composer (1809–47), a grandson of Moses Mendelssohn, was also the conductor of the Staatskapelle (state orchestra) at the opera house in Unter den Linden. His grave is found in one of the cemeteries in front of the Hallesches Tor in Kreuzberg.

Felix Mendelssohn Bartholdy

For moments in history in Berlin *see pp42–3*

Left **Ku'damm Kneipe** Centre **Obst & Gemüse** Right **Tables outside Zwiebelfisch**

🔟 Kneipen (Pubs)

1 Obst & Gemüse

A classic among the new drinking establishments in Berlin Mitte, this pub is always full to bursting with its never-ending stream of guests. Obst & Gemüse (fruit & vegetables), which thrives on nostalgia for life in the former East Germany, is based in a former grocer's shop selling "southern fruits". Most of the patrons sit at long tables outside or stand in large crowds in the street. 🅢 *Oranienburger Str. 48–49 • Map J4/5 • from 8:30am daily • (030) 282 96 47*

2 Mitte-Bar

Despite its name, this bar is a Kneipe, where in the summer you can enjoy a cold beer or one of the inexpensive cocktails outdoors. Frequented by a young and trendy crowd who love to make a noise, the bar serves some of the best cocktails in Berlin. 🅢 *Oranienburger Str. 46–7 • Map J4/5 • summer: 10am–6am, winter 1pm–6am daily • (030) 283 38 37*

3 Hackbarths

Berliner Weiße

Friendly Hackbarths is a corner pub frequented by trendy students, local artists and tourists. From

At Hackbarth's

6pm, the locals gather here in jovial mood and are always ready to strike up conversation over a glass of Berliner Weiße (sour beer with a shot of raspberry or woodruff syrup). In the summer, the pavement serves as a makeshift extension of the pub. 🅢 *Auguststr. 49a • Map G2/3 • 9am–3am daily • (030) 282 77 06*

4 E. & M. Leydicke

This slightly dated winery is still a big hit with tourists as well as groups of pupils and students. Try the sweetish strawberry and raspberry wines. 🅢 *Mansteinstr. 4 • Map E6 • 6pm–1:30am daily • (030) 216 29 73*

5 Morena-Bar

With its walls completely covered with Spanish tiles, this bar draws an upmarket Kreuzberg crowd as well as students who like to meet here for a beer. At weekends it is full to bursting and gets livelier by the hour. 🅢 *Wiener Str. 60 • 9pm–4am daily • (030) 611 47 16*

6 Zum Nußbaum

One of only a few traditional pubs in the historic Nikolaiviertel worth checking out, the Nußbaum serves draught beer and traditional Berlin food. 🅢 *Am Nußbaum 3 • Map K6 • from noon daily • (030) 242 30 95*

Diener, favoured by actors

7 Zwiebelfisch
A classic of the ageing Charlottenburg scene, this is where the last survivors of the 1968 generation prop up the bar and reminisce about the great days of the revolution in West Berlin. The artists in the photographs on the walls are all past clients, many of them from the 1968 generation. In the summer, there are tables outdoors on Savignyplatz – great for people-watching and taking in the scene. ✆ *Savignyplatz 7–8 • Map N3 • noon–6am daily • (030) 312 73 63*

8 Diener-Tattersaal
An atmospheric pub popular with local actors, serving draught beers and traditional German and Austrian fare. The pub bears the name of Franz Diener, the legendary boxer who knocked out the erstwhile boxing world champion, Max Schmeling. ✆ *Grolmanstr. 47 • Map P3 • 6pm–3am daily • (030) 881 53 29*

9 Café am Neuen See
The only Berlin Kneipe that is also a café – except that you cannot order any coffee here. In summer, crowds gather in the vast beer garden. Customers bring their own food to grill and sit at the long tables, chatting over a local beer. ✆ *Tiergarten, Neuer See, Lichtensteinallee 1 • Map M5 • Mar–Oct: 10pm–11pm; Nov–Feb: 10am–8pm daily • (030) 254 49 30*

10 Dralle's
One of the pub hotspots in the 1980s, Dralle's has become more sedate in recent years, but media people and trendy business students still meet up in this rockabilly pub, which is decorated entirely in red. ✆ *Schlüterstr. 69 • Map N3 • 9am–2am Mon–Sat, 10am–2am Sun • (030) 313 50 38*

Outside Dralle's

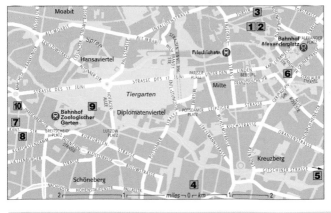

For Berlin bars **see pp54–5**

Left **Inside 925 Loungebar** Centre **The Bar am Lützowplatz** Right **The Reingold bar**

🔟 Bars & Lounges

1 Newton-Bar
The best cocktails in town are mixed at this elegant bar in Gendarmenmarkt. Service is charming and the fastest in town, and in summer there's even a fold-down bar on the pavement outside. Heavy leather armchairs make for comfortable sitting, and the walls are adorned with enlarged photographs of nudes by Helmut Newton, after whom the bar is named. Highly recommended: the Caribbean and Latin-American cocktails – Chin-Chin! Ⓢ *Charlottenstr. 57 • Map L4 • 10am–3am daily • (030) 20 61 29 99*

In the Newton-Bar

2 925 Loungebar
The Trenta Sei Lounge, part of the Italian restaurant next door, is elegant and completely furnished in red. The cocktails are slightly less expensive here than in other bars in the area. It's a particularly pleasant place in summer, when you can enjoy your drink outside, overlooking Gendarmenmarkt. Ⓢ *Taubenstr. 19 • Map L4 • summer: 11am–4am; winter: 5pm–4am daily • (030) 20 18 71 77*

3 Le Bar du Paris Bar
Despite its name, the Paris Bar was until quite recently only a French restaurant. Now this trendy celebrity haunt has its own bar, and although the cocktails are not quite as good as those of the competition, it is easy to forget this when you are enjoying one of their wonderful French wines or champagnes. Ⓢ *Kantstr. 152 • Map N3 • from 6pm daily • (030) 31 01 50 94*

4 Harry's New York Bar
Sip your tropical concoctions and champagne cocktails while seated underneath the portraits of 43 US Presidents in this bar, a sister venue of the famous bar in Venice. The clientele is more sedate than in other Berlin bars, but the ambience is upmarket, and evening entertainment (jazz singers and piano) is more stylish than elsewhere. Ⓢ *Grand Hotel Esplanade, Lützowufer 15 • Map N6 • from noon daily • (030) 25 47 88 21*

5 Trompete
This new bar, which belongs to the actor Ben Becker, has very quickly established itself as *the* place to be. The bar, with its soft leather armchairs and settees and completely black walls, is relaxed and comfortable. At weekends, Trompete hosts live concerts ranging from jazz and salsa to house. Ⓢ *Lützowplatz 9 • Map P6 • from 9pm daily • (030) 23 00 47 94*

6 Bar am Lützowplatz

For a long time, this was the favourite bar for the "beautiful people" but, although it is now a little quieter than it used to be, this venue still boasts the longest bar in Berlin. The interior is truly astounding, and the well-dressed barmen with their white dinner jackets, as well as the outstanding cocktails they mix make this a "must" for any visitor.
◎ Lützowplatz 7 • Map M6 • from 2pm daily • (030) 262 68 07

Ice-cold Mojito cocktail

7 lore.berlin

One of the youngest "hip" bars in Berlin, lore.berlin is themed as a relaxing lounge bar: soft music, occasional live concerts, and easy chatting at the long bar are guaranteed. The bar's unusual name harks back to its location in a former coal cellar – 1 lore is an old unit of measurement which equals 10,000 kg (22,000 lb) of coal.
◎ Neue Schönhauser Str. 20 • Map J6 • 7pm–4am daily • (030) 28 04 51 34

LE BAR DU
Paris Bar
Expensive but good: the Paris Bar

8 Galerie Bremer

This small bar, personally designed by Hans Scharoun, is the meeting point for Berlin's cultural elite, the lobby doubling as a highly regarded gallery space. Here you can enjoy a discussion about art while sipping a cool drink and listening to excellent jazz. ◎ Fasanenstr. 37 • Map C5 • 8pm–1am daily • (030) 881 49 08

9 Reingold

Portraits of 1930s radicals Erika and Klaus Mann adorn the walls of this bar, which is friendlier and more intimate than most other bars in Berlin. The cocktails are excellent.
◎ Novalisstr. 11 • Map F2 • 6pm–2am daily • (030) 28 38 76 76

10 Café M

The (in)famous Café M Kneipe in Schöneberg is today even noisier than before. If you find the rock music inside too loud, you can always escape to the tables outside. ◎ Goltzstr. 33 • Map E6 • 8am–2am Mon–Thu, from 9am Fri–Sun • (030) 216 70 92

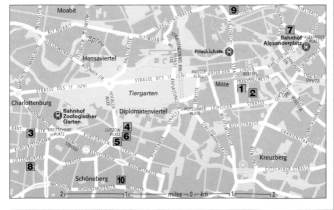

For pubs see pp52–3

Left **Deutsches Theater** Centre **Friedrichstadtpalast** Right **Inside the Tanztheater in Berlin**

🔟 Performing Arts Venues

1 Staatsoper Unter den Linden

Both the theatre troupe and the orchestra of the venerable Berlin Opera – now ably directed by Daniel Barenboim – enjoy top reputations. Nowhere else can you see so many top stars of classical music *(see pp12–15)*. ✆ *Unter den Linden 5–7 • Map K4 • (030) 208 28 61*

Claudio Abbado and Philharmonic Orchestra

2 Philharmonie

Germany's "temple" of classical music still presents the best conductors and orchestras in the world. Designed by Scharoun, the concert hall boasts unique acoustics that are much appreciated by artists and audience alike. Concerts by the Berlin Philharmonic Orchestra are very popular and are often sold out for weeks ahead *(see pp32–5).* ✆ *Herbert-von-Karajan-Str. 1 • Map L2 • 8pm daily, Sun also 4pm • box office (030) 25 48 81 26*

3 Wintergarten Varieté

Berlin's largest variety show relates back to the traditions of its famous predecessor from the 1920s. Every evening, André Heller and

Wintergarten

Bernhard Paul direct a varied classical cabaret show in the former cinema, which has been transformed into an amazingly beautiful theatre. The shows change three or four times a year, but there is always a mix of acrobatics, comedy and song on offer. ✆ *Potsdamer Str. 96 • Map E5 • 8pm Mon–Fri, 6pm and 10pm Sat, 6pm Sun • (030) 25 00 88 88*

4 Chamäleon-Varieté

The lack of technology is more than made up for with much wit and ingenuity by the small, alternative Chamäleon stage. If you are seated in the front row, you are likely to get pulled onto the stage. ✆ *Rosenthaler Str. 40–1, Hackesche Höfe • Map J5 • 8pm daily, midnight performances Fri, Sat • (030) 282 71 18*

5 Bar jeder Vernunft

This venue, whose name means "devoid of all reason", is Berlin's most popular comedy theatre. The cabaret offers a humorous and, at times, romantic programme of songs and chansons, reviews, cabaret, slapstick and comedy, all based in an amazing mirror tent dating from the 1920s. Many stars of the international and German cabaret scene can be seen regularly among the performers here: for example Tim Fischer, Georgette Dee, the Pfister Sisters and Gayle Tufts, as well as older stars such as

Berlin Philharmonic Orchestra: www.berlin-philharmonic.com

Otto Sander or Brigitte Mira.
Ⓢ Schaperstr. 24 (car park Freie Volks-
bühne) • Map C5 • 7pm daily
• (030) 883 15 82

Theater des Westens

Inside the mirror tent: Bar jeder Vernunft

6 Deutsches Theater
Performances at the German
Theatre, one of the best German-language venues, include
mainly classic plays in the tradition of Max Reinhardt. Experimental theatre by young playwrights is performed at the DT
Baracke. Ⓢ Schumannstr. 13 • Map J3
• 8pm daily • (030) 28 44 12 25

7 Theater des Westens
For two decades, this theatre has been producing its own
shows, such as La Cage aux
Folles, and promoting German
musicals around the world. Now
its future hangs in the balance.
Ⓢ Kantstr. 12 • Map N4 • 8pm Tue–Sat,
6pm Sun • (030) 599 89 99

8 Friedrichstadtpalast
The long-legged dancers in
Friedrichstadtpalast are as popular today as they were in the
1920s in their legendary former
venue, which was damaged during World War II. Long celebrated
as the "world's greatest variety
show," the performances have
today become even more spirit-
ed and entertaining. Ⓢ Friedrichstr.
107 • Map J4 • box office (030) 25 00 25

9 Hebbel-Theater
The Hebbel-Theater has
attained cult status in Berlin,
thanks to its modern and varied
programme of concerts, dance
and song. Top performers from
around the world appear here.
Ⓢ Stresemannstr. 29 • Map F5 • 8pm
daily • (030) 25 90 04 27

10 Volksbühne
Frank Castorf has trans-
formed this former Socialist
stage into a theatre, which has
become famous for its classy,
and at times controversial performances. Ⓢ Rosa-Luxemburg-Platz
• Map H2 • (030) 247 67 72

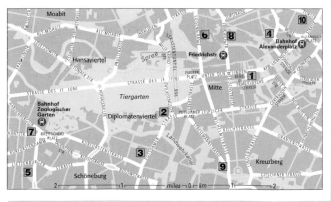

Left **Tom's Bar** Centre **Façade of the Connection** Right **The Mann-o-Meter**

Gay & Lesbian Attractions

Christopher Street Day on Ku'damm

1 Christopher Street Day

Every summer, Germany's largest gay festival, Christopher-Street Day, transforms Berlin into a giant street party, with thousands of gays and lesbians parading from Kurfürstendamm down the Straße des 1. Juni to Siegessäule. At night, the party continues in the city's many gay clubs and Kneipen.
✆ *Kurfürstendamm, Straße des 17. Juni • Map P3/4 • 4th weekend in June*

2 Siegessäule

Berlin's oldest and best-selling gay newspaper is named after the Victory Column, Berlin's landmark. This colourful monthly magazine includes all sorts of useful information, a round-up of what's on, small ads and interviews from the city's gay scene. ✆ *Free in gay cafés and shops.*

Siegessäule front covers

3 Mann-o-Meter

Berlin's best-known advice centre for gays offers help and advice of all kinds. Apart from psychological support in relation to Aids, safe sex and coming out, its counsellors offer help in finding accommodation, give support to those in troubled relationships and provide legal advice. Mann-o-Meter is also a good starting point for gay visitors to Berlin, who wish to find out abut the gay scene – and, last but not least, the café is also a good place to meet people.
✆ *Bülowstr. 106 • Map E5 • 5–10pm daily • (030) 216 80 08*

4 SchwuZ

"SchwuZ" in Kreuzberg is one of the best venues for gay parties in Berlin. At weekends, this is where a young crowd hangs out, dancing, chatting, drinking and enjoying the entertainment. The parties are often themed – details can be found in gay magazines such as "Siegessäule" or "Sergej".
✆ *Mehringdamm 61 • Map F5 • from 11pm Fri,. Sat • (030) 693 70 25 • Admission charge*

5 Tom's Bar

One of the traditional pubs in Berlin, in the centre of the city's gay heart in Motzstraße, Tom's Bar is not for those who are shy and timid; Tom's Bar is in fact a well-known pick-up joint. Below the (rather dark and dingy) Kneipe is a darkroom.

Ⓢ *Motzstr. 19 • Map D5 • from 7pm daily • (030) 213 45 17*

Inside the Prinz-Eisenherz bookstore

6 Prinz-Eisenherz-Buchhandlung

Germany's oldest, openly gay bookstore stocks the entire range of German and international gay and lesbian publications. Its knowledgeable bookshop assistants will track down rare or out-of-stock titles at your request. The bookshop also hosts frequent literary readings.

Ⓢ *Bleibtreustr. 52 • Map N3 • 10am–7pm Mon–Fri, 10am–4pm Sat • (030) 313 99 36*

7 Connection

Connection is perhaps not the best, but certainly one of the most popular gay discos in Berlin. Late at night, this is where gays mainly from the scene meet and dance to house and techno rhythms. In the base-ment under the club is a labyrinth of darkrooms. Ⓢ *Fuggerstr. 33 • Map D5 • from 11pm Fri, Sat • (030) 218 14 32 • Admission charge*

8 Café Anderes Ufer

One of the oldest gay pub-cafés, the "café of the other bank" has often been written off, but it continues to survive. The atmosphere is boisterous and there's a lively chat-up scene.

Ⓢ *Hauptstr. 157 • Map E6 • 8am–1am Sun–Thu, 8am–2am Fri, Sat • (030) 78 70 38 00*

9 Schwules Museum

The small Gay Museum is situated in Kreuzberg. It documents, through temporary exhibitions, the high and low points of gay and lesbian life since the 19th century. Next to the museum is an archive, a small library and a venue for cultural events.

Ⓢ *Mehringdamm 61 • Map F5 • 2–6pm Wed–Sun • (030) 69 59 90 50 • Admission charge*

10 SO 36

This famous – and infamous – dance venue for young gays has been extremely popular for many years. The Sunday night club "Café Fatal" is legendary, when old German chart hits and dance tunes are played.

Ⓢ *Oranienstr. 190 • Map H5 • from 10pm Wed, Fri, from 9pm Sat, from 7pm Sun • (030) 61 40 13 06*

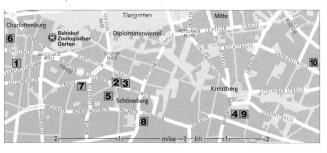

Left **Inside Quartier 206** Centre **Food department Galeries Lafayette** Right **In Winterfeldtplatz**

Shops & Markets

1 Kaufhaus des Westens (KaDeWe)

Whatever you are looking for, you will find it here, in Europe's

The KaDeWe

largest temple of consumption. On eight floors, the venerable KaDeWe (department store of the West) offers more than three million products. On its gourmet floor, West Berlin's former "shop window", you can choose from 1,800 cheeses, 1,400 breads and pastries and 2,000 cold meats. The window displays and inner courtyards are also worth a visit (see also p170). ✎ Tauentzienstr. 21–24 • Map D4, P5 • (030) 22 13 24 55

2 Galeries Lafayette

This small French department store specializes in classic womens- and menswear. The French delicacies on sale in the food department make many a heart beat faster, not just those of Francophiles (see also p119).

3 Kunst- und Antikmarkt Straße des 17. Juni

Berlin's largest art and antiques market specializes in genuine antique furnishings and fittings, cutlery and porcelain, books, paintings, clothing and jewellery. The traders are professionals and demand high prices, but in return you are assured of buying something splendid. With its street artists and buskers, the market is an ideal spot for browsing, dawdling and people-watching (see p85). ✎ Straße des 17. Juni • Map M4 • 10am–5pm Sat, Sun

4 Department Store Quartier 206

Berlin's most recent fashion store is also the most expensive in town. Here, the man-about-town can purchase his Gucci or DKNY ties, while the lady tries on Versace or Calvin Klein gear on three floors in the Friedrichstadtpassagen (see p119). ✎ Friedrichstr. 71 • Map L4 • (030) 20 94 62 40 • 10am–8pm Mon–Fri, 10am–4pm Sat

5 Stilwerk

Style is writ large in this trendy shop. Stilwerk is not a department store, however, but a shopping centre, specializing in designer furniture, lamps and fittings – basically anything good

The famous glass cone at Lafayette

Façade of the Stilwerk shopping centre

and expensive *(see also p85)*.
⊗ *Kantstr. 17, 71 • Map C4 • (030) 31 51 50 • 10am–8pm Mon-Fri, 10am–4pm Sat*

6 Gipsformerei der Preußischen Gärten und Schlösser

If you fancy a Schinkel statue for your home or an elegant Prussian sculpture from the palace gardens, you'll find moulded plaster reproduction in all shapes and sizes here. ⊗ *Sophie-Charlotten-Str. 17–18 • Map A3 • (030) 326 76 90 • 9am–4pm Mon–Fri, till 6pm Wed*

7 Königliche Porzellan-Manufaktur (KPM)

Prussia's glory and splendour to take away – traditional KPM porcelain for your dining table at home. Apart from elegant porcelain dinner services, figures and

accessories made in the Berlin factory are also on sale.
⊗ *Kurfürstendamm 27 • Map P4 • (030) 886 72 10 • 10am–8pm Mon–Fri, 10am–4pm Sat* ⊗ *Unter den Linden 35 • Map F/G3, K3/4 • (030) 206 41 50 • 10am–8pm Mon–Fri, 10am–4pm Sat*

8 Markt am Winterfeldtplatz

The trendiest and also the most attractive weekly food and clothing market in Berlin has developed into a hotspot of the Schöneberg crowd. This is the place for meeting up on Saturday mornings *(see p107)*.

9 Türkenmarkt am Maybachufer

Berlin's largest weekday Turkish market lures visitors with its smells and dishes of a thousand-and-one-nights. Bartering is expected *(see p107)* ⊗ *Maybachufer • Map H5 • 10am–8pm Wed, Thu, noon–6:30pm Tue, Fri*

10 Berliner Antik- und Flohmarkt

Numerous antique and junk shops are hidden underneath the S-Bahn arches at Friedrichstraße Station. Much of it is overpriced, but occasionally you will find a bargain. ⊗ *Friedrichstr., S-Bahn arches • Map J4 • (030) 208 26 45 • 11am–6pm daily exc Tue*

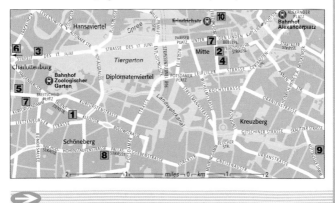

Left **Love Parade** Centre **Christopher Street Day Parade** Right **The Berlin Marathon**

Festivals & Fairs

1 Berliner Filmfestspiele
The Berlinale is the only top German film festival, and is attended by Hollywood stars and German starlets alike. Until 1999, the film festival took place all around the Zoo-Palast cinema; today the traditional festival draws thousands of cinema fans to the area around Potsdamer Platz. *Filmhaus Potsdamer Platz • Map L2 • (030) 25 92 00 • 2nd and 3rd week in February*

Zoo-Palast cinema during the Berlinale

2 Internationale Funkausstellung (IFA)
The latest in entertainment technology from around the world and high-tech toys for young and old are on show at the IFA (International Broadcasting Exhibition) in the ICC. *Messe Berlin, ICC • Map A5 • (030) 303 80 • every 2 years in Aug • Admission charge*

3 Love Parade
Although it has lost some of its original fun, the largest techno-party in the world still attracts a crowd of nearly one million visitors every year to ear-shattering beats in Tiergarten. *Großer Tiergarten • Map M5/6 • (030) 28 46 20 • 2nd or 3rd weekend in July*

4 Christopher-Street-Parade
This gay parade openly and brashly celebrates alternative lifestyles. At the end of June, up to 500,000 gays and lesbians from around the world boisterously dance, drink and celebrate in the streets of Central Berlin *(see also p58). Kurfürstendamm and Straße des 17. Juni • Map P3/4 • (030) 216 80 08 • 4th weekend in June*

5 Berliner Festwochen
Classical concerts, exhibitions and events organized around a particular theme form the cultural highpoint of the year. *Various venues • September*

6 Lange Nacht der Museen
For one night, entrance to many of Berlin's museums is free. Many institutions also put on special events for that weekend, and the street artists and

IFA, ITB and Grüne Woche at the Messe

Karneval der Kulturen

Sports Highlights

1 Berlin-Marathon
The most exuberant marathon in the world attracts thousands of runners.
Straße des 17. Juni • 2nd or 3rd Sunday in September

2 Berlin Parade
Inline-skaters from around the world meet for "blading".
Straße des 17. Juni • June

3 Sechstagerennen
The Six Day Race is one of Berlin's most venerable sports events. Velodrom
• first half January

4 German Open
Top-quality ladies' tennis, usually sold out.
Tennisclub Rot-Weiß • May

5 Berliner Neujahrslauf
The New Year's Day Run is a race for those who are fit and not afraid of the cold.
Brandenburger Tor • Map K3
• 1st January

6 Internationales Stadionfest (ISTAF)
Germany's biggest athletics festival.
Olympiastadion
• 1st week in September

7 DFB-Pokalfinale
German's soccer Cup Final is played to a crowd of 76,000 fans every year.
Olympiastadion

8 Deutsches Traberderby
The derby for professional trotter races. Trabrennbahn Mariendorf • 1st week in August

9 Internationales Reitturnier
German show-jumpers meet.
Trabrennbahn Mariendorf
• 3rd week in November

10 Berliner Motorradtage
The international meeting of bikers is a noisy event.
Kurfürstendamm • end March

---

sellers entertain the public, who normally wait in long queues.
Berlin museums • (030) 28 39 74 77
• last weekends in January and August

7 Grüne Woche
The largest gourmet feast in the world, Green Week is a tasty agricultural and gastronomical fair for everyone. Nowhere else can you enjoy a culinary journey around the world in such a condensed space.
Messe Berlin, ICC • Map A5
• (030) 303 80 • 2nd half of January
• Admission € 11

8 Theatertreffen Berlin
Since 1963, the most interesting theatre productions from around Germany have been performed annually here in Berlin. Various venues • May
• Admission charge

9 Karneval der Kulturen
Multicultural Berlin celebrates for three days in the colourful Kreuzberg district in a cheerful street carnival parade.
Kreuzberg • Map G/H5/6 • Whitsun

10 Internationale Tourismusbörse (ITB)
The world's largest tourism fair offers up-to-date information to the general public, often at elaborately designed stalls. The nighttime shows put on by many of the exhibiting countries are especially popular.
Messe Berlin • Map A5 • (030) 303 80
• March • Admission € 11.50

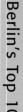

Left **Filmpark Babelsberg** Centre **Roller-skating in Berlin** Right **In Museumsdorf Düppel**

🔟 Children's Attractions

1 Deutsches Technikmuseum

The technology museum is a giant playground for children, excellent for learning through play. There are locomotives to clamber over, windmills to play with and the exhibition "Spektrum", where older children can conduct their own physics and chemistry experiments *(see p103)*.

2 Labyrinth Kindermuseum

Berlin's only Museum for Children is particularly suitable for children at the preschool stage and in the early school years. Three or four themed exhibitions each year deal with subjects in a child-friendly and entertaining way – for example "Snoops and Detectives". Every exhibition is interactive, allowing children to join in and become independent through their experiences in play.
⊛ *Osloer Str. 12 • 9am–1pm Mon; 9am–4pm Tue, Thu, Fri; 9am–6pm Wed; 1–6pm Sat; 11am–6pm Sun • (030) 49 30 89 01 • Admission € 4, families € 8*

3 Grips-Theater

This famous Berlin theatre for children and young people has been showing the hit musical "Linie 1" for over ten years. The play, which is best suited to older children and adolescents, tells of the exciting life in the big city, using a U-Bahn line running from East to West as a metaphor. ⊛ *Altonaer Str. 22 • Map D3 • Phone for performance times • (030) 39 74 74 77 • Admission charge*

4 Museumsdorf Düppel

A visit to the historical museum village of Düppel is like time travel back to the Middle Ages. Children can watch activities such as sowing, harvesting and feeding *(see p91)*.

5 Zoologischer Garten

If you are visiting Berlin with children you should not miss out on the Zoo. Particular favourites are the Monkey House (with baby gorillas and chimpanzees) and the Baby Zoo, where children are allowed to touch and feed the young of various animal species *(see pp36–7)*.

Giraffe House in the Zoo

6 Filmpark Babelsberg

Exciting shoot-outs, a walk-on film set with a U-boat, a town on an island and a small town in the Wild West are the most popular attractions at the film park – and not just with the children. A tour of the former UFA-Film studios lets visitors look behind the scenes: children try out make-up and costumes and admire the "sandman", a TV figure popular with children in East Germany since 1959. Everywhere in the park you will encounter props and figures from well-known German films. "Special Effects" are demonstrated on the visitors in an imaginative exhibition. The "World of Horror" chills more than just children's spines.

The Sandman in Filmpark Babelsberg

🕲 Großbeerenstr., Potsdam • mid-Mar–Nov: 10am–6pm daily; Jul–Aug: 10am–8pm daily • (01805) 34 66 66 • Admission charge

ZEISS-Großraum-planetarium
7
Artificial stars, planets and nebulae take you to far-away galaxies under the silvery dome of the Planetarium (see p142).

blub-Badeparadies
8
After a long day, the ideal place for resting and reviving tired children's feet and legs – and those of their parents – is a visit to the blub Swimming Paradise, one of Germany's largest water parks with water slides, outdoor pool, saunas and children's pool. 🕲 Buschkrugallee 64 • 10am–11pm daily • (030) 606 60 60 • Admission charge

Puppentheater-museum
9
This small but excellent and inspirational Puppet Museum specializes in dolls and puppets. Children are allowed to perform their own puppet shows and have a go at being puppet theatre directors.
🕲 Karl-Marx-Str. 135 • Map H6 • 9am–4pm Mon–Fri, 11am–5pm Sun • (030) 687 81 32 • Admission charge

Domäne Dahlem
10
This old manor house, built in 1680, offers a rare insight into rural life in the Berlin area 100 years ago. Next door is a farm with animals, fields and a vegetable garden. This historical farm is very popular, not just with city children. A small market creates a genuinely rural atmosphere, and children can try out country activities such as sowing and harvesting for themselves, watch cows being milked and horses being shoed, and get close to beehives. 🕲 Königin-Luise-Str. 49 • 10am–6pm Wed–Mon • (030) 831 59 00 • Admission charge

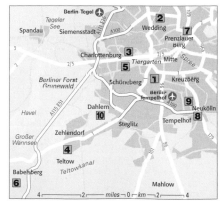

At the Domäne Dahlem

Left **Neuer See** Centre **Landwehrkanal** Right **The 'Moby Dick" ferry on Wannsee**

🔟 Lakes, Rivers & Canals

1 Großer Wannsee

Wannsee has long been a popular destination for Berliners, and it is well worth visiting Strandbad Wannsee. Europe's largest inland beach, it attracts some 40,000 visitors a day who sunbathe on its beautifully white, artificial beach and swim in the lake. This is also a great place for people-watching, and in the summer you will see yachts, wind surfers and jet skis. In the middle of the large lake is Pfaueninsel (Peacock Island), which can be reached on the whale-shaped "Moby Dick" ferry.
🚲 *Am Großen Wannsee*

2 Teufelssee

The dark green waters of the Devils' Lake may conjure up evil, yet this is actually one of Berlin's cleanest lakes. It is also one of the most relaxed and easy-going places – nudists, gay Berliners and dog lovers enjoy peace and tranquillity on the reed-covered banks in the middle of the Grunewald woods.
🚲 *Teufelsberg, Grunewald*

3 Großer Müggelsee

Covering 766 ha (1,900 acres), Berlin's largest lake is situated in the far southeast of the city. Berliners have nicknamed it the "large bathtub" – a good description, for thousands of Berliners congregate here in the heat of summer for a refreshing dip. You can also row, sail or surf on the lake *(see p146)*.

4 Schlachtensee

After Wannsee, Schlachtensee is the second most popular lake in Berlin. The small, elongated lake attracts mainly young people. To avoid the crowds on the sunbathing lawn right next to Schlachtensee S-Bahn station, just follow the embankment path around to the right. There you will find many small and slightly concealed green spaces perfect for sunseekers. The best time to go is during the week.
🚲 *Am Schlachtensee*

5 Spree River

One of Berlin's many epithets is that of "Athens on the Spree", so named because of its cultural heritage and the slowly meandering river. In total, the Spree measures 398 km (249 miles), of which 46 km (29 miles) run through Berlin. Its banks are attractive for rest and recreation, and guided boat tours, romantic evening cruises and walks along the riverside are pleasant ways to spend the day.
🚲 *Mitte, Tiergarten • Map J/K 1–6*

Boat trip to the Spree bend

Houseboats on Landwehrkanal

6 Lietzensee

The Bohemian population of Charlottenburg considers this their "local lake". It is not suitable for swimming, but idyllic meadows around the lake are ideally suited for sunbathing and snoozing. The shaded lakeside walks in the middle of the city are also popular with dog owners. In the evening, the few cafés on the east side offer a great view of the illuminated Funkturm.
🗺 *Am Kaiserdamm • Map A4*

7 Krumme Lanke

Although Krumme Lanke is commonly thought not to be clean enough for bathing, some people now think otherwise. In fact, it seems cleaner (though also colder) than the water in Schlachtensee.
🗺 *Am Fischerhüttenweg*

8 Landwehrkanal

Built in 1845–50, this is Berlin's oldest artificial waterway. The canal connects the Upper and Lower Spree, running east to west through the western part of the centre. Take a boat trip along the canal and you will see some of Berlin's most attractive bridges. At some places, it is possible to lie on the green banks of the canal in the middle of the city, for example at the Paul-Lincke-Ufer in Kreuzberg.
🗺 *Am Fischerhüttenweg • Map M/N5*

9 Tegeler See

The northernmost lake in Berlin is situated in an elegant residential area. A particularly attractive

walk is Greenwich Promenade, from Tegeler Hafen (harbour) to Schwarzer Weg. A small, slightly hidden lakeside path leads from here to the other side of the lake and to a peninsula. Here stands the Villa Borsig, built in 1905 for a family of industrialists. Today it is owned by a foundation and is closed to the public. If you continue southward along Schwarzer Weg, you will get to the Tegeler See lido. 🗺 *Alt-Tegel*

Ship's bell

10 Neuer See

Visitors will be surprised to discover the tranquil New Lake in the middle of the city, well hidden at the western end of the vast Großer Tiergarten park. On its banks is the Café am Neuen See *(see p101)*. A boat trip or a walk around the lake is a pleasant way to while away the day. 🗺 *Großer Tiergarten • Map M3*

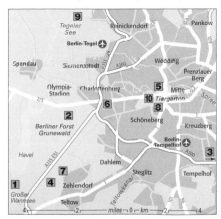

For parks and gardens in Berlin see pp70–71

Left **Inline-Skating in the Tiergarten** Centre **Trabrennbahn Mariendorf** Right **At Sport Oase**

🔟 Sport & Fitness Venues

1 Olympiastadion

The Olympic Stadium is worth a visit even if no particular sports events are scheduled. The giant edifice, constructed by Werner Mach for the Olympic Games in 1936, reflects the architectural style typical of the Nazi period. Two statues by Arno Breker flank the main entrance. Opposite the 80,000-seater stadium are the Maifeld, inspired by the architecture of ancient Rome, and a belltower from where you have fantastic views of Berlin. The stadium itself was renovated and partially covered in 2000–1. Berlin's premier-league football club, Hertha BSC, plays its home games here. An exhibition documents the history of the stadium *(see p84)*.

Hertha BSC playing in the Olympiastadion

2 Galopprennbahn Hoppegarten

Horse races take place against the historical backdrop of the Union Club 1867's traditional race track, considered to be the most attractive track between Moscow and Paris. In the audience, horse- and betting-mad Berliners mingle with the city's upper classes. 🕲 *Goetheallee 1, Dahlwitz-Hoppegarten • races 2pm Sun • (03342) 389 30*

3 Trabrennbahn Mariendorf

Exciting trotting races such as the annual derby for the "Blue Ribbon" take place on the Trabrennbahn in Mariendorf. 🕲 *Mariendorfer Damm 222 • races 6pm Wed, 1:30pm Sun • (030) 740 12 12*

4 Velodrom

This futuristic, silvery sports arena is the focal point for Berlin's cyclists. Every year in January, this is where the legendary Sechstagerennen (Six Day Race) takes place. 🕲 *Paul-Heyse-Str. 26 • times vary depending on event • (030) 44 30 44 30*

5 Cycling

The large green spaces in Berlin and Potsdam are ideal for cycling excursions. Districts such as the Scheunenviertel or Dahlem are also well suited for exploration by bike. There are several places where you can hire a bicycle – for example, in the centre at Friedrichstraße station *(see p162)*.

Hertha BSC: **www.herthabsc.de**

Interior of the Neukölln swimming baths

6 Stadtbad Neukölln

The most attractive swimming baths in Berlin date back to the late 19th century. These luxuriously fitted Art-Nouveau baths make swimming a rather special experience. Ⓢ *Ganghoferstr. 3 • 2–5pm Mon; 6:45–8am, 2:15–6pm Tue; 2:15–6:30pm Wed; 6:45–8am, 1:30–10pm Thu; 6:45–8am, 12:30–10pm Fri; 9am–4pm Sat • (030) 68 24 00 12*

7 Sport Oase

This charming badminton and squash centre is based in a former Schultheiss brewery. It has four halls with 23 courts on several levels; and there is also a bar to relax in after the game. Ⓢ *Stromstr. 11–17 • Map D3 • 8am–11pm daily • (030) 394 50 94*

8 Jopp Frauenfitness

In the western centre of the city is this Fitness Centre for Women, which guarantees a relaxed and cheerful atmosphere for exercise on standard equipment as well as many classes, away from prying eyes. The staff are very helpful. Ⓢ *Tauentzienstr. 13 • Map P5 • 7am–11pm Mon–Fri, 10am–8pm Sat, Sun • (030) 21 01 11*

9 Inline-Skating Tiergarten

The paths and tracks in the northern half of the Großer Tiergarten park, as well as around the perimeters of Straße des 17 Juni, are excellent for inline-skating away from the traffic. Skating in the busy city streets – though practised – is officially forbidden. Ⓢ *Tiergarten • Map M5/6*

10 Fitnessstudio Ars Vitalis

Berlin's friendliest and most elegant fitness studio follows a holistic approach to wellbeing. Visitors can relax, attend classes on a day ticket or enjoy a massage as well as use the pool and sauna. Ⓢ *Hauptstr. 19 • Map E6 • 7am–11:30pm Mon, Thu; 8am–11:30pm Tue, Wed, Fri–Sun • (030) 788 35 63 • Admission charge*

Relaxing in the Ars Vitalis

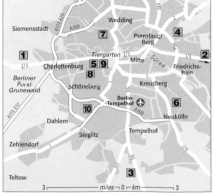

Left **Britzer Schloss and Park** Centre **Neuer See** Right **Schlosspark Charlottenburg**

🔟 Parks & Gardens

1 Großer Tiergarten

Tiergarten – the green lungs of Berlin – is the most famous park in the city. It covers an area of 203 ha (500 acres) and is situated right in the centre of town. Originally designed, in 1833–40, by Peter Joseph Lenné as a hunting estate for the Elector, in the latter half of the 19th century the park became a recreation ground for all Berliners. Today it attracts a happy crowd of cyclists, joggers, sun-bathers and Turkish families having barbecues, especially at weekends.
⊗ *Tiergarten • Map M5/6*

Statue of Luise on Pfaueninsel

2 Schlosspark Charlottenburg

The Palace Park is one of the most attractive and charming green spaces in Germany. Immediately behind Schloss Charlottenburg is a small but magnificent Baroque garden, and beyond this extends a vast park, dating back to the early 19th century. It was landscaped in the English style and boasts artificial lake and river landscapes, small hidden buildings and idyllic shaded groves on the banks of ponds and streams. The park is ideally suited for strolling, and it is also a favourite place for sunseekers *(see also pp28–31)*.
⊗ *Schloss Charlottenburg, Spandauer Damm • Map A/B3 • from sunrise to sunset daily*

3 Grunewald and Teufelsberg

The Grunewald, or "green forest" as the public woods in the southwest of Berlin were known originally, is the least built-up area of woodland in the city. Parts of Grunewald are very quiet and isolated indeed, and there are even wild boar in the woods – which can be a nuisance to people who have gardens in the nearby district of Zehlendorf. Grunewald is excellent for hiking and horse-riding. ⊗ *Grunewald*

4 Pfaueninsel

Peacock Island, an island in the middle of Wannsee that can be reached only by ferry, is probably the most romantic spot in Berlin. In the 19th century, the island served as a love nest for King Friedrich Wilhelm II. His charming folly of a palace ruin was in keeping with the tastes of the time. Today some 100 proud peacocks live in the area around the building *(see p89)*.

5 Botanischer Garten

The 19th-century Botanical Garden is a paradise of flowers and plants in the centre of town. The vast area with 15 greenhouses was built in the late 19th century around gentle hills and picturesque ponds. In the Great Palm House by Alfred Koerner you can see spectacular orchids

Botanischer Garten: **www.bgbm.fu-berlin.de**

and giant Victoria water lilies, reaching a diameter of over 2 m (6 ft). The museum introduces visitors to the world of microbiology. ◎ *Unter den Eichen 5–10 (garden), Königin-Luise-Str. 6 (museum)* • *9am to sunset daily (garden); 10am–6pm daily (museum)* • *(030) 83 85 01 00* • *Admission charge*

Flowering hibiscus in Botanischer Garten

6 Viktoriapark and Kreuzberg

The old municipal park, originally designed in 1888–94 as a recreation area for local workers, is today one of Berlin's most popular green spaces. The meadows around Kreuzberg, which rises to 30 m (98 ft), are great for sunbathing. On top of the mountain, a monument recalls the Prussian Wars of Liberation *(see p105).*

7 Volkspark Friedrichshain

The oldest park in Berlin (1840) is an artificial landscape of lakes and meadows and two heaps of rubble, one of which is jokingly called "Mount Klamott", meaning Mount Rubble. There is also a fairy-tale fountain with statues of the most popular fairy tale characters *(see pp146–7).*

8 Tierpark Friedrichsfelde

This second, smaller zoo is situated in the idyllic palace park of Friedrichsfelde. Some 950 animal species live in the park; the lions are particularly worth seeing *(see p147).*

9 Treptower Park

The 19th-century landscape garden on the banks of the Spree has become famous for the Soviet Memorial, which stands next to the graves of 5,000 Red Army soldiers *(see p146).*

10 Britzer Schloss and Park

The Palace in Britz, dating from 1706, has been furnished with historical furniture from the Gründerzeit (after 1871). It is situated in a lovely park that invites visitors for a rest.
◎ *Alt-Britz 73* • *2–5:30pm Wed (guided tours of the palace), 9am to sunset daily (garden)* • *Admission charge*

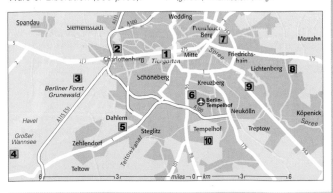

For waterside recreation grounds see pp66–7

Left **Brandenburger Hof** Centre **Inside the Bristol Kempinski** Right **Lobby of the Four Seasons**

🔟 Famous Hotels

Inside the famous Hotel Adlon

1 Hotel Adlon Berlin

Berlin's top hotel ranks as one of the finest in Europe. A reconstruction of the historic Adlon hotel, it opened in 1997 and has become popular with celebrities and politicians from around the globe. Even if you are not going to stay here, you could have a cup of tea or coffee in the magnificent lobby.
⊗ *Unter den Linden 77 • Map K3 • (030) 226 10 • www.hotel-adlon.de • €€€€*

2 Four Seasons

Concealed behind the ultra-modern façade of this hotel is a late 19th-century building with thick carpets, sparkling chandeliers and tasteful wallpaper. Comfort of an international standard and discreet service are guaranteed.
⊗ *Charlottenstr. 49*
• Map K4 • (030) 203 38
• www.fourseasons.com • €€€€

3 Grand Hyatt

Japanese minimalism is the style that was chosen for this new building on Potsdamer Platz. The

spacious rooms overlook the Marlene-Dietrich-Platz, but if this is too mundane for you, you can always enjoy the fantastic views of the entire city from the hotel's Olympus Wellness-Club.
⊗ *Marlene-Dietrich-Platz 2*
• Map F4 • (030) 25 53 12 34
• www.berlin.hyatt.com • €€€€

4 Ritz-Carlton Schlosshotel

This small and very expensive palace hotel is situated in a quiet part of Grunewald, some distance from the centre. The hotel is popular with filmstars and celebrities wishing to get away from the crowds. Karl Lagerfeld designed the interior – and for a mere € 1,500 you can even rent his permanent bedroom suite for one night.
⊗ *Brahmsstr. 10 • (030) 89 58 40*
• www.ritzcarlton.com • €€€€

5 Kempinski Hotel Bristol Berlin

The grand old lady of West Berlin hotels, the Kempinski is beginning to show her age, but the glamour is still there and no hotel in town is better. All the rooms are furnished with a timeless elegance, while the lobby and bar are panelled in dark wood. In the Kempinski-Grill you can enjoy a glass of Sekt right on the Ku'damm while watching less fortunate mortals. ⊗ *Kurfürstendamm 27 • Map P4 • (030) 88 43 40 • www.kempinski-berlin.de • €€€€*

Four Seasons porter

6 Hackescher Markt

One of Berlin's best hotels, the charming Hackescher Markt, is situated right in the popular Mitte district. Service and furnishings are of a four-star standard, yet the prices are moderate. Best of all is the hotel's central location in one of Berlin's liveliest areas: it is only a few steps away from the Hackesche Höfe and the Scheunenviertel.

Große Präsidentenstr. 8
• Map J5 • (030) 28 00 30
• www.hackescher-markt.de • €€

7 Großer Kurfürst

This hotel, part of the DeRag chain, is based in a historic building on Fischerinsel, in a slightly remote spot in the east of the city. The rooms and the lobby all boast many artistic details, while the furnishings are modern. The service is faultless and many attractive luxury extras are available here at reasonable prices. There's a well-appointed fitness area and the hotel restaurant overlooks the Spree River.

Neue Roßstr. 11-12
• Map L6 • (030) 24 60 00 •
www.deraghotels.de • €€€

8 Dorint Hotel am Gendarmenmarkt

A quiet and elegant hotel with great views over the historic square, the relatively small Dorint has real style and offers excellent service. All the rooms are first-class and feature elegant furnishings *(see p179)*.

9 Savoy Hotel

Greta Garbo used to stay at the Savoy, and the style of days gone by is celebrated throughout. Many filmstars are regulars in this hotel, which is justly proud of its service. The Savoy is famous for its Times Bar.

Fasanenstr. 9–10 • Map N4 • (030) 20 37 50 • www.hotel-savoy.com • €€€

Times Bar, Savoy

10 Brandenburger Hof

An elegant town hotel, based in a 19th-century manor house. The lobby is traditionally furnished and the rooms are in a sobre Bauhaus-style. The Michelin-starred Quadriga restaurant specializes in French cuisine.

Eislebener Str. 14
• Map P4 • (030) 21 40 50
• www.brandenburger-hof.com
• €€€

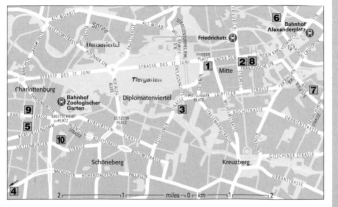

For hotel price categories see p173

Left **Inside First Floor** Centre **Outdoor tables at Lutter & Wegner** Right **The super-trendy Vau**

🔟 Best Places to Eat

1 Vau
The best of international and Austrian cooking is served by Kolja Kleeberg at the stylishly designed Vau. The restaurant has been awarded a well-deserved Michelin star *(see p121)*. 🍴 *Jäger-str. 54–55 • Map L4 • noon–2pm, 7–10:30pm Mon–Sat • (030) 202 97 30*

2 Kaiserstuben
Opposite the Pergamon-museum, this restaurant is one of the best new upmarket restaurants in Berlin, offering traditional German fare of the highest quality, but at top prices. Try one of the set menus – they are more reasonably priced and still of the highest standard.
🍴 *Am Kupfergraben 6a • Map K4 • from 6pm Tue–Sat • (030) 20 45 29 80*

3 Margaux
A newcomer among the gastronomical stars, the Margaux is Berlin's most elegant restaurants, popular with celebrities as well as food-lovers who enjoy its French or German nouvelle cuisine and its successful new interpretations of classic dishes. Michael Hoffmann, the chef, is particularly renowned for his fish and seafood dishes. The wine list includes over 800 top wines *(see p121)*.
🍴 *Unter den Linden 78 • Map K3 • 6pm–1am Mon–Sat • (030) 22 65 26 11*

Inside the Margaux

4 E.T.A. Hoffmann
Based in the Hotel Riehmers Hofgarten, this restaurant has risen to the top of Berlin's gastronomical establishments – largely due to its surprising new creations *(see p109)*.

5 Borchardt
Everyone of importance, including the Chancellor himself, dines at Borchardt. The historic room is furnished in Wilhelminian style (featuring tall columns, wall mosaics and tiles flooring) – an appropriate setting for the classic French cooking. Without a reservation, however, even top politicians can't get a table *(see p121)*. 🍴 *Französische Str. 47 • Map K4 • 11:30am–1am daily • (030) 20 38 71 10*

6 First Floor
This top gourmet restaurant, specializing in the creation of new German dishes, is a well-guarded secret. The menu features traditional Berlin fare such as *eisbein mit sauer-kraut* (pork knuckle with sauerkraut) as well as new creations using fish, langoustines and truffles. The specials of the day are more moderately priced; you are well advised to book a table in advance.
🍴 *Hotel Palace, Budapester Str. 45 • Map N5 • noon–2:30pm and from 6pm Son–Fri, only from 6pm Sat • (030) 25 02 10 20*

borchardt RESTAURANT

The popular Borchardt restaurant

7 Seasons

This elegant dining room with an open fireplace provides an enjoyable setting for a meal. The kitchen specializes in French-inspired and vegetarian dishes *(see p121)*. ✪ *Four Seasons Hotel, Charlottenstr. 49 • Map K4 • 6:30am–11:30am, noon–2:30pm, 6–11:30pm daily • (030) 20 33 63 63*

8 Adermann

An elegant restaurant on the first floor of an old town house in the centre of Scheunenviertel. Note the dressers and the parquet flooring. Especially worth trying are the light, French-style fish dishes *(see p129)*. ✪ *Oranienburger Str. 27 • Map J4 • noon–midnight Tue–Sun • (030) 28 38 73 71*

9 Lutter & Wegner Gendarmenmarkt

In this old building, formerly the Berliner Sektkellerei (supposedly the place where sparkling wine, or *sekt*, was invented), Austrian cuisine is the star. Try the best *wiener schnitzel* in town, accompanied by a classic warm potato salad, at consistently low prices. In the summer, there are tables outdoors. ✪ *Charlottenstr. 56 • Map L4 • 9am–2am daily • (030) 202 95 40*

10 Ana e Bruno

Ana e Bruno's is one of the best restaurants in Berlin, and certainly serves the best Italian food in the city. Don't be shocked when you see the menu: the numbers refer to the calories in a dish rather than to the price – although these are also at the top end *(see p87)*. ✪ *Sophie-Charlotten-Str. 101 • Map A3 • 6:30pm–midnight Tue–Sat • (030) 325 71 10*

At Ana e Bruno's

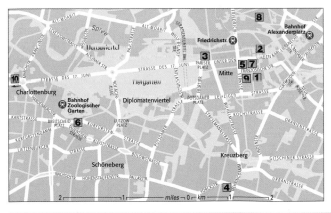

For restaurants in Berlin districts **see pp87, 93, 101, 109, 121**

AROUND
TOWN

BERLIN'S TOP 10

Left **On Savignyplatz** Centre **Front door in Charlottenburg** Right **On Breitscheidplatz**

Charlottenburg & Spandau

CHARLOTTENBURG IS THE ESSENCE OF BERLIN. *Here, the capital is more urbane and more cosmopolitan, more bohemian and more elegant than anywhere else. The historical streets off Ku'damm feature small cafés, restaurants, art galleries and boutiques, based in stout residential houses from the beginning of the 20th century. These streets and Charlottenburg's proud town hall remind us that this district was once the richest town in Prussia, which was only incorporated into the city of Berlin in 1920. Spandau, on the other hand, is rural in comparison, a part of Berlin with a special feel. Spandau's Late Medieval old town and the citadel make this district on the other side of the Spree and Havel seem like a small independent town.*

Prussian Eagle in Spandau

10 Sights

1. Kurfürstendamm
2. Schloss Charlottenburg
3. Zoologischer Garten
4. Zitadelle Spandau
5. Spandau Old Town
6. Savignyplatz
7. Fasanenstraße
8. Funkturm and Messegelände
9. Erotik-Museum
10. Käthe-Kollwitz-Museum

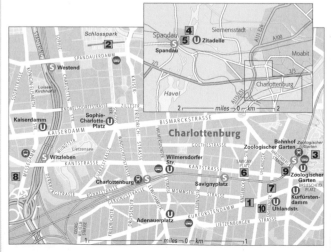

1 Kurfürstendamm

The famous Berlin boulevard, the pride of Charlottenburg, is today more elegant than ever *(see pp24–5)*.

2 Schloss Charlottenburg

The English-style gardens of this Hohenzollern summer residence are ideal for a stroll *(see pp28–31)*. ◐ *Spandauer Damm • Map A/B3 • opening hours see p28 • (030) 20 90 55 55 • Admission charge*

Inside Nikolaikirche, Spandau Old Town

3 Zoologischer Garten

Germany's largest and oldest zoological gardens are a must for all families on a visit to Berlin *(see pp36–37)*.

4 Zitadelle Spandau

The only surviving fortress in Berlin, the citadel, at the confluence of the Havel and Spree Rivers, is strategically well placed. The star-shaped moated fortress, built in 1560 by Francesco Chiaramella da Gandino, was modelled on similar buildings in Italy. Its four powerful corner bastions, named Brandenburg, König (king), Königin (queen) and Kronprinz (crown prince) are especially remarkable. A fortress stood on the same site as early as the 12th century, of which the Juliusturm survives – a keep that served as

a prison in the 19th century. At the time, Berliners used to say, "off to the Julio", when they sent criminals to prison. Later the imperial war treasures were kept here – the reparations paid by France to the German Empire after its defeat in the Franco-Prussian War of 1870–1. The Bastion Königin houses a museum of municipal history. ◐ *Am Juliusturm • 9am–5pm Tue–Fri, 10am–5pm Sat, Sun • (030) 354 94 40 • Admission charge*

5 Spandau Old Town

When walking around Spandau Old Town, it is easy to forget that you are still in Berlin. Narrow alleyways and nooks and crannies around Nikolaikirche are lined by Late Medieval houses, a sign that Spandau was founded in 1197 and is thus older than Berlin itself. Berlin's oldest house, the Gothic House, dating back to the early 16th century, stands here, in Breite Straße 32. ◐ *Breite Straße, Spandau*

Spandau and Berlin

West Berliners consider the Spandauers to be rather different sorts of people, provincial and rough, and not "real" Berliners at all. But the Spandauers can reassure themselves that Spandau is 60 years older than Berlin, and proudly point to their independent history. The mutual mistrust is not just a consequence of Spandau's geographical location, isolated from the remainder of the city by the Havel and Spree Rivers. It is also due to the recent incorporation of Spandau in 1920. Today, still, Spandauers say they are going "to Berlin", even though the centre of the city is only a few stops away on the U-Bahn.

Zitadelle Spandau

Left **A plaque in Savignyplatz** Centre **Literaturhaus Fasanenstraße** Right **Villa Grisebach**

6 Savignyplatz

One of Berlin's most attractive squares is right in the heart of Charlottenburg. Savignyplatz, named after a 19th-century German legal scholar, is the focal point of Charlottenburg's reputation as a district for artists and intellectuals and as a trendy residential area for dining out and entertainment. The square has two green spaces, either side of Kantstraße. It was built in the 1920s as part of an effort to create parks in the centre of town.

Balconies in Savignyplatz

Small paths, benches and pergolas make it a pleasant place for a rest. Dotted all around Savignylatz are restaurants, street cafés and shops, especially in Grolman-, Knesebeck-, and Carmerstraße, all three of which cross the square. Many a reveller has lost his way here, after a night's celebrating, which is why the area is jokingly known as the "Savignydreieck" (the Savigny Triangle). North of Savignyplatz it is worth exploring some of the

most attractive streets in Charlottenburg – Knesebeck-, Schlüter- and Goethestraße. This is still a thriving Charlottenburg community; the small shops, numerous bookstores, cafés and specialist retailers are always busy, especially on Saturdays. South of the square, the red-tiled S-Bahn arches also lure visitors with their shops, cafés and bars; most of all the Savignypassage near Bleibtreustraße and the small passageway between Grolman- and Uhlandstraße on the opposite side of the square.

🔊 *An der Kantstraße • Map N3*

7 Fasanenstraße

This elegant street is the most attractive and the trendiest street off Ku'damm. Designer shops, galleries and restaurants are tucked away here, a shoppers' paradise for all those who regard Kurfürstendamm as a mere retail strip catering for the masses. The junction of Fasanenstraße and Ku'damm is one of the liveliest spots in Berlin. One of the best known places

The Jewish House, in Fasanenstraße

Statue in Savignyplatz

Hotel Bristol Berlin Kempinski, Fasanenstraße

is the "Bristol Berlin Kempinski" *(see p72)* at the northern end of Fasanenstraße. The Lübbecke & Co bank opposite cleverly combines a historic building with a new structure. Next to it are the Jüdisches Gemeindehaus (Jewish Community House, *see p84)* and a little farther along, at the junction with Kantstraße, is the Kant-Dreieck *(see p41)*. Berliner Börse (stock exchange), based in the ultra-modern Ludwig-Erhard-Haus *(see p40)*, is just above, at the corner of Hardenbergstraße. The southern end of the street is dominated by residential villas, some of which may seem a little pompous, as well as the Literaturhaus, Villa Grisebach, one of the oldest art auction houses in Berlin, and the Käthe-Kollwitz-Museum *(see p83)*. There are also some very expensive fashion stores here, as well as a few cosy restaurants. At its southern end, the street leads to picturesque Fasanenplatz, where many artists lived before 1933.
🏵 *Charlottenburg • Map N/P4*

Shops in Fasanenstraße

A Day in Charlottenburg

Morning

🚏 Begin your tour of Charlottenburg at Breitscheidplatz and stroll down **Kurfürstendamm** *(see pp24–5)* in a westerly direction. Turn left into **Fasanenstraße** to visit the **Käthe-Kollwitz-Museum** *(see p83)* and to see the **Literaturhaus**. You could stop for a mid-morning breakfast at **Café Wintergarten** *(see p86)* in the Literaturhaus, before going back up Fasanenstraße in a northerly direction. On the left you will pass the Hotel **Bristol Berlin Kempinski**, and on the right you can see the Jewish House and the Ludwig-Erhard-Haus. Diagonally opposite, on the other side of Kantstraße, stands the **Theater des Westens** *(see p57)*. Continue along Kantstraße on the left side until you reach the shopping centre **Stilwerk** *(see pp60–61)*, a place no one has ever been known to leave without buying something!

Afternoon

🍴 A good place for lunch is the **Restaurant Stil** *(see p87)* in the Stilwerk shopping centre. Afterwards, continue along Kantstraße to **Savignyplatz.** Now explore the small streets around the square, Grolman-, Carmer-, Knesebeck- and Mommsenstraße. Small shops invite you to browse and spend your money, and the **Café Savigny** *(see p86)* is a good place for a fruit flan with whipped cream and a cup of coffee. For the early evening, **Schell** *(see p87)* is recommended; here you could try fresh pike-perch or one of the Mediterranean dishes.

Around Town – Charlottenburg & Spandau

Ehrenhalle in the Messegelände

8 Funkturm and Messegelände

The 150 m (492 ft) high Funk-turm (TV tower), reminiscent of the Eiffel Tower in Paris, is one of the landmarks of Berlin that can be seen from afar. Built in 1924 to plans by Heinrich Straumer, it served as an aerial and as an air-traffic control tower. The viewing platform at 125 m (410 ft) pro-vides magnificent views, while the restaurant, situated at 55 m (180 ft), overlooks the oldest part of the complex, the exhibition centre and the surrounding pavil-lions. The giant building in the

The Berliner Funkturm

The History of Charlottenburg

The magnificent Charlottenburger Rathaus (town hall) on Otto-Suhr-Allee is a reminder of the time when this district of 200,000 people was an independent town. Charlottenburg, named after the eponymous palace, arose in 1705 from the medieval settlement of Lietzow. Towards the end of the 19th century, Charlottenburg – then Prussia's wealthiest town – enjoyed a meteoric rise following the construction of the Westend colony of villas and of Kurfürstendamm. Thanks to its numerous theatres, the opera and the Technical University, the district developed into Berlin's west end during the 1920s.

east is the Hall of Honour built to designs by Richard Ermisch in 1936, in the colossal Fascist architectural style.

On the opposite side rises the shiny silver ICC, the International Congress Centrum, built in 1975–9 by Ralf Schüler and Ursulina Schüler-Witte. The ICC is still considered one of the advanced conference centres in the world, with 80 rooms for up to 5,000 visitors. Berlin's vast exhibition grounds are among the largest in the world, covering an area of 160,000 sq m (40 acres). These play host to, among others, Grüne Woche (green week, an agricultural fair), Internationale Tourismusbörse (international tourism fair) and Internationale Funkausstellung (international TV fair). ◎ *Messedamm 22 • Map A4/5 • 11am–9pm Mon; 10am–10pm Tue–Sun • (030) 30 38 29 96 • Admission charge*

9 Erotik-Museum

Beate Uhse, who headed an empire of erotica until her death

in 2001, set a monument to herself with this unusual museum. Erotic art and kitsch, hailing from all cultures and all periods of history, and which normally remain hidden away in private bedrooms, are on public display here. Next door is a cinema and a Beate Uhse sex shop.
🔹 *Kantstr. 5 • Map N4 • 9am–midnight daily • (030) 886 06 66 • Admission charge (over 18 years only)*

10 Käthe-Kollwitz-Museum
The museum is dedicated to the work of the Berlin artist Käthe Kollwitz (1897–1945), who documented the misery of workers' lives in 1920s Berlin in numerous prints, graphics and sketches. After losing a son and a grandson in World War I, she concentrated on the themes of war and motherhood. The museum holds some 200 of her works, including several self-portraits.
🔹 *Fasanenstr. 24 • Map P4*
• 11am–6pm Wed–Mon • (030) 882 52 10
• Admission charge

Mother and Child by Käthe Kollwitz

A Day in Spandau

Morning

⏱ Start with a journey on the U-Bahn. From the centre of town, take a U2 train in the direction of Ruhleben, and at Bismarckstraße station change to the U7 train in the direction of Rathaus Spandau. Ten minutes later you will have reached the centre of **Spandau Old Town** *(see p79)*, where you can visit Breite Straße and Nikolaikirche.

Before returning to Charlottenburg, make sure you visit the **Zitadelle Spandau**. There, in the museum café, you can also enjoy a late breakfast. Return by U-Bahn. This time, get off the train at the Wilmersdorfer Straße station, one of the few pedestrianized areas in Berlin. This is a particularly good area for shopaholics and bargain hunters.

Afternoon

From Wilmersdorfer Straße a 20-minute walk along Kaiserdamm in a westerly direction will take you to the **Funkturm** and the **Messegelände** with the "Ehrenhalle". You could have lunch at the **Funkturm-Restaurant**, and enjoy the magnificent views. Nearby, the Haus des Rundfunks (broadcasting house) and the **Georg-Kolbe-Museum** *(see p84)* are worth visiting. After your museum visit, if you still have some time and energy, you could take bus No. 218 from here to the **Olympiastadion** *(see p68)*. In the evening, return to Charlottenburg and Savignyplatz by bus No 149. Here you can enjoy the justly famed, delicious Franconian cooking at **Florian's** *(see p87)*.

Left **In the Deutsche Oper** Centre **Denkmal Benno Ohnesorg** Right **In the Theater des Westens**

Best of the Rest

1 Olympiastadion
The stadium built for the Olympic Games in 1936 is typical of the Fascist style of architecture *(see p68)*. ◈ Olympischer Platz • Apr–Oct: 9am–6pm daily • (030) 305 81 23

2 Georg-Kolbe-Museum
Sculptures by Georg Kolbe (1877–1947) are exhibited in his home and workshop. ◈ Sensburger Allee 25 • 10am–5pm Tue–Sun • (030) 304 21 44 • Admission charge

3 Le-Corbusier-Haus
The apartment block where the French architect Corbusier lived was built for the 1957 Interbau trade fair. Designed to alleviate the acute housing shortage after World War II, it was highly innovative in its day. ◈ Flatowallee 16

4 Jüdisches Gemeindehaus
Berlin's Jewish community house stands on the site of the Charlottenburg synagogue. Damaged during "Reichskristallnacht" on 9 November 1938, it was mostly destroyed during World War II. Only the portal remains. ◈ Fasanenstr. 79–80 • Map P4 • 10am–6:30pm daily • (030) 88 02 82 23

5 Theater des Westens
This theatre is based in an attractive building from 1895–6. Renowned for its fare of light entertainment, it is regarded as one of Germany's best musical theatres *(see p57)*. ◈ Kantstr. 12. • Map N4 • 8pm Tue–Sat, 6pm Sun • (01 80) 599 89 99

6 Deutsche Oper
The German Opera, opened in 1961, specializes in Italian and German classics. ◈ Bismarckstr. 34–37 • Map B4 • (030) 343 84 01 • Admission charge

7 Denkmal Benno Ohnesorg
Alfred Hrdlicka's sculpture from 1971 commemorates the student Benno Ohnesorg, who was shot dead here during a demonstration on 2 April 1967. ◈ Bismarckstr. • Map B4

8 Technische Universität
Berlin's Technical University was founded in 1879. ◈ Straße des 17. Juni • Map C4 • 8am–8pm Mon–Fri • (030) 31 40

9 Universität der Künste
The School of Art is one of the best German universities for the fine arts, architecture and design. ◈ Hardenbergstr. 32–33 • Map N4 • 8am–8pm Mon–Fri • (030) 318 50

10 Straße des 17. Juni
An east–west axis through Berlin, the road is named after the workers' uprising in 1953. ◈ Charlottenburg • Map M4/5

Deutsche Oper: **www.deutsche-oper.berlin.de**

Left **Zille-Hof** Centre **Butter Lindner** Right **Herr Schmitt in King's Teagarden**

Shops & Markets

1 Stilwerk
A shopping centre, specializing in stylish designer goods *(see p60).* ✆ *Kantstr. 17. • Map C4*
• *(030) 31 51 50*

2 Antik- und Flohmarkt Straße des 17. Juni
Berlin's largest antiques, art and flea market, selling excellent items *(see p60).* ✆ *Straße des 17. Juni • Map M4 • 10am–5pm Sat, Sun*

3 KPM
Delicate Berlin porcelain with Prussian subjects *(see p61).*
✆ *Kurfürstendamm 27 • Map P4*
• *(030) 886 72 10*

4 Kiepert
Berlin's largest bookseller sells anything from books and maps to CDs and PC games in its main store. In front of the shop, the book bazaar offers second-hand and reduced books at low prices. ✆ *Hardenbergstr. 4–5 • Map M3 • (030) 31 18 80*

5 Bucherbogen
Berlin's leading arts and photography bookseller is tucked away within three arches under the S-Bahn viaduct. ✆ *Savignyplatz • Map N3 • (030) 31 86 95 11*

6 Jil Sander
Simple, elegant designer fashions for men and women are for sale at this upmarket, stylishly cool boutique.
✆ *Kurfürstendamm 185 • Map P4*
• *(030) 343 82 50*

7 Butter Lindner
This traditional Berlin store specializes in fresh, home-made foods and delicatessen. Of its numerous branches the most attractive one is in Charlottenburg. ✆ *Knesebeckstr. 92 • Map P3*
• *8:30am–8pm Mon–Fri, 8.30am–4pm Sat*
• *(030) 313 53 75*

8 Patrick Hellmann
Ladies' and gentlemen's fashions made from the best materials, including Hellmann's own collection and clothes from well-known designers.
✆ *Kurfürstendamm 53 & Bleibtreustr. 20*
• *Map P3 • 10am–8pm Mon–Fri, 10am–4pm Sat • (030) 882 25 65*

9 King's Teagarden
Tea retailer Werner Schmitt personally advises his customers on the many teas available in Berlin's best tea shop. ✆ *Kurfürstendamm 217 • Map P4 • 9:30am–7pm Mon–Fri, 9:30am–4pm Sat • (030) 883 70 59*

10 Zille-Markt
Bric-à-brac market, with a vast albeit expensive selection. ✆ *Fasanenstr. 15 • Map P4 • 10am–6pm Mon–Fri, 10am–4pm Sat • (030) 313 43 33*

Left **Café Wintergarten** Centre **Café Leysieffer** Right **Café Filmbühne am Steinplatz**

🔟 Cafés

1 Café Wintergarten im Literaturhaus
One of Berlin's most beautiful cafés is based in the conservatory of an old town house. In summer guests can sit outside, in the Literaturhaus garden. ✪ *Fasanenstr. 23 • Map P4 • 9:30am–1am daily • (030) 882 54 14 • no credit cards*

2 Café Savigny
This gay and lesbian café, with traditional interior, has a relaxed atmosphere; the fruit flans are particularly worth trying. ✪ *Grolmanstr. 53–54 • Map N3 • 9am–1am daily • (030) 312 81 95*

3 Café Leysieffer
Café Leysieffer, one of Berlin's oldest patisseries, is based in the former Chinese embassy. ✪ *Kurfürstendamm 218 • Map P4 • 10am–8pm Mon–Sat, 11am–7pm Sun • (030) 885 74 80 • no credit cards*

4 Café Kranzler
The new Café Kranzler is very different from the historic café of pre-World War II fame, yet the views over Ku'damm are just as amazing. ✪ *Kurfürstendamm 18 • Map P4 • 9:30am–midnight daily • (030) 887 18 39 25*

5 Café Filmbühne am Steinplatz
Other cafés may sell better cakes, but this coffee shop excels thanks to its student atmosphere. ✪ *Hardenbergstr. 12 • Map N3 • 9am–2am Sun–Thu, 9am–3am Fri, Sat • (030) 312 65 89*

6 Café Hardenberg
The Technical University's student café has a great atmosphere and reasonable prices. ✪ *Hardenbergstr. 10 • Map N3 • 9am–1am daily • (030) 312 26 44 • no credit cards*

7 Café Balzac
One of several modelled on the US Starbucks chain, this café is based in Kiepert bookstore. ✪ *Hardenbergstr. 4–5 • Map M3 • 10am–8pm Mon–Fri, 10am–6pm Sat • (030) 31 80 01 82 • no credit cards*

8 Café Aedes
This modern café, based in an S-Bahn arch, forms part of an architectural gallery. ✪ *Savignyplatz-Passage • Map N3 • 9am–midnight daily • (030) 31 50 95 35*

9 Café Wellenstein
Viennese coffee shop with a great outdoor terrace. ✪ *Kurfürstendamm 190 • Map P3 • 9am–1am daily • (030) 881 78 50*

10 Schwarzes Café
Alternative rock café, offering all-day breakfasts. ✪ *Kantstr. 148 • Karte N4 • Open around the clock • (030) 313 80 38 • no credit cards*

Note: *All restaurants accept credit cards and offer vegetarian dishes unless stated otherwise.*

Left **Entrance of Stil** Centre **The Schell, near Savignyplatz**

🔟 Restaurants

Price Categories

For a three-course
meal for one with half
a bottle of wine (or
equivalent meal), taxes
and charges included

€ under € 20
€€ € 20–30
€€€ € 30–45
€€€€ € 45–60
€€€€€ over € 60

1 Paris-Bar
Berlin's most famous French restaurant boasts sophisticated cuisine and a fantastic atmosphere with many celebrities. ⊗ *Kantstr. 152 • Map N3 • noon–2am daily • €€*

2 Alt-Luxemburg
Chef Karl Wannemacher (one Michelin star) dishes up good international and German food. ⊗ *Windscheidstr. 31 • 5pm–midnight Mon–Sat • (030) 323 87 30 • €€€€*

3 Stil
Sophisticated fish and game dishes, often in creative new combinations, served in stylish surroundings. ⊗ *Kantstr. 17 • Map N3 • 10am–1am Mon–Sat, 11am–1am Sun • (030) 315 18 60 • €€€*

4 Lubitsch
A small, elegant restaurant, serving German and Italian "fusion" food. ⊗ *Bleibtreustr. 47 • Map N/P3 • 9:30am–1am Mon–Sat, 6pm–1am Sun • (030) 882 37 56 • €€*

5 Florian
Trendy and popular with film lovers; food from southern Germany. ⊗ *Grolmanstr. 52 • Map N3 • 6pm–3am daily • (030) 313 91 84 • €€*

6 First Floor
A 1920s-style restaurant, serving traditional Berlin and French food. ⊗ *Budapester Str. 45 • Map N5 • noon–2:30pm and 6–10:30pm Sun–Fri, 6–10:30pm Sat • (030) 25 02 10 20 • €€*

7 Dressler
Everything at Dressler's looks, smells and tastes as it would in a real French brasserie. In winter, the game and poultry dishes are well worth trying. ⊗ *Kurfürstendamm 207–208 • Map C5 • 10am–1am daily • (030) 883 35 30 • €€*

8 Bovril
The tables of regulars are marked with brass plaques, but anyone will enjoy the French menu and outstanding wine list. ⊗ *Kurfürstendamm 184 • Map C5 • 11am–2am Mon–Sat • (030) 881 84 61 • €€*

9 Schell
This French-Italian restaurant serves an amazing breakfast and light fish dishes in the evening. ⊗ *Knesebeckstr. 22 • Map N3 • 10am–midnight daily • (030) 312 83 10 • €€€*

10 Ana e Bruno
The best, friendliest and most tasteful Italian restaurant, Ana e Bruno is the best – and most expensive – Italian restaurant in Berlin ⊗ *Sophie-Charlotten-Str. 101 • Map A3 • 6:30pm–midnight Tue–Sat • (030) 325 71 10 • €€€€*

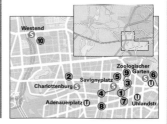

Around Town – Charlottenburg & Spandau

Left **Landing stage Wannsee** Centre **Castle ruins on Pfaueninsel** Right **Jacobsbrunnen Pfaueninsel**

Grunewald & Dahlem

BERLIN'S *green south, which includes the districts of Grunewald and Dahlem, is dotted with numerous lakes, rivers, small castles, private estates and residential villas, leafy roads and cafés for daytrippers. Grunewald and Dahlem have managed to preserve their rural character, although affluent and famous Berliners have always built their houses here. There are many attractions in Berlin's southwest: visitors can enjoy extensive walks in the Grunewald forest, or ferry across the picturesque lake to Pfaueninsel, an island with romantic castle ruins – and a favourite destination for locals. The swimming baths at Wannsee, Europe's largest inland beach, welcomes up to 40,000 visitors a day for fun, games and a dip in the water and on its beautiful white beaches. The museum complex in Dahlem, too, with its outstanding ethnographic and art collections, is worth visiting. Meanwhile, the Alliiertenmuseum and the Haus der Wannsee-Konferenz recall a more painful period in Berlin's history.*

A peacock on Pfaueninsel

🔟 Sights

1. Dahlem Museums
2. Pfaueninsel
3. Schloss Klein-Glienicke
4. Gedenkstätte Haus der Wannsee-Konferenz
5. Strandbad Wannsee
6. Alliiertenmuseum
7. Mexikoplatz
8. Dahlem Villas
9. Jagdschloss Grunewald
10. Museumsdorf Düppel

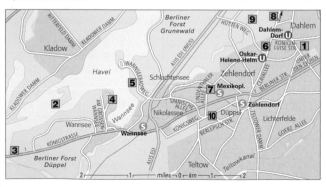

1 Dahlem Museums

These four museums in south Berlin, dedicated to foreign cultures and peoples, feature one of Germany's best ethnocultural collections. The Ethnological Museum holds around one million items from around the world, especially artistic and cult objects from Africa, as well as exhibits from North-American Indians. Full-scale wooden huts and boats from the island populations of the South Pacific as well as a large collection of ceramic and stone sculptures from the Mayas, Aztecs and Incas are particularly impressive.

Exhibit in a Dahlem Museum

The Museum für Ostasiatische Kunst, focusing on 1,000 years of Far-Eastern culture, displays mainly objects in porcelain and lacquer from Korea, China and Japan. The shiny green jade exhibits from ancient China are just as amazing. 🔊 *Lansstr. 8 (Museum Europäischer Kulturen: Im Winkel 6–8)* • *10am–6pm Tue–Fri, 11am–6pm Sat, Sun* • *(030) 830 11* • *Admission charge*

2 Pfaueninsel

Visitors are enchanted by the romantic palace ruins and the eponymous peacocks that run around here. The Wannsee island, which can only be reached by ferry, is one of the most charming spots for a walk in Berlin *(see also p70)*. 🔊 *Pfaueninselchaussee* • *10am–1pm & 1:30–5pm Tue–Fri* • *(030) 80 58 68 32* • *ticket*

Gryffin at Schloss Klein-Glienicke

3 Schloss Klein-Glienicke

One of the most beautiful Hohenzollern palaces in Berlin, this romantic castle with its extensive park was built by Schinkel in 1824–60 as a summer residence for Prince Carl of Prussia. The landscape garden, designed by Peter Joseph Lenné, hides many secrets – for example pavilions called "Große" and "Kleine Neugierde" (large and small curiosity), a garden house and a teahouse, a casino right on the water (a former apartment for guests) as well as the Orangerie (a greenhouse). 🔊 *Königstr. 36* • *mid-May–mid-Oct: 10am–5pm Sat, Sun* • *(030) 805 30 41* • *Admission charge*

4 Gedenkstätte Haus der Wannsee-Konferenz

It is hard to believe that something as abhorrent as the Holocaust could have been planned at this elegant villa in a picturesque spot on Wannsee. Built in 1914–15 by Paul Baumgarten in the style of a small Neo-Baroque palace for the businessman Ernst Marlier, it was here that the

Wannsee Conference memorial

Nazi elite, among them the infamous Adolf Eichmann, met on 20 January 1942 to discuss the details of the mass extermination of Jews. An exhibition at the memorial documents both the conference and its consequences as well as the history of the villa. 🔊 *Am Großen Wannsee 56–58* • *10am–6pm daily* • *(030) 805 00 10* • *Admission charge*

Prussia and Antiquity

From 1821, the landscape designer Peter Joseph Lenné and the architect Karl Friedrich Schinkel tried to turn the Potsdam countryside and its woods and lakes into an "island paradise". Their concept was based on Classical ideas of the harmonious ensemble of architecture and landscape, in accordance with the idealized views of antiquity prevalent in the Neo-Classical period. The architectural style of Prussian palaces thus harks back to Greek and Roman models and the Italian Renaissance.

Villa Seebergsteig No. 23

flanked by elegant semi-circular Art-Nouveau apartment blocks, and in front of these stands Berlin's last remaining Art-Deco-style S-Bahn station. The yellow buildings are covered in green shingles and, in summer, the balconies are richly decked with greenery and flowers. Some of Berlin's most magnificent mansion houses line both sides of Argentinische and Lindenthaler Allee. Many celebrities live in the area around the square. ✎ *Mexikoplatz*

5 Strandbad Wannsee

Europe's largest inland beach is a surprisingly picturesque spot in the middle of the large city, attracting up to 40,000 visitors a day. The swimming baths were built in 1929–30 as a recreation area for workers in the neighbouring districts *(see p66)*. ✎ *Wannseebadeweg 25 • Apr–Oct: 10am–7pm Mon–Fri, 8am–8pm Sat, Sun • (030) 803 56 12 • Admission charge*

6 Alliiertenmuseum

Visitors stroll around this museum reminiscing and recalling the 50 or so years of partnership between Western Allies and West Berliners. The museum, based in a former US-barracks, employs uniforms, documents, weapons and military equipment to tell the story of Berlin's postwar history, though not only from the military point of view. ✎ *Clay-allee 135 • 10am–6pm daily exc Wed • (030) 818 19 90 • Admission charge*

7 Mexikoplatz

Idyllic Mexikoplatz in the southern district of Zehlendorf is one of the most atmospheric and architecturally fascinating squares in Berlin. The two round green spaces in the centre are

8 Dahlem Villas

Some of Berlin's most attractive villas, dating back to the 19th century, are found in the streets surrounding the Grunewald S-Bahn station. Especially worth seeing are Nos. 15 and 11 in Winklerstraße, the latter of which was built by Hermann Muthesius in the style of an English country mansion. Villa Maren, at No. 12 next door, is a beautiful example of the Neo-Renaissance style. The villas in Seebergsteig No. 23 and in Furtwänglerstraße are also worth a detour. ✎ *Am Großen Wannsee*

Villa at No. 11 Winklerstraße

Alliiertenmuseum: **www.alliiertenmuseum.de**

Jagdschloss Grunewald

9 Jagdschloss Grunewald

The small gleaming white palace in Grunewald, dating back to 1542, served as a hunting lodge for the Electors. The castle, built in the Renaissance and Baroque styles, houses a small collection of German and Dutch paintings. ◈ *Hüttenweg 100, Grunewaldsee • May–Oct: 10am–5pm Tue–Sun; Nov–Apr: 10am–4pm Sat, Sun • (030) 969 43 18 • Admission charge*

10 Museumsdorf Düppel

The open-air museum at Düppel is a reminder of the fact that Berlin once consisted of a series of villages, with one of the oldest settlements dating back to the 13th century. The lively museum is animated by actors, who are dressed and act out daily life as it would have been during the Middle Ages – at least during opening hours. There are fascinating live demonstrations of ancient crafts such as bread-baking, pottery and basket-weaving. Plants are grown as in medieval times for their various uses. ◈ *Clauertstr. 11 • Apr–Oct: 10am–5pm Sun, 3pm–7pm Thu • (030) 802 33 10 • Admission charge*

At Museumsdorf Düppel

A Day in the South

Morning

Start your morning walk through Berlin's southern districts by taking the S-Bahn (lines S7 and S1) to **Mexikoplatz**. Here you can admire the beautiful villas and the lovely green square before dropping in to **Café Krone** in Argentinische Allee for a late breakfast. After refreshments continue on foot or by bus (No. 211) southwards to the open-air museum **Museumsdorf Düppel**. From there return by bus via Argentinische Allee to the **Alliiertenmuseum**. From the museum you can stroll across Königin-Luise-Straße and through the picturesque streets right up to the beer garden **Luise** *(see p93)* at the Free University, where you may like to have lunch.

Afternoon

Start your afternoon walk at the **Dahlem Museums** *(see p89)*. One you have enjoyed this cultural break, continue by U-Bahn (U2, Dahlem-Dorf) to Krumme Lanke, and from there, on foot, to the S-Bahn station Mexikoplatz. The S-Bahn will take you to Wannsee S-Bahn station, from where you can reach all the sights in the southwestern corner of Berlin. When the weather is right, visit **Strandbad Wannsee**, or visit the **Haus der Wannsee-Konferenz** *(see p89)* and then admire the **Dahlem Villas** around Grunewald station. After your walk allow yourself to be tempted by coffee and cake or supper at the **Remise in Schloss Klein-Glienicke** *(see p93)*. Your best option for the return journey is the S-Bahn.

Left **Onkel-Tom-Siedlung** Centre **St.-Annen-Kirche** Right **Outside the Free University Berlin**

₁₀ Best of the Rest

1 Stolpe
This small village has managed to retain its original character to the present day.

2 Grunewaldturm
Fantastic views can be had from the red Neo-Gothic brick tower, built in 1897 as a memorial to Kaiser Wilhelm I. It now houses a restaurant. ◈ *Havelchaussee*

3 Onkel-Tom-Siedlung
The "Uncle Tom's Hut" settlement, developed in 1926–32 according to designs by Bruno Taut and others, was intended to create a modern housing estate for workers, unlike their old narrow, dark tenement blocks.
◈ *Argentinische Allee*

4 Free University
The campus of Berlin's largest university, founded in 1948 as a rival to East-Berlin Humboldt University, covers large parts of Dahlem. It is worth looking at the 1950s Henry-Ford-Bau and the so-called *Rostlaube* (rusting hut), at present being redesigned by Sir Norman Foster. ◈ *Garystr.*

5 Teufelsberg
Both the hill and the lake, the dark green Teufelssee, are popular destinations for a day out at the weekend, for flying kites, biking and sunbathing.

6 Kirche St. Peter und Paul
This wooden church, built in 1834–7 by F. A. Stüler, resembles Russian-Orthodox churches. This church is a popular venue for marriage ceremonies.
◈ *Nikolskoer Weg • 9am–6pm Mon–Sat • (030) 805 21 00*

7 Blockhaus Nikolskoe
The log cabin, built in 1819, was a present from King Friedrich Wilhelm III to his daughter Alice (Alexandra) and his son-in-law, future Tsar Nicholas I. The wooden Russian-style *dacha* was restored after a fire in 1985.
◈ *Nikolskoer Weg 15 • from 10am Fri–Mon • (030) 805 29 14*

8 Heinrich von Kleist's Tomb
The German playwright Kleist and his lover Henriette Vogel committed suicide by shooting themselves in 1811; they are buried here together (Königstraße at the S-Bahn overpass).
◈ *Bismarckstr. 3, Am Kleinen Wannsee*

9 St.-Annen-Kirche
The 14th-century Gothic church is a typical Berlin country church. Attractive murals depict scenes from the life of Saint Anna. Also on display are 11 late-Gothic figures of saints and a Baroque pulpit. ◈ *Königin-Luise-Str./Pacelliallee*

10 Teltower Damm
The main shopping street in the district of Zehlendorf has managed to preserve its charming village character. ◈ *Zehlendorf, at S-Bahn station Zehlendorf*

Price Categories

For a three-course	€	under € 20
meal for one with half	€€	€ 20–30
a bottle of wine (or	€€€	€ 30–45
equivalent meal), taxes	€€€€	€ 45–60
and charges included	€€€€€	over € 60

Left **Sign of the Wirtshaus Paulsborn** Right **Enjoying an outdoor meal at Blockhaus Nikolskoe**

Restaurants & Beer Gardens

1 Loretta am Wannsee
This restaurant, a favourite with day trippers to Wannsee, attracts visitors with its giant beer garden, shaded by chestnut trees, and a great atmosphere.
⊗ *Kronprinzessinnenweg 260*
• *9am–midnight daily* • *(030) 803 51 56*
• *no credit cards* • *€*

2 Forsthaus Paulsborn
A rustic restaurant next to Jagdschloss Grunewald, based in an old hunting lodge.
⊗ *Hüttenweg 90* • *summer: 11am–11pm Tue–Sun; winter: 11am–6pm Tue–Sun*
• *(030) 818 19 10* • *€€*

3 Wirtshaus Schildhorn
Nouvelle cuisine in Grune-wald. In summer you can enjoy your *bratwurst* outside, in a pic-turesque spot right on Wannsee.
⊗ *Havelchaussee/Straße am Schildhorn 4a*
• *summer: 11am–midnight daily; winter: 11am–10pm Sat, Sun*
• *(030) 305 31 11* • *€€*

4 Blockhaus Nikolskoe
Traditional German fare is served in this historic log cabin, built as a Russian *dacha*. ⊗ *Nikols-koer Weg 15* • *from 10am Fri–Wed* • *(030) 805 29 14* • *no credit cards* • *€€*

5 Wirtshaus zur Pfaueninsel
A small venue, serving rustic German food in the open air. This is an ideal place for refresh-ments before a visit to Pfauenin-sel. ⊗ *Pfaueninselchaussee 100*
• *summer: 9am–8pm daily; winter: 10am–6pm daily* • *(030) 805 22 25* • *€€*

6 Alter Krug Dahlem
Large beer garden with a lengthy menu, offering excellent wines and desserts.
⊗ *Königin-Luise-Str. 52* • *11am–midnight daily* • *(030) 84 31 95 40* • *€€*

7 Luise
One of Berlin's nicest beer gardens, on the Free University campus, Luise's is crowded even at lunchtime and always boasts a good atmosphere. The salads and sandwiches are particularly worth trying. ⊗ *Königin-Luise-Str. 40*
• *10am–1am daily* • *(030) 841 88 80*
• *no credit cards* • *€*

8 Grunewaldturm-Restaurant
A great place for mushroom and game dishes, with views of Wann-see. ⊗ *Havelchaussee 61* • *summer: 10am–midnight daily; winter 10am–6pm daily* • *(030) 304 12 03* • *€€*

9 Remise in Schloss Klein-Glienicke
Sophisticated cuisine and sur-roundings; light fish dishes and salads in summer, game and roasts in winter. ⊗ *Königstr. 36*
• *Apr–Oct: noon–10pm daily, Nov–Mar: noon–10pm Tue–Sun* • *(030) 805 40 00*
• *no credit cards* • *€€€*

10 Chalet Suisse
Swiss hospitality and a cosy atmosphere in Grunewald. Apart from local dishes, exquisite Swiss cooking predominates.
⊗ *Clayallee 99* • *from 11:30am daily*
• *(030) 832 63 62* • *€€€*

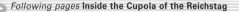
Following pages **Inside the Cupola of the Reichstag**

Left **Haus der Kulturen der Welt** Centre **In Tiergarten** Right **Shell-Haus**

Tiergarten & Federal District

IN 1999, BERLIN'S GREEN *centre became the government district. Around Tiergarten, Berlin's largest and most popular park, stand the Reichstag, the Bundeskanzleramt and Schloss Bellevue, seat of the President of the Federal Republic of Germany. Tiergarten itself is a great place for strolling and cycling, and it also boasts the Neuer See, the Spree River and Berlin's Zoo. In summer, its lawns are used for soccer games and barbecue parties.*

The renovated Reichstag

🔟 Sights

1 Reichstag

2 Kulturforum

3 Großer Tiergarten

4 Siegessäule

5 Diplomatenviertel

6 Hamburger Bahnhof

7 Sowjetisches Ehrenmal

8 Gedenkstätte Deutscher Widerstand

9 Hansa-Viertel

10 Villa von der Heydt

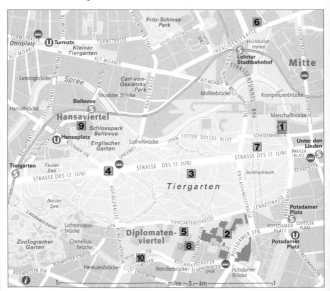

1 Reichstag

More than any other Berlin landmark, the Reichstag - seat of the German parliament – has come to symbolize German history (see pp10–11).

2 Kulturforum

This unique complex of buildings features the best museums and concert halls in Berlin (see pp32–5).

3 Großer Tiergarten

The Großer Tiergarten is Berlin's largest park, straddling an area of 200 hectares (494 acres) between the eastern and western halves of the town. Formerly the Elector's hunting grounds, it was redesigned in the 1830s as a park by Peter Joseph Lonné. At the end of the 19th century, the Siegesallee was established in the east of the park, more than 500 m (1640 ft) in length, lined by the statues of monarchs and politicians. After World War II, the starving and freezing population chopped down nearly all the trees for firewood and dug up the lawns to grow food. Thanks to reforestation work since the 1950s, Tiergarten today has become Berlin's favourite green space and the lungs of the city.

🌑 Tiergarten • Map M5/6

4 Siegessäule

In the middle of Tiergarten stands the 62-m (203-ft) high Victory Column, erected to commemorate Prussian victory against Denmark in the war of 1864. After victory over Austria in 1866 and France 1871, the structure was crowned by a 35-ton gilded statue of the goddess Victoria. There are excellent views from the viewing platform (see p39).

Statue on Siegessäule

🌑 Großer Stern • Map M6
• 1–6pm Mon, 9am–6pm Tue–Sun
• Admission charge

5 Diplomatenviertel

In the late 19th century, an embassy district sprang up. Its extent is still marked today by two pompous Fascist buildings (Italian and Japanese embassies of 1938 and 1943 respectively). Most structures were destroyed during World War II, and until the reunification of Germany the diplomatic buildings were left to decay. Since 1999, new life has been breathed into the diplomats' quarter and, thanks to its adventurous architecture, it has been transformed into one of the most interesting parts of Berlin. Especially worth seeing are the Austrian and Indian embassies on Tiergartenstraße as well as, on Klingelhöferstraße, the embassies of the Nordic countries (see p41) and of Mexico.

🌑 Between Stauffenbergstr. and Lichtensteinallee as well as along Tiergartenstr.
• Map E4

Left **Roof of the Japanese Embassy** Right **The Austrian Embassy**

For more on modern architecture **see pp40–41**

Peter Joseph Lenné

Lenné (1789–1866), regarded as Germany's most important landscape architect, was born into a family of gardeners in Bonn. He studied in Paris and joined the Royal Gardens in Potsdam as an apprentice in 1816. There he met Schinkel and, together, these two men set out to design the parks of Berlin and Potsdam in the harmonious style of the time.

Main entrance Bendlerblock

6 Hamburger Bahnhof

The former Hamburg railway station, now the "Museum of the Present Day", holds a cross-section of conetmporary paintings and the latest multi-media works of art and installations. One of the highlights is the private collection of Erich Marx, including works by Beuys and others. Apart from well-known artists such as Andy Warthol, Jeff Koons and Robert Rauschenberg, it also shows works by Anselm Kiefer and Sandro Chiao. ◎ *Invalidenstr. 50–51• Map F2 • Map10am–6pm Tue-Fri, 11am–6pm Sat, Sun • Admission charge*

7 Sowjetisches Ehrenmal

The giant Soviet Memorial near Brandenburg Gate was officially opened on 7 November 1945, the anniversary of the Russian October Revolution. It is flanked by two tanks, supposedly the first ones to reach Berlin. The memorial commemorates 300,000 Red Army soldiers who died during World War II in the struggle to liberate Berlin. The large column was constructed from marble blocks from Hitler's Reich Chancellery, which had just been torn down. The column itself, designed by Nicolai Sergijevski, is crowned by the huge bronze statue by Lev Kerbel. Behind the memorial, 2,500 Russian soldiers are buried. ◎ *Straße des 17. Juni • Map K2*

Sowjetisches Ehrenmal

8 Gedenkstätte Deutscher Widerstand

The 1930s complex, which is today known as Bendlerblock, lies behind the former Prussian Ministry of War. During World War II it served as army headquarters. It was here that a group of officers planned the assassination of Adolf Hitler. When the attempt failed on 20 July 1944, Claus Schenk Count von Stauffenberg and the others involved were arrested in the Bendlerblock, and many of them were shot in the courtyard during the night. A memorial, created by Richard Scheibe in 1953, commemorates these events. On the upper floor is a small exhibition documenting the German resistance against the Nazi regime. Today, the Bendlerblock has been incorporated into the official headquarters of the Federal Ministry of Defence. ◎ *Stauffenbergstr. 13–14 • Map E4 • 9am–6pm Mon–Wed, Fri, 10am–6pm Sat, Sun • (030) 26 99 50 00 • Admission charge*

Lortzing Memorial in Tiergarten

9 Hansa-Viertel

The Hansa estate west of Schloss Bellvue was built for the "Interbau" trade fair in 1957. World War II bombs had flattened Tiergarten, and 36 residential complexes were erected in the park, designed by distinguished architects from around the world, including Walter Gropius (Händelallee 3–9), Alvar Aalto (Klopstockstr. 30–32) and Oscar Niemeyer (Altonaer Str. 4–14). ◈ *Tiergarten, Hanseatenweg • Map D3*

10 Villa von der Heydt

The late-Neo-Classical Villa von der Heydt is one of the few surviving examples of the architectural villa style typical of Tiergarten. It was built in 1860–61, according to plans by Hermann Ende and G. A. Linke, for one of the most elegant residential areas in Berlin at the time. Since 1967, the Prussian Heritage Foundation has had its headquarters here. ◈ *Von-der-Heydt-Str. 18 • Map E4*

Villa von der Heydt

A Day Out

Morning

Star your tour of Tiergarten at the **Reichstag** *(see pp10–11)*. Explore the government district from here starting with the Bundeskanzleramt (the Federal Chancellor's Office, diagonally opposite). Stop at **Restaurant Käfer** *(see p101)* in the Reichstag for breakfast. Via John-Foster-Dulles-Allee you will pass the Carillon and the Haus der Kulturen der Welt on the way to **Großer Tiergarten** *(see p97)*. Continue along one of the paths into the park, directly opposite the old Kongresshalle, until you reach Straße des 17. Juni. If you turn right here, you will be heading directly towards **Siegessäule** *(see p39)*. From there continue along Fasanenallee in a southwesterly direction until you get to the **Café am Neuen See** *(see p101)*, where you could have lunch.

Afternoon

A stroll through the **Diplomats' Quarter** *(see p97)*. from Neuer See, it is only a few steps along Lichtensteinallee and Thomas-Dehler-Straße in an easterly direction until you get to Klingelhöferstraße with its Scandinavian Embassies. On Tiergartenstraße you will pass, among others, the Embassies of Japan, Italy, India and Austria. From here you could continue south along Klingelhöferstraße, making a small detour for refreshments at **Café Einstein** *(see p101)*. Continue along Lützowufer until you reach the **Kulturforum** *(see pp32–3)* via Potsdamer Brücke. A good place for an evening meal would be the **Vox** *(see p101)*.

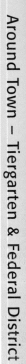

Left **On Neuer See** Centre **The Löwenbrücke** Right **Estonian Embassy; Greek Embassy ruins**

TOP 10 Hidden Treasures

1 Neuer See
Shimmering in a mysterious emerald green, the largest lake in Tiergarten is perfect for rowing. Afterwards you can recover in the Café am Neuen See. Ⓢ *S-Bahn station Tiergarten • Map M5*

2 Löwenbrücke
The Lion Bridge, which leads across a small stream near Neuer See, is "suspended" from the sculptures of four lions. This idyllic spot is a favourite meeting point for gays in Berlin. Ⓢ *Großer Weg • Map M5*

3 Lortzing-Denkmal
There are 70 statues of philosophers, poets and states-men in Tiergarten. The statue of the composer Lortzing, at one end of Neuer See, is one of the most beautiful. Ⓢ *Östlicher Großer Weg • Map M5*

4 Houseboats
Docked on the banks of the Spree are some of the remaining few houseboats in Berlin – an idyllic haven in the middle of the city. Ⓢ *Straße des 17. Juni, Tiergarten-ufer • Map M3*

5 Carillon
The carillon, officially dedi-cated in 1987, is the largest of its kind in Europe. The 68 bells are rung every day at noon and 6pm in the 42-m (138-ft) high black tower. Ⓢ *John-Foster-Dulles-Allee (Haus der Kulturen der Welt) • Map E3*

6 Englischer Garten
The landscaped English-style garden near Schloss Bellevue is ideal for strolling. Ⓢ *An der Klopstockstr. • Map M5*

7 Estonian Embassy
The restored Estonian Embassy and the ruined Greek Embassy, next to each other in a quiet side street, are characteris-tic of the diplomats' quarter. Ⓢ *Hiroshimastr. • Map E4*

8 Locks
The two canal locks behind the zoo, taking visitors across the dammed Landwehrkanal, are popular resting places. Ⓢ *At the Zoo, S-Bahn station Tiergarten • Map M5*

9 Gaslights in Tiergarten
With 80 historic gaslights along the paths, an evening stroll in Tiergarten is very romantic. Ⓢ *At S-Bahn station Tiergarten • Map M5*

10 Landwehrkanal
The sloping, grass-covered banks of Landwehrkanal are ideal spots to chill out. Ⓢ *Corneliusstr. • Map M/N5/6*

Price Categories		
For a three-course	€	under € 20
meal for one with half	€€	€ 20–30
a bottle of wine (or	€€€	€ 30–45
equivalent meal), taxes	€€€€	€ 45–60
and charges included	€€€€€	over € 60

Left **In the Café am Neuen See** Right **Restaurant Am Karlsbad**

🔟 Restaurants & Cafés

1 Café am Neuen See
Not a place of pilgrimage for gourmets but Berlin's most popular beer garden, serving salads, pasta and pizza *(see p53)*.
⊗ *Lichtensteinallee 1 • Map M5 • (030) (03) 254 49 30 • no credit cards • €€*

2 Schleusenkrug
This small café, right next to a lock, has a rustic beer garden and is very popular with students.
⊗ *Tiergarten-Schleuse • Map M5*
• 10am–1am daily • (030) 313 99 09
• no credit cards • €

3 Café Einstein
Based in the villa belonging to the film star Henny Porten, Café Einstein is the ultimate in Viennese elegance, serving Austrian food and boasting the best strawberry torte in town.
⊗ *Kurfürstenstr. 58 • Map E5 • 9am–2am daily daily• (030) 261 50 96 • €€€*

4 Käfer im Reichstag
Ambitious restaurant, better known for its view than its food.
⊗ *Platz der Republik • Map K2*
• (030) 22 62 99 33 • €€€

5 Am Karlsbad
Mediterranean food, creatively prepared and stylishly presented, dominates the menu at this elegant eaterie. ⊗ *Am Karlsbad 11 • Map E4 • (030) 264 53 49 • €€€*

6 Harlekin
A gourmet restaurant, influence by Californian cooking and firmly on the way to receiving its first Michelin star. ⊗ *Lützowufer 15 (Grand Hotel Esplanade) • Map N6 • (030) 254 78 86 30 • €€€€€*

7 Zum Hugenotten
This restaurant offers double enjoyment: great views and Michelin-starred Mediterranean food. ⊗ *Budapester Str. 2 • Map N4/5 • (030) 26 02 12 63 • €€€€€*

8 Vox
Asian "fusion" food in stylish surroundings – you can watch the food being prepared. ⊗ *Marlene-Dietrich-Platz 2 (Grand Hyatt Hotel) • Map L2 • (030) 25 53 17 72 • €€€€€*

9 Paris-Moskau
A classic Berlin restaurant, in a timber-frame house, serving French food – especially game dishes. ⊗ *Alt-Moabit 141 • Map J1 • (030) 394 20 81 • no credit cards • €€€*

10 Alte Pumpe
There is always an excellent atmosphere in this old Berlin restaurant, based in a pumping station and serving rustic German fare. ⊗ *Lützowstr. 42 • Map F5 • (030) 26 48 42 65 • €€*

Note: All restaurants accept credit cards and offer vegetarian dishes unless stated otherwise.

101

Left **Martin-Gropius-Bau** Centre **Above a door in Schöneberg** Right **Shield, Jüdisches Museum**

Kreuzberg & Schöneberg

REUZBERG IS POSSIBLY *Berlin's most famous district, and it definitely qualifies as its most colourful area. Here, in historic tenement blocks that are slowly but surely being renovated, Turkish families live next door to drop-outs and alternatives, artists and students. Social tensions, still characteristic of Kreuzberg today, makes this a varied and interesting district – but at the same time a problematic one. The neighbouring district of Schöneberg is markedly quieter; this part of town is not as experimental as Kreuzberg, nei-ther is it as elegant as Charlottenburg – here Berlin is simply enjoyed by its*

inhabitants. Winterfeldtplatz is surrounded by many inviting pubs, and in the area around Nol-lendorfplatz, entire roads have been taken over and transformed by Berlin's gay scene, with their shops, bars and night clubs.

Statue on Mehringplatz

🔟 Sights

1. Deutsches Technikmuseum
2. Jüdisches Museum
3. Checkpoint Charlie
4. Topographie des Terrors
5. Anhalter Bahnhof
6. Oranienstraße
7. Nollendorfplatz
8. Viktoriapark
9. Martin-Gropius-Bau
10. Riehmers Hofgarten

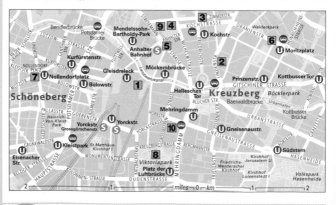

1 Deutsches Technikmuseum

The history of technology and crafts are the themes of this fascinating museum, located in the grounds of a former station. In a new building, visitors can learn about developments in aviation and admire 40 planes, including a Junkers Ju 52 and a "raisin bomber", the planes used for the Berlin airlift. Old ships and steam locomotives bring back the days of the Industrial Revolution.
Trebbiner Str. 9 • Map F5 • 9am–5:30pm Tue–Fri, 10am–6pm Sat, Sun • (030) 902 54 0 • Admission charge

2 Jüdisches Museum

The Jewish Museum is not only unique architecturally, but it is also one of Berlin's most fascinating museums. Its collections present an overview of almost 1,000 years of German-Jewish cultural history; a special exhibition is devoted to everyday Jewish life in Berlin from the end of the 19th century *(see p46).*
Lindenstr. 14 • Map G5 • 10am–8pm daily • (030) 25 99 34 10 • Admission charge

3 Checkpoint Charlie

The Haus am Checkpoint Charlie, next to the former crossing point for the Alllied forces, has an exhibition on the history of the Berlin Wall and the various means people used when trying

The old sign at Checkpoint Charlie

to escape from East to West Berlin, ranging from a hot-air balloon to a car with a false floor-pan. Only a control hut remains of the former border. *Friedrichstr. 43–44 • Map G4 • 9am–10pm daily • (030) 253 72 50 • Admission charge*

4 Topographie des Terrors

After 1934, three terrifying Nazi institutions had their headquarters in this area: the security service (Sicherheitsdienst, SD) was based at Wilhelmstraße 102 in the Prinz Albrecht-Palais; the school of arts and crafts at Prinz-Albrecht-Straße 8 was occupied by the Gestapo; while Heinrich Himmler, head of the SS, resided next door at No. 9, at the Hotel Prinz Albrecht. After World War II, all the buildings were bulldozed except for the cellers where, in 1933–45, prisoners had been interrogated and tortured. An exhibition and a documentation centre (under construction) chronicle the history of the area.
Stresemannstr. 110, entrance Nieder kirchner Str • Map F4 • 10am–6pm daily • (030) 25 40 67 03 • Admission charge

Left **Inside Deutsches Technikmuseum** Right **Exhibition of Nazi crimes at Topographie des Terrors**

Left **Plaque on Nollendorfplatz** Centre **Façade of the Metropol** Right **Ruins of Anhalter Bahnhof**

5 Anhalter Bahnhof

Only pitiful fragments remain of the railway station that was once the largest in Europe. The giant structure was erected in 1880 by Franz Schwechten as a showcase station: official visitors to the Empire were meant to be impressed by the splendour and glory of the German capital as soon as they reached the railway station. In 1943 the station was badly damaged by bombs and in 1960 it was pulled down. The waste ground behind the façade was meant to become a park; today the Tempodrom is based here, hosting concerts and cabaret shows. ◈ *Askanischer Platz 6–7 • Map F5*

6 Oranienstraße

Oranienstraße is the heart of Kreuzberg. It is the wildest, most colourful and most unusual street of the district, where alternative shops and pubs jostle for space with doner kebab take-aways and Turkish greengrocers. All aspects of life and politics in Kreuzberg are centred around this road. ◈ *Between Lindenstr. and Skalitzer Str. • Map H5*

Flower stall on Winterfeldtmarkt

7 Nollendorfplatz

Nollendorfplatz and neighbouring Winterfeldtplatz are right in the centre of Schöneberg. The former square has always been a focal point for the gay scene in Berlin, and a plaque at U-Bahn station Nollendorfplatz commemorates approximately 5,000 homosexuals killed in concentration camps by the Nazis. Today, gay life is concentrated more in the surrounding streets. Before World War II, Nollendorfplatz was also a centre of entertainment. The Metropol-Theater, today a discotheque, then boasted Erwin Piscator as its innovative director. And next door lived the writer Christopher Isherwood, whose novel formed the basis of the famous musical "Cabaret". ◈ *Map E5*

Turkish Berlin

In the 1960s, thousands of Turkish *gastarbeiters* ("guest workers") came to Berlin in response to a shortage of labour. Today the Turkish community numbers around 190,000 and it is mainly their children who leave their mark on life in the city. There are few "guest workers" left; most Turkish Berliners own their own shops and consider themselves to be true Berliners. The rate of naturalization is still fairly low, and many German Berliners have no contact with everyday life in the Turkish community. At 40 per cent, the rate of unemployment among Turkish Berliners is depressingly high.

Memorial by Schinkel in Viktoriapark

8 Viktoriapark

This rambling park was set up as a recreational space for workers in Kreuzberg in 1888–94 to plans by Hermann Mächtig. It has an artificial waterfall, and the Neo-Gothic Schinkel memorial at the top of Kreuzberg, 66 m (216 ft) high, commemorates Prussian victory in the Wars of Liberation against Napoleon. ✪ *Kreuzbergstr.*
• *Map F6*

9 Martin-Gropius-Bau

The richly ornamented former museum of arts and crafts is one of Berlin's most attractive exhibition centres (see pp46–7). ✪ *Niederkirchnerstr. 7 • Map F4*
• *changing exhibitions 10am–8pm Tue–Fri, Sun; 10am–10pm Sat • (030) 25 48 60*
• *Admission charge*

10 Riehmers Hofgarten

Over 20 buildings make up this elegant estate, built as officers' quarters in the Gründerzeit

(after the founding of the German Empire in 1871). Attractively restored in recent years, there is also a pleasant hotel with restaurant. ✪ *Yorckstr. 83–86*
• *Map F6*

Riehmers Hofgarten

A Day in Kreuzberg

Morning

 Start from the famous ruins of **Anhalter Bahnhof**, which you can reach by S-Bahn. From here continue along Stresemannstraße in a north-westerly direction to the **Martin-Gropius-Bau**. It is easy to while away a few hours in this impressive building if there is a special exhibition. You could take a break for refreshments in the museum café. A visit to the neighbouring exhibition, the **Topographie des Terrors** *(see p103)* afterwards will bring you face to face with the dark Nazi past of this area. Continue along Niederkirchnerstraße, past an original section of the Berlin Wall, to Wilhelmstraße. Then turn into Kochstraße to visit **Checkpoint Charlie** and the museum at the former border *(see p103)*.

Afternoon

You can buy a tasty lunch at **Sale e Tabacchi** *(see p109)* in Kochstraße. Continue along Kochstraße in an easterly direction and you will get to the heart of Kreuzberg. Make a detour south on Lindenstraße to the **Jüdisches Museum** *(see p103)* or carry on into **Oranienstraße**. Take the U-Bahn U6 from U-Bahn station Kottbusser Tor to Platz der Luftbrücke. The **Viktoriapark** nearby is a good place for a rest, while shopaholics prefer a stroll up and down Bergmannstraße. At the end, turn north into Baerwaldstraße and continue to Carl-Herz-Ufer, where you will be able to round off the day with a delicious evening meal at the **Altes Zollhaus** *(see p109)*.

Left **Rathaus Schöneberg** Centre **Oberbaumbrücke** Right **On Mariannenplatz**

🔟 Best of the Rest

1 Rathaus Schöneberg
It was from this Town Hall, on 26 June 1963, that the US President John F. Kennedy made his famous speech, declaring "I am a Berliner" and expressing his commitment to the freedom of West Berlin.
Ⓢ John-F.-Kennedy-Platz

2 Mehringplatz
Once Kreuzberg's prettiest square, Mehringplatz was destroyed in World War II and is today surrounded by modern residential buildings. Ⓢ Map G5

3 Flughafen Tempelhof
Tempelhof, built in 1939 by Ernst Sagebiehl and then Germany's biggest airport, survives as the largest Fascist structure in Europe. In front of it, a monument, nicknamed "the starving claw", recalls the airport's role during the Berlin Airlift in 1948–9.
Ⓢ Platz der Luftbrücke • Map G6

4 Mariannenplatz
This square is dominated by the Gothic-style artists' house Bethanien. A former hospital, it is today used as studio space by experimental artists. Ⓢ Map H5

5 Oberbaumbrücke
Pedestrians and cyclists can cross to the other side of the Spree River from Kreuzberg to Friedrichshain on this red-brick bridge, one of Berlin's loveliest, which was erected in 1894–6.
Ⓢ Warschauer/Skalitzer Str.

6 Altes Mosse-Palais
One of Berlin's most important publishing houses was based in this Art Nouveau corner house in the former newspaper district. Ⓢ Kochstr. • Map G4

7 Friedhöfe Hallesches Tor
Numerous celebrities lie buried in the four cemeteries, including the composer Felix Mendelssohn Bartholdy. Also the writer E.T.A. Hoffmann, whose work inspired Offenbach to write *The Tales of Hoffmann*.
Ⓢ Mehringdamm • Map G5

8 Lapidarium
The former pumping station is open for visits; the sculptures in the garden once decorated the Siegesallee (alley of triumph).
Ⓢ Hallesches Ufer 78 • Map F5

9 Kottbusser Tor
Kreuzberg in the raw: social misery tucked away in between new buildings in the Turkish heart of the district. • Map H5

10 Kammergericht
In 1947–90, the magnificent supreme court, built in 1909–13, was used as Allied Control Council. Ⓢ Potsdamer Str. 186 • Map E6

Rathaus Schöneberg: **http://www.engr.psu.edu/ deutschlandsarchitektur/berlin/rathaeuser/schoeneberg.html**

Left **A stall in Winterfeldtmarkt** Centre **Marheineke-Markthalle** Right **At Grober Unfug Comics**

Shops & Markets

1 Winterfeldtmarkt
At Berlin's largest and most wonderful weekday market you can buy fresh fruit and vegetables as well as other goods from around the world, such as clothes and New-Age items. ⊛ *Winterfeldtplatz • Map E5 • 8am–2pm Sat*

2 Türkenmarkt Maybachufer
No other market in Berlin is quite as exotic. This is where Berliners and Turks alike buy their unleavened bread and fresh sheeps' cheese. ⊛ *Maybachufer • Map H5 • noon–6:30pm Tue, Fri*

3 Molotow
Funky and trendy fashion from Berlin designers – perhaps not to everyone's taste, but guaranteed to cause a stir. ⊛ *Gneisenaustr. 112 • Map G6 • (030) 692 08 18*

4 Oranienplatz and Oranienstraße
Kreuzberg's main square and unofficial high street specialize in all things alternative. ⊛ *Oranienstr./ corner Oranienplatz • Map G5*

5 MaaßenZehn
Designer jeans or trendy belts – all with minor faults – at heavily reduced prices. ⊛ *Maaßenstr. 10 • Map E5 • (030) 215 54 56*

6 bizzi
This is the place to find the unusual and the downright weird to take home, including porcelain, ceramics and everything for the home. ⊛ *Grimmstr. 19 • Map H5/6 • (030) 69 81 95 51*

7 High-Lite
If you're worried about standing out in the alternative crowd in Kreuzberg, this is the place to get your shades, body piercings and other essentials. ⊛ *Bergmannstr. 99 • Map F/G6 • (030) 691 27 44*

8 Ararat
One of the best stocked and trendiest stationery shops in Berlin, Ararat has many designer items for sale. ⊛ *Bergmannstr. 99a • Map F/G6 • (030) 694 95 32*

9 Marheineke-Markthalle
One of the last remaining market-halls in Berlin. Visit the colourful fruit and vegetable stores for a genuine taste of Old Berlin. ⊛ *Marheinekeplatz • Map G6 • 8am–6pm Mon–Sat*

10 Grober Unfug Comics
This store sells comic books of all periods and in various languages – its name means "complete rubbish". ⊛ *Zossener Str. 32 • Map G6 • (030) 69 40 14 90*

Left **The bar at Mister Hu** Centre **Inside Kumpelnest 3000** Right **At Café Adler**

Pubs, Bars & Discos

1 Kumpelnest 3000
A super-popular venue, based in a former brothel, complete with chintz wallpaper. Apart from the delicious Caipirinhas, the cocktails are not particularly special. ◎ *Lützowstr. 23* • *Map E5* • *(030) 261 69 18*

2 Yorckschlösschen
A pub-restaurant with a great Old Berlin feel. Live jazz concerts at the weekend.
◎ *Yorckstr. 15* • *Map F6* • *(030) 215 80 70*

3 Mister Hu
The locals would like to keep this secret to themselves: Mister Hu serves some of the greatest cocktails in town. ◎ *Goltzstr. 39* • *Map E5* • *(030) 217 21 11*

4 Van Loon
Enjoy a snack surrounded by nautical artifacts on this old barge moored in Urbanhafen. In summer you can sit on the green banks to drink your beer.
◎ *Carl-Herz-Ufer 5–7* • *Map G5* • *(030) 615 31 22*

5 Blue Note Bar
Young-at-heart couples in their late thirties sip cocktails in this classic bar and hit the tiny dance floor to funk and soul tunes. ◎ *Courbièrestr. 13* • *Map P6* • *(030) 218 72 48*

6 90 Grad
Rising with the ebb and flow of popularity in the Berlin club scene, this discotheque is always popular thanks to its changing club nights and great house music. ◎ *Dennewitzerstr. 37* • *Map E5* • *(030) 21 47 41 00*

7 Golgatha
A popular pick-up venue for students, this classic beer garden on the Kreuzberg also attracts an older clientele, bopping to funk on the small dance floor. ◎ *Dudenstr. 48-64 (Viktoriapark)* • *Map F6* • *(030) 785 24 53*

8 Wirtschaftswunder
The "Economic Miracle" is a 1950s-revival venue, fitted with formica furniture and kidney-shaped tables. ◎ *Yorckstr. 82* • *Map F6* • *no telephone*

9 Würgeengel
The drinks at the "Angel of Death" are not in fact, lethal, but bar and clientele are straight out of a Buñuel film. ◎ *Dresdner Str. 122* • *Map H5* • *(030) 615 55 60*

10 Café Adler
Time seems to have stood still at this pub–café, next to the former border crossing at Checkpoint Charlie. ◎ *Friedrichstr. 206* • *Map G4* • *(030) 215 89 65*

Price Categories

For a three-course meal for one with half a bottle of wine (or equivalent meal), taxes and charges included

€	under € 20
€€	€ 20–30
€€€	€ 30–45
€€€€	€ 45–60
€€€€€	over € 60

Left **In Storch** Right **The sign outside Sale e Tabbacchi**

🔟 Restaurants & Cafés

1 Altes Zollhaus
International and German cuisine, served in a former border control point on the banks of the Landwehrcanal. Try the house speciality: "Brandenburger Landente aus dem Rohr" – a roast duck dish or dishes with wild mushrooms, when in season. ◊ *Carl-Herz-Ufer 30 • Map G5 • (030) 692 33 00 • €€€*

2 E.T.A. Hoffmann
Shooting star among Berlin's gourmet restaurants, specializing in surprising presentations of German nouvelle cuisine. ◊ *Yorckstr. 83 • Map F6 • (030) 78 09 88 09 • €€€*

3 Osteria No. 1
The Italian local par excellence: noisy and expensive, but serving unique pizzas and excellent pasta dishes. Later you can just decamp to the wine bar next door. ◊ *Kreuzbergstr. /1 • Map F6 • (030) 786 91 62 • €€*

4 Hasir
One branch of the Turkish-Arabic fast food chain, serving falafels and other delicacies till late into the night. ◊ *Maaßenstr. 10 • Map E5 • (030) 215 60 60 • no credit cards • €*

5 Sale e Tabbacchi
Italian restaurant with elegant interior, popular with the media crowd. In summer, be sure to reserve a table in the central courtyard. ◊ *Kochstr. 18 • Map G4 • (030) 25 29 50 03 • €€€*

6 Thymian
One of the best – and most expensive – vegetarian eateries in town. ◊ *Gneisenaustr. 57 • Map G6 • (030) 69 81 52 06 • €€€€*

7 Le Cochon Bourgeois
Top-quality French cooking at moderate prices, attracting a Bohemian local crowd and others. ◊ *Fichtestr. 24 • Map H6 • (030) 693 01 01 • no credit cards • €€*

8 Merhaba
One of the best Turkish restaurants in Berlin, dishing up great lamb kebabs and other Turkish specialities. ◊ *Hasenheide 39 • Map H6 • (030) 692 17 13 • €€*

9 Storch
The best dishes from the Alsace are served at this reliable, classic wood-panelled restaurant. Try one of the Flammkuchen. ◊ *Wartburgstr. 54 • Map D5 • (030) 784 20 59 • €€€*

10 Pranzo e Cena
Unbeatable pizzas from the clay oven are the speciality in this Italian venue, popular with students and always busy. ◊ *Goltzstr. 32 • Map E5 • (030) 216 35 14 • no credit cards • €€€*

Following pages: **Gendarmenmarkt at night**

109

Left **Portal of Kronprinzenpalais** Centre **Opernpalais** Right **Inside the Komische Oper**

Central Berlin: Unter den Linden

MOST VISITORS TO BERLIN *regard the magnificent boulevard of Unter den Linden as the heart of the small historic Mitte district. Many of Berlin's sights are concentrated along the grand avenue and around Bebelplatz, creating an impressive picture of Prussian and German history from the early 18th century until the present day. South of Unter den Linden is Gendarmenmarkt, one of Europe's most attractive squares. In recent years, many varied and elegant restaurants and cafés have appeared around the Neo-Classical square. Not far away, chic Friedrichstraße is lined with luxury shops and department stores as well as modern offices and apartments.*

Sculpture on Schlossbrücke

Sights

1. Brandenburger Tor
2. Deutsche Guggenheim
3. Forum Fridericianum
4. Gendarmenmarkt
5. Museumsinsel
6. Friedrichstraße
7. Holocaust-Denkmal
8. Wilhelmstraße
9. Schlossplatz
10. Museum für Kommunikation

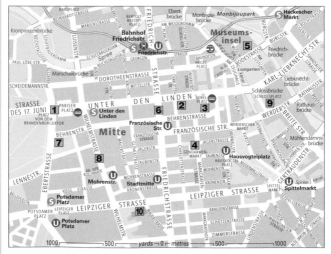

1 Brandenburger Tor

Berlin's best-known landmark on Pariser Platz leads through to Unter den Linden *(see pp8–9)*.

🕭 *Pariser Platz • Map K3*

2 Deutsche Guggenheim

This branch of the American Guggenheim museum, together with the Deutsche Bank branch Unter den Linden, show changing exhibitions of modern art of the highest standard from the US. During recent years, Deutsche Guggenheim has thus managed to become one of the most successful and popular art venues in the city, with an emphasis placed on installations. In 1999, the retrospective of works by Dan Flavin was a particular highlight. Treasures from the Deutsche Bank archives are also shown here. Pop into the small museum shop and refresh yourself with a coffee from the museum café.

🕭 *Unter den Linden 13–15 • Map K4*
• 10am–6pm Tue–Sun • (030) 202 09 30
• Admission charge, free on Mon

3 Forum Fridericianum

The historic structures of this architectural complex in Unter den Linden are among the finest attractions in Berlin. From 1740, Frederick the Great commissioned the prestigious Early-Neo-Classical buildings for the

Altes Palais at Forum Fridericianum

area around today's Bebelplatz, and personally influenced their design: Deutsche Staatsoper, the first free-standing opera house in Europe; Catholic St. Hedwigskathedrale, Alte Bibliothek and Prinz-Heinrich-Palais, later the Humboldt University. Bebelplatz itself is particularly interesting. A memorial set into the ground reminds of its dark past – in 1933, it was the venue for the Nazi book burning. Frederick's successors commissioned Altes Palais and a memorial statue of "old Fritz", surrounded by "his" buildings. Christian Daniel Rauch created the 13.5-m (44-ft) high equestrian bronze figure in 1840. It portrays Frederick the Great wearing his trademark tricorn hat and coronation mantle and carrying a walking stick. The statue had always turned its back to the east – but wags claim that the East German government had mistakenly set up the figure the wrong way around.

🕭 *Unter den Linden and Bebelplatz*
• Map K4

Frederick as Architect

Forum Fridericianum was not only Frederick the Great's memorial to himself, it also ensured that Unter den Linden became one of the greatest boulevards in Europe. The king, who favoured a strict Neo-Classical style, drew up the plans for the Staatsoper and other buildings himself, and Knobbelsdorff executed his ideas.

Deutsche Guggenheim Unter den Linden

For more on Unter den Linden see pp12–15

Left **Inside the Konzerthaus** Centre **Deutscher Dom** Right **Front view of Altes Museum**

4 Gendarmenmarkt

This square, whose strict layout is strongly reminiscent of an Italian Renaissance *piazza*, is probably the most beautiful in Berlin. To the left and right of Schauspielhaus – today's Konzerthaus – stand the twin towers of Deutscher and Französischer Dom (German and French cathedrals), dating back to the late 18th century. Gendarmenmarkt, named after a regiment of *gens d'armes* stationed nearby, was built at the end of the 17th century, as a market square. The Schauspielhaus (theatre) on the north side of the square, built by Schinkel in 1818–21, was used as a theatre until 1945. Heavily damaged in World War II, it was reopened as Konzerthaus (concert hall) in 1984. A statue of the playwright Friedrich Schiller stands in front of the building. Französischer Dom, to its right,

Figure of Athena in Pergamonmuseum

is a prestigious Late-Baroque building; concealed behind it is the French Friedrichstadtkirche, a church serving Berlin's Huguenot community. The Deutscher Dom opposite, built in 1708 on the south side of the square for the Reformed Protestant Church, did not receive its first tower until 1785. Today it houses an exhibition on democracy in Germany. ✆ *Mitte • Map L4*

5 Museumsinsel

Museum Island, a UNESCO World Heritage Sight, is one of the most important complex of museums in the world, holding major arts collections and imposing full-scale ancient structures. Based here are the Pergamonmuseum, the Alte Nationalgalerie (the old national gallery), Bodemuseum and Altes and Neues Museum. The latter three will remain closed until 2004–5 *(see pp20–23 and 46–9)*. ✆ *Pergamonmuseum, Bodestr. 1–3 • Map J5 • 10am–6pm Tue–Sun, till 10pm Thu • (030) 20 90 55 55* ✆ *Alte Nationalgalerie • Bodestr. 1–3 • Map J5 • 10–6pm Tue–Thu • (030) 20 90 55 55 • Admission charge*

The Huguenots in Berlin

In 1685, the Great Elector issued the famous Edict of Potsdam, granting asylum in Berlin to around 20,000 Huguenots, who were persecuted in their native France because of their Protestant faith. Skilled academics and craftsmen, they moulded the social and cultural life of the city and enriched Berlin with the French art of living. Today, still, the French community worships in the Friedrichstadtkirche on Gendarmenmarkt.

Antique vase in Altes Museum

Konzerthaus in Gendarmenmarkt: www.konzerthaus.de

Quartier 206 in Friedrichstraße

Friedrichstraße
6 Friedrichstraße has again risen to the glamour and vibrancy it possessed before World War II. Today, Berlin's Fifth Avenue once again boasts elegant shops, and some upmarket restaurants and cafés which have opened here in recent years. Especially worth visiting are the three Quartiers 205, 206 and 207 within the Friedrich-stadtpassagen, containing the Galeries Lafayette store and Department Store 206 respectively. At the northern end of the street is the famous Dussmann store, S-Bahn station Friedrich-straße as well as the former entertainment district with the Friedrichstadtpalast, today housing the Metropoltheater.
Ⓝ *Mitte • Map J–L4*

Holocaust-Denkmal
7 After years of debate, construction of a memorial for the murdered Jews of Europe was begun in 2001. The US architect Peter Eisenmann designed the memorial to stand next to Brandenburger Tor. It is comprised of a large field with 2-m (6-ft) steles, meant to recall the six million Jews and others murdered by the Nazis in their concentration camps between 1933 and 1945. Underneath the memorial is a documentation centre, which will record the causes leading to the genocide, its course and consequences. It is planned for opening in 2003.
Ⓝ *Ebertstr. • Map L3*

A Day of Culture

Morning

🕐 Unter den Linden runs from **Pariser Platz** to **Brandenburger Tor** *(see pp8–9)*. Stroll eastwards along the wide avenue, past Hotel Adlon Berlin. Then turn right into **Wilhelmstraße** *(see p116)*, the former political nerve centre in Nazi Berlin. On the right-hand side you will pass the new building of the British Embassy. In Behrenstraße you can assess progress in the construction of the **Holocaust-Denkmal**. Turn left into Französische Straße, which will take you to **Friedrichstraße**. Here you can shop at the **Galeries Lafayette** *(see p119)* or in the **Department Store 206** *(see p119)*. After your shopping expedition, you may wish to recover over a snack lunch in the gourmet food department, which is situated in the store's basement.

Afternoon

Before you continue your exploration of Friedrich-straße, make a detour to **Gendarmenmarkt** with its Konzerthaus as well as Deutscher and Französi-scher Dom. From here return to **Friedrichstraße** and its modern buildings. Walk down the street to Leipziger Straße. Turn left into Leipziger Straße, and on the left you will see the giant structure of the former Ministry of Aviation. Today the Federal Ministry of Finance is based here. From there you can retrace your steps to Unter den Linden or return to Gendarmenmarkt. An evening meal at the Asian restaurant **Langhans** *(see p121)* is highly recommended.

Left **The former Ministry of Aviation, Wilhelmstraße** Centre **Hotel Adlon** Right **Stadtschloss**

Nazi Architecture

One of few surviving examples of the monumental architectural style favoured by Fascists is the former Reichsluftfahrtministerium (Ministry of Aviation), commissioned by Hermann Göring in 1934–6 from Ernst Sagebiehl. At the time, the monotonous sandstone building was the world's largest and most modern office block, strengthened by steel girders against aerial attack. After reunification, the Treuhandanstalt was based here; today it houses the Federal Ministry of Finance.

8 Wilhelmstraße

In imperial Berlin, the centre of the German Empire's governmental power was based in Wilhelmstraße. Around 100 years later, nothing remains of the prestigious historic buildings. Representing the equivalent of No. 10 Downing Street in London or Quai d'Orsay in Paris, all political decisions were made at Wilhelmstraße: both Chancellor (No. 77) and President (No. 73) of the German Reich lived here in old town houses. Their gardens became known as "ministerial gardens". Adolf Hitler had the street systematically developed into the nerve centre of Nazi power. The Neue Reichskanzlei (the Chancellor's office) was built in 1937–9 to plans by Albert Speer, at the cor-

British Embassy, Wilhelmstraße

ner of Vossstraße and Wilhelmstraße. It was blown up in 1945. Behind the Reichskanzlei was the so-called "Führerbunker" where Adolf Hitler committed suicide on 30 April 1945 (today it is a playground). Of the historic buildings, only the former Reichsluftfahrtministerium (Ministry of Aviation) remains. Today, Wilhelmstraße is lined by modern office buildings; and the British Embassy, built in 2000 by Michael Wilford, creates a link with the international importance of this street. ◈ *Between Unter den Linden and Leipziger Str. • Map K/L3*

9 Schlossplatz

Today Schlossplatz seems deserted, but once the Stadtschloss (town residence) of the Hohenzollerns stood here. It was blown up by the East German government in 1950–51, and today just a few historic fragments remain.

The debate about the reconstruction of the palace began in the early 1990s and, in 1993, a spectacular model was built; however the costs are prohibitive and make it unlikely that this venture will ever succeed. Remains include the façade of the doorway where Karl Liebknecht supposedly proclaimed the Socialist Republic in 1918. The portal has been incorporated into the former Staatsratsgebäude on the

Portal of the Staatsratsgebäude

south side of the square. On its eastern side, Schlossplatz is bordered by the Palast der Republik (palace of the republic), the former seat of the East German parliament. The future plans for this building, dating from 1976, are still uncertain. ◈ *Mitte • Map G3, K5*

10 Museum für Kommunikation

The world's largest Post Office Museum was opened as early as 1872. Its excellent displays document the history of communication from the Middle Ages via the first postage stamps to today's satellite technology. Particularly worth seeing are a blue and a red Mauritius stamp, one of the first telephone installations (dating back to the year 1863) and three talking robots who interact with the visitors. Children – young and old – always enjoy the Computergalerie, where they can learn and gain new insights while playing.
◈ *Leipziger Str. 16 • Map L4 • 9am–5pm Tue–Fri, 11am–7pm Sat, Sun • (030) 20 29 40 • Admission charge*

Museum für Kommunikation at night

A Day of Culture

Morning

Start your stroll on Unter den Linden, at the corner of Friedrichstraße. Once this spot was one of Berlin's liveliest street junctions, and there is still plenty to see today. For breakfast or refreshments, pop into **Café Einstein** *(see p121)*. Afterwards continue eastwards along the boulevard; you will pass numerous fascinating buildings, for example, on the right, the Deutsche Bank with the Kunstmuseum in **Deutsche Guggenheim** *(see p49)*. From here you can already see the equestrian statue of Frederick the Great, which marks the centre of **Forum Fridericianum** *(see p113)*. This area as well as Bebelplatz are right in the centre of Old Berlin, with Staatsoper, St Hedwigskathedrale, Altes Palais and Humboldt-Universität. You could have lunch in one of the restaurants based in the **Opernpalais**.

Afternoon

In the afternoon continue your stroll along Unter den Linden and, if you like, make a detour to the north to **Museumsinsel** *(see p114)*. Afterwards, if you still feel energetic enough, you could visit **Berliner Dom**. Opposite the cathedral you will see **Schlossplatz** *(see p115)*; its architectural future is still being hotly debated. You could round off your day of sightseeing in Mitte with a delicious evening meal at **Dressler Unter den Linden** *(see p121)*. To get there, just retrace your steps and return along Unter den Linden in a westerly direction.

Museum für Kommunikation Berlin:
www.museumsstiftung.de/berlin/d211_rundgang.asp

Left **The "Tränenpalast"** Centre **At the Mohrenkolonnaden** Right **Admiralspalast**

Best of the Rest

1 Tränenpalast
The Palace of Tears witnessed much heartbreak, when Western visitors parted from family or friends in the East after a visit. Today, the former checkpoint at S-Bahn station Friedrichstraße is a concert hall. ✆ *Friedrichstr./Reichstagsufer 17 • Map J4 • (030) 20 61 00 11*

2 Russian Embassy
This giant building, typical of Stalinist "wedding cake" style, was erected in 1948–53 on the site of the old Tsarist embassy. ✆ *Unter den Linden 63–65 • Map K3*

3 WMF-Haus
The former headquarters of the porcelain and cutlery manufacturer WMF has remarkable façades, decorated with beautiful mosaics. ✆ *Leipziger Str., corner Mauerstr. • Map L3*

4 Alte Bibliothek
The old Library, nicknamed "chest of drawers" by locals, is based in a magnificent Baroque building dating from 1775. ✆ *Bebelplatz • Map K4*

5 Maxim-Gorki-Theater
The renowned theatre was once Berlin's Singakademie, or singing school. Paganini and Liszt, among others, performed here. ✆ *Am Festungsgraben 2 • (030) 20 22 11 29 • Map K5*

6 S-Bahnhof Friedrichstraße
Remodelled several times, this has always been one of Berlin's most famous stations. In 1961–89, it was the principal crossing point between East and West. ✆ *Friedrichstr. • Map J4*

7 Admiralspalast
The old Admirals' Palace is the only remaining theatre in Berlin's erstwhile entertainment district. Today it is the home of the Metropoltheater. ✆ *Friedrichstr. 101–102 • Map J4*

8 Palais am Festungsgraben
The Baroque palace of 1753 has maintained its original elegant interior. ✆ *Am Festungsgraben 1 • Map K5 • (030) 208 40 00*

9 Komische Oper
One of Germany's most magnificent opera houses, dating from 1892, is concealed behind a modern façade. All performances are in German. ✆ *Behrenstr. 55–57 • Map K3 • (030) 47 99 74 00*

10 Mohrenkolonnaden
The Neo-Classical arcades, designed in 1787 by Carl G. Langhans, originally adorned a bridge across the city moat. ✆ *Mohrenstr. 37b u. 40–41 • Map L4*

Tränenpalast: www.traenenpalast.de

Around Town – Central Berlin: Unter den Linden

Left **Outside Kunstsalon** Centre **Fashion at Galeries Lafayette** Right **In Quartier 206**

🔟 Shops

1 Galeries Lafayette
Berlin's most attractive shop is the only branch of the luxury French store in Germany. Here you will find elegant fashion and gourmet foods on the lower level. ✪ *Friedrichstr. 76–78 • Map L4 • 9am–8pm Mon–Fri, 9am–4pm Sat • (030) 20 94 80*

2 Department Store 206
Stylish Berliners shop here for up-to-the-minute and top-of-the-range designer clothes. ✪ *Friedrichstr. 71 • Map L4 • (030) 20 94 62 93*

3 Quartier 206
Apart from the department stores, many top designer shops, such as Gucci and DKNY, are based in Friedrichstadtpassagen. ✪ *Friedrichstr. • Map L4*

4 Kunstsalon
Art to touch and take home, including all sorts of paraphernalia (old costumes, for example), make ideal souvenirs. ✪ *Unter den Linden 41 • Map K4 • (030) 20 45 02 03*

5 Fassbender & Rausch
Giant chocolate sculptures of Reichstag and Brandenburger Tor adorn the windows and tempt visitors into this shop, a chocaholic's paradise. ✪ *Charlottenstr. 60 • Map L4 • (030) 20 45 84 40*

6 Berlin Story Wieland Giebel
Almost anything you've ever wanted to read about Berlin as well as photographs and souvenirs are available from Herr Giebel, who knows the town like no one else. ✪ *Unter den Linden 10 • Map K4 • (030) 20 45 38 42*

7 Kulturkaufhaus Dussmann
This multi-media store is a mecca for culture-junkies, offering everything from good books to computer games, and also boasting a large section of classical music on CD. The store is open in the evening. ✪ *Friedrichstr. 90 • Map K4 • (030) 202 50*

8 Budapester Schuhe
Small branch of a chain, selling quality men's shoes. ✪ *Friedrichstr. 81 • Map L4 • (030) 20 38 81 10*

9 Escada
Stylish (and expensive) bespoke tailors for gentlemen, boasting a fantastic selection of luxurious materials. ✪ *Friedrichstr. 200 • Map L4 • (030) 22 33 55 01*

10 Juwelier Christ
Well-known jeweller, selling quality watches and jewellery in this luxury outlet. ✪ *Friedrichstr. 176–179 • Map L4 • (030) 204 10 49*

Left **Café LebensArt** Centre **925 Loungebar** Right **Brauerei Lemke in an S-Bahn arch**

🔟 Pubs & Bars

1 Newton Bar
One of the trendiest bars in town. Sink into the deep leather armchairs and sip your cocktails, surrounded by Helmut Newton's photographs of proud women.
⊗ Charlottenstr. 57 • Map L4
• 10am–3am daily • (030) 20 61 29 99

2 925 Loungebar
Everything inside this bar on Gendarmenmarkt is red. Clients, however, are unlikely to "see red" thanks to the friendly staff who serve delicious cocktails.
⊗ Taubenstr. 19 • Map L4 • 5pm–4am daily • (030) 20 18 71 77

3 Opernschänke
Completely furnished in leather, this small but elegant bar in the historic Opernpalais is an ideal stopping-off point for night owls, after an evening at the opera. ⊗ Unter den Linden 5 • Map K3
• 8am–1am Wed–Sun • (030) 20 26 83

4 Emil
Café, pub and restaurant, especially popular with actors.
⊗ Schumannstr. 15 • Map J3
• 3pm–1am Mon–Fri, 5pm–1am Sat
• (030) 559 74 54

5 LebensArt
A café rather than a pub or bar, offering breakfast and afternoon cakes, this is one of the few places open at night on Unter den Linden. ⊗ Unter den Linden 69a
• Map K4 • 7am–11pm Mon–Thu, 7am–midnight Fri, 9am–midnight Sat, 9am–11pm Sun • (030) 229 00 18

6 Café Einstein
Small and cosy branch of the Café in the eastern city, serving excellent wines and Austrian specialities. ⊗ Unter den Linden 42 • Map K4 • 8pm–3am Mon–Thu, 8pm–4pm Fri, Sat • (030) 204 36 32

7 Ständige Vertretung
The name harks back to the permanent West German representation in East Berlin, but the drinks are bang up to date.
⊗ Schiffbauerdamm 8 • Map J3
• 11am–2am daily • (030) 282 39 65

8 Ganymed Brasserie
Well-run French bistro, overlooking the boulevard. ⊗ Unter den Linden 14 • Map J3 • 3pm–1am Sun–Fri
• (030) 285 99 46

9 Brauerei Lemke
Atmospheric pub under the S-Bahn arches; courtyard. ⊗ Dirksenstr. S-Bahn arch No. 143 • Map J5
• noon–1am daily • (030) 24 72 87 27

10 Windhorst
Trendy cocktail bar – classy, elegant, good. ⊗ Dorotheenstr. 65
• Map K3 • from 5pm Mon–Fri, from 9pm Sat • (030) 20 45 00 70

Price Categories

For a three-course		
meal for one with half	€	under € 20
a bottle of wine (or	€€	€ 20–30
equivalent meal), taxes	€€€	€ 30–45
and charges included	€€€€	€ 45–60
	€€€€€	over € 60

Left **Outside Dressler Unter den Linden** Right **Trenta Sei in Gendarmenmarkt**

🔟 Restaurants & Cafés

1 Margaux
A newcomer among Berlin's top restaurants, Margaux serves sophisticated French-German nouvelle cuisine. ◈ *Unter den Linden 78 • Map K3 • Noon–2pm, 7–11pm Mon–Sat • (030) 22 65 26 11 • €€€€€*

2 Borchardt
No.1 of Berlin's trendy new restaurants, offering good French food in an historic setting. ◈ *Französische Str. 47 • Map K4 • 11:30am–1am daily • (030) 20 38 71 10 • €*

3 Vau
The chef, Kolja Seeberg, deserves his Michelin star with his top-class German food. Attractive interior. ◈ *Jägerstr. 54–55. • Map L4 • noon–2:30pm, 7–10.30pm Mon–Sat • (030) 202 97 30 • €€€*

4 Seasons
The unimaginative name of this restaurant in the Four Seasons Hotel does little justice to the sophisticated dishes that are served here. The crackling open fire in the dining room makes each meal a special experience. ◈ *Charlottenstr. 40 • Map K4 • 6:30am–2:30pm, 6–11:30pm daily • (030) 20 33 63 63 • €€€*

5 Dressler Unter den Linden
In season, this French brasserie is an excellent place for oysters. At other times, the inexpensive three-course set menu is recommended. ◈ *Unter den Linden 39 • Map K3 • 8am–1am daily • (030) 204 44 22 • €€€*

6 Lutter & Wegner
Try this Austrian restaurant for the tastiest Wiener Schnitzel and potato salad in Berlin. ◈ *Charlottenstr. 56 • Map L4 • 9am–2am daily • (030) 202 95 40 • €€€*

7 Trenta Sei
Super pasta dishes, enjoyed by the Chancellor and most other guests. ◈ *Markgrafenstr. 36 • Map L4 • noon–midnight daily • (030) 20 45 26 30 • €€€€*

8 Langhans
Asian "fusion" food in stylish, minimalist surroundings. ◈ *Charlottenstr. 59 • Map L4 • noon–11:30pm Mon–Sat, 4–11:3-pm Sun • (030) 20 94 50 70 • €€€*

9 Kaiserstuben
German gourmet food opposite the Pergamonmuseum. ◈ *Am Kupfergraben 6a • Map J4 • 6pm–1am Tue–Sat • (030) 20 45 29 80 • €€€€*

10 Aigner
Original Viennese restaurant serving typically Austrian food. ◈ *Französische Str. 25 • Map K4 • (030) 203 75 18 50 • €€*

Note: All restaurants accept credit cards and offer vegetarian dishes unless stated otherwise.

121

Left **Hackesche Höfe** Centre **Tacheles, Oranienburger Straße** Right **In the Hackesche Höfe**

Central Berlin: Scheunenviertel

THE SCHEUNENVIERTEL, *literally the "barn quarter", Berlin's former Jewish quarter, has experienced a unique revival in recent years. Originally, the* thriving Jewish community lived in neighbouring Spandauer Vorstadt, beyond the city limits, while the Scheunenviertel was better known as a red-light district. The Nazis, however, applied the name of "Scheunenviertel" to both areas, in order to tarnish the Jews. After World War II the district was much neglected and gradually fell into decay. Today, many of the historic merchants' yards and narrow side streets have been restored, reviving the Scheunenviertel's unique and lively character. Many pubs and restaurants, galleries and shops are now based here and the area has become very fashionable with locals and visitors alike, especially at night. The tragic history of its former inhabitants, however, remains unforgotten.

Neue Synagoge

🔟 Sights

1. Oranienburger Straße
2. Neue Synagoge
3. Hackesche Höfe
4. Sophienstraße
5. Tacheles
6. Museum für Naturkunde
7. Dorotheenstädtischer Friedhof
8. Brecht-Weigel-Gedenkstätte
9. Gedenkstätte Große Hamburger Straße
10. Postfuhramt

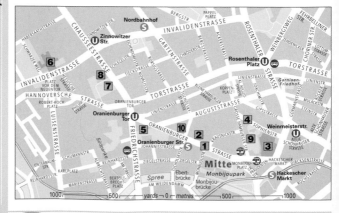

1 Oranienburger Straße

Like no other street, Oranienburger Straße, in the centre of the old Scheunenviertel, symbolizes the rise and fall of Jewish culture in Berlin. Traces of its Jewish past are visible all along the street, such as the Neue Synagoge and several Jewish cafés and restaurants *(see p129)*. Some 18th- and 19th-century buildings bear witness to the street's former splendour – the Postfuhramt *(see p125)*, for example, or the house at No. 71–2, built in 1789 by Christian Friedrich Becherer for the Grand Lodge of the Freemasons of Germany. ◈ *Mitte, between Friedrich-str. and Rosenthaler Str. • Map J4/5*

2 Neue Synagoge

The New Synagogue, built in 1859–66, was once the largest in Europe. In 1938, it survived "Reichskristallnacht" thanks to the vigilance of a brave guard, but it was damaged by bombs during World War II. Behind the Moorish façades are a prayer room and the Centrum Judaicum. ◈ *Oranienburger Str. 29–30 Str. 40–41 • Map J4/5 • 10am–6pm Sun–Thu, 10am–2pm Fri • (030) 28 40 13 16 • Admission charge*

3 Hackesche Höfe

Berlin's largest and most attractive group of restored commercial buildings, Hackesche Höfe extends between Oranienburger and Rosenthaler Straße and up to Sophienstraße in the east. The complex of buildings, comprised of nine interconnecting courtyards, was designed around the turn of the 20th century by Kurt Berndt and August Endell, two leading exponents of Art Nouveau. The first courtyard especially features elements that are typical of this style: geometric patterns are laid out in vibrant colours on glazed tiles, covering the entire building from the foundations to the guttering. What had lain in ruin after 1945 has now been carefully restored, and forms today one of the most popular nightlife centres in the city. Restaurants and cafés *(see p128–9)*, the Varieté Chamäleon *(see p56)*, galleries and small shops have all settled in this area. ◈ *Rosenthaler Str. 40–41 • Map I5*

4 Sophienstraße

Narrow Sophienstraße has been beautifully restored and now looks exactly as it did in the late 18th century. A number of shops and arts and crafts workshops are now based in the modest buildings and courtyards. Closeby stands Sophienkirche, the first Protestant parish church, founded by Queen Sophie Luise in 1712. Next to the Baroque church is a small cemetery with some 18th-century tombs. ◈ *Große Hamburger Str. 29 • Map I5*

The old Sophienkirche

Left **Bertolt Brecht's study** Right **Memorial on Große Hamburger Straße**

5 Tacheles

The ruins of the former Wilhelm-Einkaufspassagen, one of Berlin's most elegant shopping centres dating back to the turn of the 20th century, have been transformed by artists into an alternative arts centre. It now houses workshops and cafés and offers a regular programme of events. ✪ *Oranienburger Str. 54–56a • Map F3 • (030) 28 09 68 35*

6 Museum für Naturkunde

The Museum of Natural History – one of the largest of its kind – has the world's largest dinosaur skeleton: a brachiosaurus, found in Tanzania. Also displayed are fossils, meteorites and minerals *(see also p47)*. ✪ *Invalidenstr. 43 • Map F2 • (030) 20 93 85 91 • Admission charge*

7 Dorotheenstädtischer Friedhof

Many celebrities have found their final resting place in this charming cemetery, dating back to 1762. To the left of the entrance are the graves of Heinrich Mann (1871–1950) and Bertolt Brecht (1898–1956); further along stand the pillar-like tombstones of the philosophers Johann Gottlieb Fichte (1762–1814) and Georg Wilhelm Friedrich Hegel (1770–1831). On Birkenallee (left off the main path) you can see the graves of master builder Karl Friedrich Schinkel (1781–1841) and the

architects Friedrich August Stüler (1800–65) and Johann Gottfried Schadow (1764–1850). ✪ *Chausseestr. 126 • Map F2 • summer: 8am–8pm daily; winter: 8am–4pm daily*

Schinkel, Dorotheenstädtischer Friedhof

8 Brecht-Weigel-Gedenkstätte

Bertolt Brecht, one of the 20th century's greatest playwrights, lived here with his wife, Helene Weigel, from 1953–6. The original furnishings, some documents and photographs are on display. ✪ *Chausseestr. 125 • Map F2 • 10–11:30am Tue–Sat exc Thu; 10–11:30am & 5–6:30pm Thu; 9:30am–1:30pm Sat; 11am–6pm Sun • (030) 283 05 70 44 • Admission charge*

Jewish Berlin

In the 19th century, Berlin had a population of 200,000 Jews, the largest such community in Germany. Apart from wealthier Jews in the west of the city, it also attracted many impoverished Jews from Poland and Russia who settled in Spandauer Vorstadt. One part of the district, the criminal red-light district, was also known as Scheunenviertel. Nazi propaganda used the name to denote the entire Spandauer Vorstadt, in order to tarnish the Jews by association. Today, the Jewish quarter is still known under its "wrong" name as "Scheunenviertel", although very few Jews live here now. Only some 5,000 Jewish Berliners managed to survive between 1933–45 in hide-outs.

---

9 Gedenkstätte Große Hamburger Straße

Before 1939, this was one of the most important Jewish streets, with several Jewish schools, the oldest Jewish cemetery in Berlin and an old people's home. The latter achieved tragic fame during the Nazi period – the SS used it as a detention centre for Berlin Jews before transporting them to the concentration camps. A simple monument commemorates thousands of Jews who were sent to their death from here. To the left of the home is a Jewish school, on the site of an earlier school founded in 1778 by the Enlightenment philosopher Moses Mendelssohn (1729–86). To the right of the monument is the Jewish cemetery, where some 12,000 Berlin Jews were buried between 1672 and 1827. In 1943, the Nazis almost completely destroyed the cemetery. Only a few Baroque tombs, or *masebas*, survived; these are now embedded into the small original cemetery wall. The place presumed to be Moses Mendelssohn's tomb is marked by a new monument. ✆ *Große Hamburger Str.* • *Map J5*

10 Postfuhramt

The richly ornamented Postfuhramt (post office transport department) dates back to the 19th century. It is now an exhibition hall for alternative photography and art shows and a centre for performance art.

Frieze on the Postfuhramt façade

✆ *Oranienburger Str.* • *Map J4*

A Day in Scheunenviertel

Morning

🕐 Take the S-Bahn to Friedrichstraße and explore this road, Berlin's former entertainment district. Walk north along the street up to Reinhardstraße, and turn left here towards Bertolt-Brecht-Platz. Continue south to Albrechtstraße to the **Berliner Ensemble** *(see p126)*. Once you have admired the theatre where the great playwright used to work, you could make a detour to visit his home, **Brecht-Weigel-Gedenkstätte** in Chausseestraße. The best way to get there is on foot – walk along Chausseestraße. If you remain in Friedrichstraße and turn right behind Friedrichstadtpalast into **Oranienburger Straße** *(see p123)*, you will get to the heart of the fashionable Scheunenviertel. At the corner of the street rises the arts centre **Tacheles**, and a few steps to the east the shiny golden dome of the **Neue Synagoge** will come into view *(see pp45 and 123)*.

Afternoon

Before exploring the Scheunenviertel district, you should take some refreshments; not far from the Synagogue is the **Adermann** restaurant *(see p129)*. Walk along Tucholskystraße, then turn right into Auguststraße. Here you will find some of the most attractive courtyards, for example **Kunsthof** at the corner of Gartenstraße. Return along Auguststraße to **Gedenkstätte Große Hamburger Straße** and the **Hackesche Höfe** *(see p123)* to shop and for an evening meal.

Left **Inside Sophienkirche** Centre **The Berliner Ensemble** Right **The Deutsches Theater**

Best of the Rest

1 Charité
Many important physicians, such as Rudolf Virchow and Robert Koch, worked and taught at this world-famous hospital, founded in 1710. A Museum of Pathology has some 23,000 remarkable exhibits on display. ◈ Schumannstr. 20–21 • Map J3 • Museum für Pathologie 10am–5pm Tue–Sun, 10am–6pm Wed, 1pm–4pm Thu, Fri • (030) 450 53 61 56

2 Alte and Neue Schönhauser Straße
Alte Schönhauser Straße is one of the oldest streets in Spandauer Vorstadt. The lively road is still characterized by a colourful jumble of traditional and trendy new shops. ◈ Hackescher Markt • Map J5

3 Deutsches Theater
Once Max Reinhardt's place of work, the theatre – widely considered the best German-language theatre – shows mainly German classics, often in new interpretations. ◈ Schumannstr. 13a • Map J3 • (030) 28 44 12 25

4 Berliner Ensemble
This theatre, established in 1891–2 by Heinrich Seeling, was the main venue for Bertolt Brecht's plays. ◈ Bertolt-Brecht-Platz 1 • Map J3 • (030) 28 40 81 55

5 Hochbunker
One of the last surviving World War II bunkers. ◈ Albrechtstr. corner of Reinhardtstr. • Map J3

6 Monbijoupark
A small park, in which once stood the little Monbijou palace. It is now an attractive green space for a rest. ◈ Oranienburger Str./Spree • Map J5

7 Auguststraße
The area round this road is one of the closest to the original old Scheunenviertel, featuring old interior courtyards and many buildings that have not yet been restored. ◈ Between Oranienburger and Rosenthaler Str. • Map G2

8 Koppenplatz
In this small square, a monument of a table and upturned chair recall the expulsion of the Jews. ◈ Map G2

9 Sophienkirche
This parish church, built in 1712, has managed to preserve its traditional Old Berlin charm. Be sure to see the Baroque pulpit. ◈ Große Hamburger Str. 29 • Map G2

10 Tucholskystraße
This narrow street is typical of the transformation of Scheunenviertel – trendy shops next to decaying façades. ◈ Map J4

Left **Heckmann-Höfe** Centre **Sophienhöfe** Right **The alternative Kunstwerke gallery**

🔟 Old Courtyards

1 Sophie-Gips-Höfe
Famous for the Hoffman art collection, which is based here, this former sewing machine factory is a popular meeting place for locals. ◈ *Sophienstr. 21–22 • Map G3*

2 Sophienhöfe
The 19th-century red-brick artisans' workshops have been transformed into artists' studios. ◈ *Sophienstr.17–18 • Map G3*

3 Heckmann-Höfe
These lavishly restored yards, the most elegant in Berlin, attract visitors today with a restaurant and fashionable clothes shops. ◈ *Between Rosenthaler and Tucholskystr. 34 • Map J4*

4 Kunstwerke
Large-scale installations by the resident artists are regularly on display at the alternative gallery space – a recent example was an entire artificial reed garden. The courtyard also has a café in the conservatory. ◈ *Auguststr. 69 • Map G2*

5 Rosenthaler Straße 37
This narrow unrestored alleyway and courtyard gives a good impression of how the entire area once looked. Just enter via the archway – you will be able to stroll around and drink a beer at the tables on the left. Until 1933, a Jewish school for the blind was based in these buildings. ◈ *Rosenthaler Str. 37 • Map G2*

6 Schulhof
Time seems to have stood still around 1900 in this courtyard, today part of the district's Kulturamt (cultural office). ◈ *Auguststr. 21 • Map G2*

7 Hof Joachimstraße
The extensive courtyard of the former Postfuhramt permits a glimpse of the original façade of the building. ◈ *Joachimstr. 11 • Map G2*

8 Auguststraße 83
A café and an art gallery are now based in the yard of a former sewing machine factory. ◈ *Auguststr. 83/Linienstr. 147 • Map G2*

9 Kunsthof
A courtyard full of nooks and crannies, which is today occupied by a number of workshops, offices and cafés. Take a look at the richly ornamented staircases. ◈ *Oranienburger Str. 27 • Map J4/5*

10 Sophienstr. 22 and 22a
Two small inner courtyards, partially planted, are surrounded by yellow and red brick walls. ◈ *Sophienstr. 22–22a • Map G3*

Left **In the 808 Bar & Lounge** Centre **Drinks at Yosoy** Right **Clärchen's Ballhaus**

🔟 Pubs, Bars & Discos

1 Riva
An elegant, cool and trendy bar free from hooligans, named after an Italian soccer player.
◈ Dircksenstr., arch 142 • Map J5
• 8pm–4am daily • (030) 24 72 26 88

2 Strecker's Bar
A cosy English-style pub, serving dark beer. ◈ Oranienburger Str. 33 • Karte J4/5 • 10am–1am daily
• (030) 24 62 89 68

3 808 Bar & Lounge
Modern bar with a colourful aquarium and curved bar. A trendy place for stylish people.
◈ Oranienburger Str. 42–43 • Map J4/5
• 5pm–4am daily • (030) 28 04 67 27

4 Cox Orange
This offshoot of the trendy Architekturcafé in Hackesche Höfe attracts media people, all dressed in existentialist black.
◈ Dircksenstr. 40 • Map J5 • from 7pm Sun–Fri, from 10pm Sat • (030) 281 05 08
• Admission charge

5 VEB Ostzone
Many souvenirs decorate this bar, celebrating nostalgia for the "good old days" under the East German regime.
◈ Auguststr. 92 • 6pm–2am daily
• (030) 28 39 14 40

6 b-flat
Live jazz and occasionally dance are on offer at this small venue. ◈ Rosenthaler Str. 13 • Map J5
• from 8pm daily • (030) 280 63 49
• Admission charge

7 Delicious Doughnuts
An old favourite among the hip new clubs of the district, promising to take you "back to the roots". Hot funk and soul rhythms are played. ◈ Rosenthaler Str. 9 • Map J5 • 10pm–5am Thu–Sun
• (030) 28 09 93 74 • Admission charge

8 Clärchen's Ballhaus
One of Berlin's last remaining dancehalls, where dance-crazy Berliners of an uncertain age dance the waltz and sing along. ◈ Auguststr. 24 • Map G2 • from 7:30pm Wed, Fri, Sat
• (030) 282 92 95

9 Yosoy
This attractively furnished Spanish restaurant serves tasty tapas, good wines and exciting cocktails – which is why it is crowded till late into the night.
◈ Rosenthaler Str. 37 • Map J5 • from 11am daily • (030) 28 39 12 13 • €€

🔟 Kurvenstar
Curves rule ok in this 1960s-style bar. Strong cocktails are lovingly prepared by the friendly staff. ◈ Kleine Präsidentenstr. 3
• Map G2 • 9pm–3am Tue–Sun
• (030) 28 59 97 10

Price Categories

For a three-course meal for one with half a bottle of wine (or equivalent meal), taxes and charges included	€	under € 20
	€€	€ 20–30
	€€€	€ 30–45
	€€€€	€ 45–60
	€€€€€	over € 60

Left **Outside Oxymoron in the Hackesche Höfe** Right **The Adermann restaurant**

🔟 Restaurants & Cafés

1 Adermann
The most upmarket restaurant in the district serves French fish and game dishes; the menu changes daily. ◈ *Oranienburger Str. 27 • Map J4/5 • 7pm–midnight Tue–Sat • (030) 28 38 73 71 • €€€*

2 Café Oren
The popular friendly café serves authentic vegetarian Jewish food in the heart of the Scheunenviertel. ◈ *Oranienburger Str. 28 • Map J4/5 • noon–1am Mon–Thu, 10am–2am Fri–Sun • (030) 28 28 223 • €*

3 Schwarzenraben
Excellent pizzas and Italian specialities are on the menu at this long restaurant, frequented by East Berlin's new elite. ◈ *Neue Schönhauser Str. 13 • Map J5 • 10am–2am daily • (030) 28 39 16 98 • €€€*

4 Maxwell
A gourmet restaurant in a New-York-style loft, serving unfussy fusion food. ◈ *Bergstr. 22 • Map G2 • 6pm–midnight daily • (030) 28 59 98 48 • €€*

5 Beth-Café
Small Jewish café of the Adass-Jisrool community, serving Jewish snacks. ◈ *Tucholskystr. 40 • Map J4 • noon–8pm Thu–Sun • (030) 281 31 35 • no credit cards • €*

6 Hackescher Hof
Best restaurant in Hackesche Höfe serves traditional German fare. ◈ *Rosenthaler Str. 40 • Map J5 • 9am–3am daily • (030) 283 52 93 • €€€*

7 Oxymoron
This small café and restaurant in Hackesche Höfe, featuring chintz decoration, serves light German meals. ◈ *Rosenthaler Str. 40–41 • Map J5 • 11am–1am daily • (030) 28 39 18 85 • €€*

8 Goa
Goa serves hot curries and other regional specialities from India, China, Thailand and elsewhere in Asia. Worth trying: the three-course "Reise durch Asien" (Journey through Asia). ◈ *Oranienburger Str. 50 • Map J4/5 • 10am–1am daily • (030) 28 59 84 51 • €*

9 McBride's Brasserie
Trendy McBride's Brasserie, based in an old barn in Heckmann-Höfe, offers hearty meat dishes and light salads. ◈ *Oranienburger Str. 32 • Map J4/5 • 11:30am–1am daily • (030) 28 38 64 61 • €€€*

10 Barist
A mixture of French, Italian and Austrian dishes are on offer here. There is always a good atmosphere under the S-Bahn arches; live jazz at weekends. ◈ *Am Zwirngraben 13–14 • Map G2 • 10am–3am daily • (030) 24 72 26 13 • €€*

Note: All restaurants accept credit cards and offer vegetarian dishes unless stated otherwise.

129

Left **Altar painting in Marienkirche** Centre **Frieze on the Münze** Right **Knoblauch-Haus**

Central Berlin: Around Alexanderplatz

*T*HE AREA AROUND ALEXANDERPLATZ *is one of the oldest parts of the city; it was here that the twin towns of Cölln and Berlin merged to become one town in the 13th century. Berlin's oldest coherent quarter, the 18th-century Nikolaiviertel and its medieval Nikolaikirche, the city's oldest church, lie in the shadow of the TV tower, the pride of the "capital" of former East Germany. On the occasion of Berlin's 750th anniversary, in 1987, the East German government had the Nikolaiviertel restored. Very few of the original buildings are preserved, however; most houses were rebuilt from scratch. Only a few paces away from the alleyways of Nikolaiviertel extends Alexanderplatz, referred to by locals simply as "Alex". Before World War II, Alex defined the heartbeat of the city; after the ravages of war, it seemed vast and a little forlorn. Although the giant square is now livelier again, especially in summer, a chilly easterly wind still blows between the houses. The vibrancy of the square, as described by Alfred Döblin in his novel* Berlin Alexanderplatz, *is only slowly returning to the area. Much building and reconstruction work is planned for Alex in the coming years.*

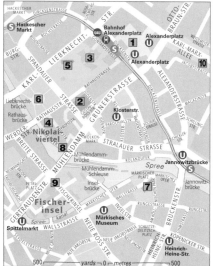

Berliner Rathaus

🔟 Sights

1. Alexanderplatz
2. Berliner Rathaus
3. Berliner Fernsehturm
4. Nikolaiviertel
5. Marienkirche
6. Marx-Engels-Forum
7. Märkisches Museum
8. Ephraim-Palais
9. Neptune Fountain
10. Karl-Marx-Allee and Frankfurter Allee

Alexanderplatz on a 24-hour webcam:
www.berlinonline.de/spass/live_kamera/.html/alex.html

Alexanderplatz

1 The vast, largely desolate square in the centre of East Berlin, called "Alex" by Berliners, was one of the most vibrant places in Berlin before World War II – and no doubt it will be again some day. Alfred Döblin beautifully captured the rhythm of the city in his world-famous novel *Berlin Alexanderplatz*. Not much remains today of the once frenzied atmosphere, although there is plenty of hustle and bustle around the Kaufhof Galleria department store *(see p135)*.

Originally, Alex was a cattle and wool market. Not many original buildings survived – only Berolinahaus and Alexanderhaus, next to the historic S-Bahn station Alexanderplatz, remain, both dating back to 1929. The square was almost completely laid to waste in World War II, and most of the surrounding soulless tower blocks were built in the 1960s. There are now plans to build skyscrapers on Alexanderplatz. ◈ *Mitte • Map I6*

Berliner Rathaus

2 Berlin's proud town hall is the office of the Governing Mayor and is the political centre of power in Greater Berlin. The

Heraldic animal at the Rathaus

Rathaus was built in 1861–9, according to plans by Hermann Friedrich Waesemann on the site of an older town hall. It was designed to demonstrate the power and the glory of Berlin, and the architect took his inspiration for the new governmental building from Italian Renaissance *palazzi*.

The building is also known as the "Red Town Hall" – not a reminder of its Socialist past, but a reference to the red bricks from Brandenburg province from which it is built *(see also p38)*. ◈ *Rathausstr. 15 • Map K6 • 9am–6pm Mon–Fri • (030) 90 26 0*

Berliner Fernsehturm

3 The 365-m (1,197-ft) high TV tower is the tallest building in Berlin, affording views of up to 40 km (25 miles) in good weather. There is a viewing platform at 203 m (666 ft). The Tele-Café above rotates once around its own axis every 30 minutes. The tower, visible from afar, was erected in 1965–9 by the East German government to signify the triumph of East Berlin, their "capital". ◈ *Panoramastr. 1a • Map I6 • Mar–Oct: 10am–1am, Nov–Feb: 10am–midnight • Tel. (030) 242 33 33 • Admission charge*

Left **Weltzeituhr (world time clock) on "Alex"** Right **Inside the Tele-Café of Fernsehturm**

Left **Nikolaikirche, Nikolaiviertel** Centre **Märkisches Museum** Right **A street in Nikolaiviertel**

4 Nikolaiviertel

Around the medieval Nikolaikirche *(see p44)*, the small Nikolaiviertel with its narrow nooks and crannies, Old Berlin restaurants and souvenir shops is one of the most charming parts of the city. The area extending between the banks of the Spree River and Mühlendamm was razed to the ground in World War II. The East German authorities restored it after the war – unfortunately not always successfully: some houses were covered in prefabricated façades.

Knoblauchhaus was one of few to escape destruction. Dating from 1835, it was the former home of the Knoblauch family (Neue Synagoge was designed by architect Eduard Knoblauch). Today it houses a museum depicting everyday life in Berlin, and includes a fully furnished apartment in the Biedermeier style. ◈ *Mitte, Knoblauchhaus: Postr. 23 • Map K6 • 10am–6pm Tue–Sat • (030) 23 45 99 91 • Admission charge*

5 Marienkirche

Originally built in 1270, Marienkirche was extensively remodelled in the 15th century. Thanks to its Baroque church tower, designed by Carl Gotthard Langhans in 1790, it is one of Berlin's loveliest churches. Inside, the alabaster pulpit by Andreas Schlüter (1703) and the main altar (1762) are particularly worth seeing. The 15th-century Gothic font and a 22-m (72-ft) long fresco, *Der Totentanz* (The Dance of Death) from 1485 are its two oldest treasures. The church was a thorn in the side for the East German government because the cross on its tower is reflected in the TV tower. ◈ *Karl-Liebknecht-Str. 8 • Map K6 • 10am–4pm Mon–Thu; noon–4pm Sat, Sun • (030) 242 44 67*

Marx and Engels

6 Marx-Engels-Forum

Shortly after German reunification in 1989, the motto "Next time it will all be different" was scrawled onto this monument to Karl Marx and Friedrich Engels, the fathers of Socialism. The bronze statues, created by Ludwig Engelhart in 1986, adorn the centre of a square. ◈ *Map K5/6*

7 Märkisches Museum

Berlin's municipal museum displays architectural treasures such as doorways and the head of one of the horses from the top of the Brandenburg Gate, plus various items relating to theatre and music in Berlin. ◈ *Am Köllnischen Park 5 • Map L6 • 10am–6pm Tue–Sun • (030) 30 86 60 • Admission charge*

Altar in Marienkirche

Ephraim-Palais

8 Ephraim-Palais
The curved Baroque palace, built in 1766 for the wealthy merchant Nathan Veitel Heinrich Ephraim, was once regarded as the city's most beautiful spot. Rebuilt after the demolition of the old palace, it is now a museum, showing paintings by local artists. ✪ *Poststr. 16*
• *Map K6* • *10am–6pm Tue–Sat*
• *(030) 24 00 20* • *Admission charge*

9 Neptune Fountain
The green Neo Baroque fountain, dating from 1895, depicts the sea god Neptune. He is surrounded by four female figures, symbolizing Germany's Rhine, Weichsel, Oder and Elb Rivers. ✪ *Am Rathaus* • *Map K6*

10 Karl-Marx-Allee and Frankfurter Allee
This road, lined by Soviet-style buildings, was built as a show-piece for Socialism in 1949–55. Known then as "Stalinallee", it provided ultra-modern apart-ments. ✪ *Mitte/Friedrichshain*

Neptune Fountain

A Day around Alexanderplatz

Morning

🕐 Start your day by going to **Alexanderplatz** *(see p131)* where you can watch the crowds in the square and perhaps do a spot of shopping before strolling to **Marienkirche**. Not far from here you can chill out at **Neptune Fountain** and then admire the statues of Marx and Engels in the **Marx-Engels-Forum**. From there it is only a few steps to the **Berliner Rathaus** *(see p131)*. The basement restaurant, or Ratskeller, is an excellent place for an early lunch, or you could stroll to the nearby historic Nikolaiviertel, and enjoy a meal, for example at **Reinhard's** *(see p137)*, which serves rustic fare.

Afternoon

Experience the historic ambience of the **Nikolai-viertel** by exploring on foot, if possible, its narrow alleyways. Nikolaikirche and the Knoblauchhaus are especially worth a visit. From here walk back to Alexanderplatz and – if the weather is nice – take the lift up to the viewing café in the **Berliner Fernsehturm** *(see p131)*. After refreshments you can continue on foot or take the U-Bahn from Alex to Strausberger Platz to admire the products of Socialist architecture in **Frankfurter Allee** *(see p133)*. On Grunerstraße you will reach the oppo-site bank of the Spree River, where you can immerse yourself in Berlin's municipal history at the **Märkisches Museum** just around the corner. In the evening, go for a posh meal at **Ermelerhaus** *(see p137)*.

Ephraim Palais and Märkisches Museum:
www.stadtmuseum.de/menu.htm

Left **Stairs of the Stadtgericht** Centre **Palais Podewil** Right **Ruins of Franziskanerkirche**

Best of the Rest

1 Stadtgericht
The imposing municipal courts building boasts extravagant stairs in the lobby area, with curved balustrades and elegant columns. ◎ *Littenstr. 13–15 • Map K6 • 8am–6pm Mon–Fri*

2 Franziskanerkirche
The ruins, remnants of a 13th-century Franciscan abbey, are surrounded by lawns, making this a picturesque spot for a rest in the city centre.
◎ *Klosterstr. 74 • Map K6*

3 Stadtmauer
A fragment of the 13th-century town wall, which once surrounded the twin towns of Berlin and Cölln. ◎ *Waisenstr. • Map K6*

4 Palais Podewil
The light yellow Baroque palace, built in 1701–4, has been transformed into Podewil, a cultural centre and one of the best places for contemporary music.
◎ *Klosterstr. 68–70 • Map K6 • 11am–10pm Mon–Sat • (030) 27 74 97 77*

5 Parochialkirche
This church, by Johann Arnold Nering and Martin Grünberg, was one of Berlin's most charming Baroque churches, but the magnificent interior was destroyed in World War II, and the bell tower collapsed.

Recently, it has become a venue for contemporary music concerts.
◎ *Klosterstr. 67 • Map K6*

6 Märkisches Ufer
This picturesque riverside promenade gives a good impression of the city in the late 18th century. ◎ *Map L6*

7 Heiliggeistkapelle
The 13th-century hospital church is a beautiful example of Gothic brick architecture.
◎ *Spandauer Str. 1 • Map K6*

8 Ribbeckhaus
The only Renaissance house in central Berlin, with a remarkable, lavishly ornamented façade.
◎ *Breite Str. 10 • Map K5*

9 Palais Schwerin and Münze
Two adjoining buildings with elegant 18th-century façades: Palais Schwerin has beautiful window cornices; Münze (the mint) is decorated with a Neo-Classical frieze. ◎ *Molkenmarkt 1–3 • Map K6*

10 Historic Port
Historic barges and tugboats that once operated on the Spree River are moored here. Boat tours of the harbour can be booked.
◎ *Märkisches Ufer • Map L6 • Apr–Oct: 2–6pm Tue–Fri; 11am–6pm Sat, Sun • (030) 21 47 32 56*

Left **Kaufhof Galleria façade** Centre **Inside Die Puppenstube** Right **Der Teeladen in Nikolaiviertel**

Shops & Markets

1 Kaufhof Galleria
The largest department store in East Berlin stocks everything your heart could desire. Its food department entices customers with a range of international gourmet foods. ◈ *Alexanderplatz 9 • Map I6 • (030) 24 74 30*

2 Die Puppenstube
Adorable dolls made from porcelain and other materials await window shopper and buyer alike, as do mountains of cute and fluffy teddy bears. ◈ *Propststr. 4 • Map K6 • (030) 242 39 67*

3 Birken-Paradies
This is the shop to visit if you are looking for decorative wood carvings, ranging from wooden toys to elaborate Christmas decorations. ◈ *Propststr. 4 • Map K6 • (030) 24 72 65 49*

4 Der Teeladen
A charming specialist tea shop opposite Nikolaikirche, always steeped in delicious scents. ◈ *Propststr. 3 • Map K6 • (030) 242 32 55*

5 Hessisches Haus (Gallery of Antiques)
One of the city's best antique shops, specializing in furniture. Expert advice is guaranteed.
◈ *Poststr. 12 • Map K5/6*
• *10am–8pm daily*
• *(030) 208 25 54*

6 Schuhtick
Schuhtick sells the best selection of shoes for today's "city-slicker", ranging from comfortable to elegant. ◈ *Alexanderplatz • Map I6 • (030) 242 40 12*

7 Berlin Carré
The snack bars based in this small shopping arcade offer delicious foods that you can buy or sample on the spot. ◈ *Karl-Liebknecht-Str. 13 • Map I6*

8 Thüringischer Weihnachtsmarkt
A vast array of stalls laden with Christmas gifts and and traditional wooden decorations at the Thuringian Christmas Market. ◈ *Propststr. 8 • Map K6 • (030) 241 12 29*

9 Wohltat'sche Buchhandlung
This large bookstore sells remainders and second-hand books, postcards and calendars of Berlin, as well as videos, CDs and DVDs. ◈ *Alexanderplatz 2 • Map I6 • (030) 242 68 54*

10 Saturn
Branch of a large multi-media chain, selling a huge range of CDs, PC games and all sorts of electronic games and entertainment at very reasonable prices.
◈ *Alexanderplatz 8*
• *Map I6 • (030) 24 75 16*

Left **Brauhaus Georgbräu** Centre **Zur letzten Instanz** Right **Zum Nußbaum**

Pubs, Cafés & Beer Gardens

1 Zur letzten Instanz
Berlin's oldest pub dates back to 1621, and former guests include Napoleon, the German artist Heinrich Zille and former Soviet leader Mikhael Gorbachev. The interior is charmingly aged. 🌑 *Waisenstr. 14–16 • Map K6 • noon–1am Mon–Fri; until 11pm Sat, Sun • (030) 24 25 528 • €€*

2 Brauhaus Georgbräu
This beer garden attracts not only Bavarians "in exile" but also many tourist groups. On offer are rustic fare and beer from both Berlin and Munich. 🌑 *Spreeufer 4 • Map K5/6 • summer: 10am–midnight daily; winter: from noon Mon–Fri • (030) 242 42 44 • €€*

3 Zum Nußbaum
A charming historic pub in Nikolaiviertel, serving draft beers and Berliner Weiße in summer. 🌑 *Am Nußbaum 3 • Map K6 • noon–11pm daily • (030) 242 30 95 • €€*

4 Sky Club
It's the gambling that draws punters to Sky Club but, at night, the views of Berlin from the 42nd floor are truly spectacular. 🌑 *Dircksenstr. 98–100 • Map I/K5/6 • from 11pm daily • no credit cards • no phone*

5 Alex Café
The Alex Café, below the TV tower, has a huge breakfast buffet – start your tour of East Berlin here. 🌑 *Panoramastr. 1a • Map K6 • 8am–3am Mon–Sat, 9am–3am Sun • (030) 24 04 76 30 • no credit cards • €€*

6 Green's
Home-made cakes make the little café diagonally opposite Nikolaikirche an irresistible stopping point. 🌑 *Poststr. 13 • Map K6 • from 11am daily • (030) 24 72 60 40 • no credit cards • €*

7 Café Ephraim's
Coffee and cakes plus views of the Spree River attract locals and tourists. 🌑 *Spreeufer 1 • Map K5/6 • (030) 24 72 59 47 • €€*

8 Telecafé Fernsehturm
Enjoy a snack in the skies above Berlin; the café does a full rotation every 45 minutes. 🌑 *Panoramastr. 1a • Map J6 • 10am–midnight daily • (030) 242 33 33 • €€*

9 Zum Fischerkietz
Atmospheric pub-restaurant, serving beer and the speciality, Berliner Weiße. 🌑 *Fischerinsel 5 • Map L6 • 11am–midnight daily • (030) 201 15 16 • €€*

10 Historische Weinstuben
A tiny wine bar/pub where you can enjoy beer and simple German food in historic surroundings. 🌑 *Poststr. 23 • Map K6 • noon–11:30pm daily • (030) 242 41 07 • €*

Left **Restaurant Zur Gerichtslaube** Right **Reinhard's in Nikolaiviertel**

Restaurants

1 Reinhard's
One of the most charming restaurants in the Mitte district. Savour the international food, surrounded by photos and paintings of famous contemporaries. ⊗ *Poststr. 28 • Map K6 • 11:30am–midnight daily • (030) 24 25 295 • €€€*

2 Ermelerhaus
Upmarket Mediterranean food in the Baroque Ermelerhaus. Try for a table in Rosenzimmer, the most attractive room. ⊗ *Märkisches Ufer 10 • Map L6 • 6pm–midnight Tue–Sat • (030) 24 06 29 00 • €€*

3 Zur Gerichtslaube
The former court building is a stylish setting for traditional Berlin specialities. ⊗ *Poststr. 28 • Map K6 • 11:30am–1am daily • (030) 241 56 98 • €€€*

4 Podewil
Pleasantly informal Italian eaterie in Kulturzentrum. Sit in the idyllic courtyard and listen to artists discussing their work. ⊗ *Klosterstr. 68–70 • Map K6 • (030) 242 67 45 • €€*

5 Zum Paddenwirt
A mecca for fans of traditional Berlin food, including fried herrings and brawn, and a strong beer. ⊗ *Nikolaikirchplatz 6 • Map K6 • 11:30am–11pm daily • (030) 242 63 82 • no credit cards • €€*

6 Raabe-Diele
Restaurant in the basement of Ermelerhaus, serving Berlin specialities such as mushy peas. ⊗ *Märkisches Ufer 10 • Map L6 • noon–11:30pm daily • (030) 24 06 20 • €€*

7 Marcellino
The best Italian restaurant in the area, with terrace and a large inviting garden, offering shade on a hot summer's day. Excellent pasta dishes and specials of the day are particularly worth trying. ⊗ *Poststr. 28 • Map K6 • noon–midnight daily • (030) 242 73 71 • €€*

8 La Riva
A more upmarket Italian venue in Nikolaiviertel, offering delicious pasta dishes, which can be enjoyed outside in summer, with a view of the Spree River. ⊗ *Spreeufer 2 • Map K6 • 11am–midnight daily • (030) 242 51 83 • €€*

9 Kartoffelhaus No. 1
At this restaurant, the menu is dominated by fish and hearty meat dishes. ⊗ *Poststr. 4 • Map K6 • (030) 24 72 09 45 • €€*

10 Mutter Hoppe
Delicious traditional German food, served in gigantic portions, makes up for the service, which is not always the friendliest. ⊗ *Rathausstr. 21 • Map K6 • 11:30am–11pm daily • (030) 241 56 25 • €*

Note: All restaurants accept credit cards and offer vegetarian dishes unless stated otherwise.

137

Left **The façades of restored houses in Hagenauer Straße** Right **The Jewish Cemetery**

Prenzlauer Berg

BERLIN'S PRENZLAUER BERG DISTRICT *attracts locals and tourists like virtually no other part of town because it has undergone the most dramatic changes in recent years. Today, the old tenement blocks in the former workers' district of East Berlin have been taken over by cafés, pubs and restaurants, and the nightlife is exciting and vibrant. Even when Berlin was still a divided city, Prenzlauer Berg was an area favoured by artists and an alternative crowd – and it exerts a similar pull today. Many houses in the quiet side streets have not yet been renovated and give a genuine impression of what Berlin once used to be like. But Prenzlauer Berg is undergoing a transformation. Since the reunification of the city, this quarter has become one of the most popular residential areas. Many West Germans, decried as "yuppies" by the locals, settle here, restore the buildings and buy up the apartments. The standard of life in the district has risen noticeably. Trendy bars, restaurants and cafés are clustered mainly around Kollwitzplatz and Husemannstraße. And so a visit to Prenzlauer Berg today is at the same time a journey back in time to the days immediately following reunification.*

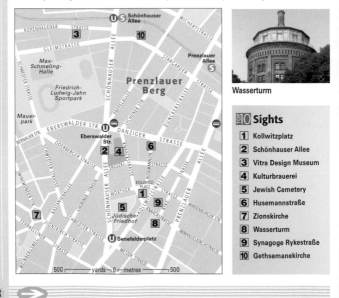

Wasserturm

🔟 Sights

1. Kollwitzplatz
2. Schönhauser Allee
3. Vitra Design Museum
4. Kulturbrauerei
5. Jewish Cemetery
6. Husemannstraße
7. Zionskirche
8. Wasserturm
9. Synagoge Rykestraße
10. Gethsemanekirche

Kollwitz monument in Kollwitzplatz

1 Kollwitzplatz

Once a quiet square, Kollwitzplatz is today the noisy and turbulent heart of the district. All around the green square, locals congregate in numerous cafés, pubs, bars and restaurants; in summer especially, the fun carries on till late at night. From the appearance of the lavishly restored façades it is hard to tell that Kollwitzplatz was once one of Berlin's poorest areas. The impoverished past of the district and its 19th-century tenement blocks is today only recalled by the name of the square. The artist Käthe Kollwitz (1867–1945) *(see p51)*, once lived and worked at Kollwitzplatz 25 and spent much of her life in the district, where she portrayed and attacked the poverty of the local workers in her drawings and sketches. ◈ *Prenzlauer Berg • Map H2*

2 Schönhauser Allee

Schönhauser Allee, 3 km (2 miles) long, is the main artery of the district. In the centre of the dual carriageway is the high-level viaduct of U-Bahn line U 2, painted green. Schönhauser Allee, which runs north-east from Rosa-Luxemburg-Platz to the edge of town, is lined with shops and a few pubs. Many buildings have not yet been restored and give

a good impression of the "old" Prenzlauer Berg – especially the buildings between Senefelderplatz and Danziger Straße. ◈ *Prenzlauer Berg • Map H1/2*

3 Vitra Design Museum

This is one of Berlin's newest museums and focuses on everything connected with style and design. Based behind the red-brick façade of a former power station, the museum presents changing exhibitions on furniture, product and interior design, with mainly contemporary themes and featuring artists such as Mies van der Rohe and Frank Lloyd Wright. Emphasis is placed on Scandinavian design, and the museum also attempts to forge links between Eastern and Western Europe. ◈ *Kopenhagener Str. 58 • Map G1 • 11am–8pm Tue–Sun • (030) 473 77 70 • Admission charge*

4 Kulturbrauerei

The giant building originally housed Berlin's Schultheiss brewery, one of the few remaining breweries that once made Prenzlauer Berg famous. The complex of buildings, parts of which are more than 150 years old, was designed by Franz Schwechten. It was completely restored in 1997–9, and has become a lively and popular meeting point for locals. Restaurants, cafes, pubs, a cinema, small shops and even a theatre have sprung up within the complex of red and yellow brick buildings and now line its numerous interior courtyards. ◈ *Schönhauser Allee 36–39 (entrance: Knaackstr. 97) • Map H1 • (030) 44 31 50*

Kulturbrauerei tower

Left **A house in Kollwitzplatz** Centre **At the Prater** Right **In Kollwitzstraße**

Jewish Cemetery

5 The small Jewish cemetery is one of the most charming cemeteries in the city. The tombstones lie or stand here amid dense scrub and high trees. The cemetery was set up in 1827, when the former Jewish cemetery in Große Hamburger Straße was closed. Two of the famous personalities who have found their final resting places here are the painter Max Liebermann (1847–1935) and the composer Giacomo Meyerbeer (1791–1864).

🔊 *Schönhauser Allee 23–25*
• *Map H2*

Husemann-straße

6 The East German regime undertook a perfect restoration of this idyllic street for Berlin's 750th anniversary celebrations. A stroll through the leafy roads lined with

houses from the Gründerzeit (the years after the founding of the German Empire in 1871) is one of the nicest ways to experience Prenzlauer Berg. Ancient-looking street lamps and signs, cobbled streets, antiquated shop signs and a few atmospheric pubs take the visitor back to the late 19th century. 🔊 *Between Wörter and Danziger Str.* • *Map H1/2*

Zionskirche

7 Zionskirche, dating from 1866–73, and the square of the same name form a tranquil oasis in the middle of the lively district. The Protestant church has always been a political centre, too. During the Third Reich, resistance groups against the Nazi regime congregated here and, during the East German period, the alternative "environment library" (an information and documentation centre) was established here. Church and other opposition groups who were active here played a decis-ive role in the political transform-ation of East Germany in 1989–90, which eventually led to reunification.

🔊 *Zionskirchplatz* • *Map G2*
• *noon–4pm Sun; noon–7pm Wed; 5–7pm Thur*
• *(030) 449 21 91*

Wasserturm

8 The unofficial symbol of the district is the giant, 30-m (98-ft) high Water Tower in Knaackstraße, built in 1856 as a water

Zionskirche

reservoir, but shut down in 1914. The engine house in the tower was used as an unofficial prison by the SA in 1933–45 – a period recalled by a commemorative plaque. The tower stands on Windmühlenberg (windmill hill), where some of the windmills that had made Prenzlauer Berg famous in the 19th century once stood. Today the yellow building has been converted into trendy apartments.

9 Synagoge Rykestraße

The synagogue, built in 1904, is one of the few Jewish places of worship to have survived "Reichskristallnacht" on 9 November 1938, the violent destruction of Jewish shop premises by the Nazis. The historic interior of the synagogue was built from red bricks in the shape of a basilica. Today it forms part of an apartment block. ◈ Rykestr. 53. • Map H2 • by prior arrangement • (030) 442 59 31

10 Gethsemanekirche

Outside this red-brick church, dating back to 1891–3, East German secret police beat up peaceful protesters. It was the starting point for the collapse of the East German regime.
◈ Stargarder Str. 77 • Map H1
• 9am–5:30pm daily • (030) 445 77 45

Entrance to Gethsemanekirche

A Day in Prenzlauer Berg

Morning

Set off from U-Bahn station Senefelderplatz – one of the lively spots in Prenzlauer Berg. From here, explore the old tenement blocks and backyards. Now continue in a westerly direction along Fehrbelliner Straße to **Zionskirchplatz** with its eponymous church. There are numerous cafés on the square, such as **Commode**, where you could stop for a cappuccino. Continue along Zionskirchstraße, then turn left into Kastanienallee. This is one of the most colourful streets in the quarter. At the end of the street you could pop into **Prater** (see p143); now turn right into Oderberger Straße, one of the best preserved streets of the district. Continue along Srzedzkistraße in an easterly direction until you reach **Husemannstraße**. Have a good look around the Old Berlin streets, you may find something interesting to buy.

Afternoon

You could have lunch at one of the many restaurants in **Kollwitzplatz** (see p139); **Gugelhof** and **Zander** are both worth recommending (for both see p143). Continue along Knaackstraße to the small **Synagoge Rykestraße**. From here it is only a few paces to the **Wasserturm** in Knaack straße. Give your feet a rest on the small green space around the tower, before continuing along Belforter and Kollwitzstraße to Schönhauser Allee. You will find perfect tranquillity there in the **Jewish Cemetery**.

Left **Senefelderplatz** Centre **Pfefferberg** Right **ZEISS-Großplanetarium**

Best of the Rest

1 Greifenhagener Straße
Not the most beautiful street of Old Berlin, but one of the best preserved. ◈ *Map H1*

2 Pfefferberg
This alternative cultural centre hosts concerts, performance art events and festivals. ◈ *Schönhauser Allee 176 • Map H2 • (030) 44 38 31 10*

3 Senefelderplatz
The wedge-shaped square is dedicated to Alois Senefelder, a pioneer of modern printing techniques. At its centre is "Café Achteck". ◈ *Map H2*

4 ZEISS-Großplanetarium
A trip to outer space – see stars, planets and galaxies under the silvery dome of the Planetarium. ◈ *Prenzlauer Allee 80 • 10am–noon Mon–Fri; 1:30–9pm Wed, Sat; 6–10pm Thu, Fri; 1:30–6pm Sun • (030) 42 18 45 12*

5 Mauerpark
The vast sporting terrain near the former border, comprising Max Schmeling Hall and Jahn Sports Park, was built for the Berlin Olympics in 2000. Today it hosts sports and music events. ◈ *Am Falkplatz • Map G1 • (030) 44 30 44 30*

6 Helmholtzplatz
All around this square, time seems to have stopped in 1925. The residential buildings are reminiscent of a social housing programme. ◈ *Map H1*

7 Prenzlauer Berg Museum
The small lively museum documents the history of the district and its poor working-class inhabitants in the 19th century. ◈ *Prenzlauer Allee 227–228 • Map H2 • 11am–5pm Tue, Wed; 1–7pm Thu; 2–6pm Sun • (030) 42 40 10 97*

8 Sammlung Industrielle Gestaltung
In this museum you can admire typically East German designs, ranging from soap powder cartons to shopping bags. Regular special exhibitions. ◈ *Kulturbrauerei, Knaackstr. 97 • Map H1 • 10am–6pm Mon–Thu • (030) 443 93 82*

9 Oderberger Straße
This tree-lined street has remain almost completely unchanged. The old municipal swimming baths of Prenzlauer Berg are also located in this road, at No. 84. ◈ *Map G/H1*

10 Thälmannpark
One of few parks in the north-east of the city, dominated by Socialist prefabricated buildings. It has a giant monument to Ernst Thälmann, a communist who was murdered by the Nazis. ◈ *Prenzlauer Allee • Map H1*

Price Categories

For a three-course
meal for one with half
a bottle of wine (or
equivalent meal), taxes
and charges included

€ under € 20
€€ € 20–30
€€€ € 30–45
€€€€ € 45–60
€€€€€ over € 60

Left **Italian restaurant BellUno** Right **Café November**

 Restaurants, Pubs & Bars

1 Drei
Yuppies and West Germans congregate at this trendy eaterie, serving international and Asian food. ◈ *Lychener Str. 20 • Map H1 • 6pm–midnight daily • (030) 44 73 84 71 • no credit cards • €€*

2 Gugelhof
Bill Clinton was once a guest at this restaurant, which draws clients from all over Berlin. The menu features an original combination of German and French dishes.
◈ *Knaackstr. 37 • Map I11/2 •10am–midnight daily • (030) 442 92 29 • €€*

3 Zander
A small restaurant, offering imaginative new interpretations of local fish specialities. The three-course set menu is particularly worth trying – it is one of the best and least expensive in the city. ◈ *Kollwitzstr. 50 • Map H2 • noon–1am daily • (030) 44 05 76 79 • €€€*

4 BellUno
Lively Italian restaurant with a large terrace – ideal for people-watching in the open air. ◈ *Kollwitzstr. 66 • Map H2 • 10am–1am daily • no credit cards • (030) 441 05 48 • €€€*

5 Prater
Surprises at the Prater include a beer garden, a rustic restaurant in the courtyard, as well as free live concerts. ◈ *Kastanienallee 7–9 • Map G2 • (030) 448 56 88 • no credit cards • €€€*

6 Knaack-Club
Almost legendary club and disco, playing rock and indie to an alternative crowd. ◈ *Greifswalder Str. 224 • Map H2 • from 9pm Fri, Sat • (030) 44 27 06 01 • no credit cards*

7 Restauration 1900
One of the oldest local restaurants in the district, it still pulls in the crowds with its deliciously light German cuisine. ◈ *Husemannstr. 1 • Map H1/2 • 8:30am–2am daily • (030) 442 24 94 • €€€€€*

8 Pasternak
Go Russian at this Moscow-style venue, with bortsch, Russian music and vodka. ◈ *Knaackstr. 22 • Map H1/2 • 10am–2am daily • (030) 441 33 99 • no credit cards • €€*

9 Café November
Popular restaurant and bar on the Prenzlauer Berg hill. ◈ *Husemannstr. 15 • Map H1/2 • 10am–2am Sun–Thu, 10am–3am Fri, Sat • (030) 442 84 25 • €€*

10 Anita Wronski
One of the district's oldest pubs, attracting students, would-be revolutionaries and locals. ◈ *Knaackstr. 26 • Map H1/2 • 10am–2am daily • (030) 442 84 83 • no credit cards*

> **Note:** All restaurants accept credit cards and offer vegetarian dishes unless stated otherwise.

Left **Normannenstraße** Centre **Schloss Friedrichsfelde** Right **Köpenick's coat of arms**

Berlin's Southeast

BERLIN'S EAST AND SOUTH *are remarkably different in character. Friedrichshain, Lichtenberg and Hohenschönhausen in the east are densely built-up, former working-class areas, while green Treptow and idyllic Köpenick in the far southeast seem like independent villages. The tenement blocks of East Berlin were steeped in history during World War II and later under the East German regime. Historic Köpenick and Großer Müggelsee, meanwhile, are popular daytrip destinations.*

🔟 Sights

1. Köpenicker Altstadt
2. Köpenicker Schloss
3. Gedenkstätte Normannenstraße
4. Deutsch-Russisches Museum
5. East Side Gallery
6. Großer Müggelsee
7. Treptower Park
8. Volkspark Friedrichshain
9. Tierpark Friedrichsfelde
10. Gedenkstätte Hohenschönhausen

Köpenick Town Hall

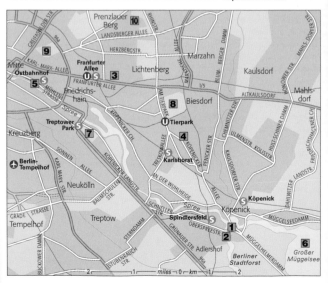

Pool in Köpenicker Altstadt

1 Köpenicker Altstadt

Köpenick is a small, quiet, self-absorbed world. This island community has a venerable history: as early as the 9th century, people had settled on Schlossinsel. The former fishing village stayed independent until 1920, and its coat of arms still features two fish, as do many of the house façades. The Old Town, on the banks of the Dahme River, is still characterized by cobbled streets and low fishermen's huts from the 18th and 19th centuries, taking the visitor back in time. Schüßlerplatz, Grünstraße and Alter Markt, too, still have some older buildings.

Old Köpenick became famous on 16 October 1906. Wilhelm Voigt, a homeless man dressed up as a captain, commanded a troop of soldiers, marched into the town hall, arrested the mayor and confiscated the municipal coffers. Today the "Hauptmann von Köpenick" (Captain of Köpenick), who later became a popular folk figure, is commemorated by a statue in front of the Rathaus (town hall). The vast red-brick structure, dating from 1901–4, is a typical example of Gothic brick architecture from Brandenburg province. ◈ Rathaus: Alt-Köpenick 21
• 8am–6pm Mon–Fri • (030) 65 68 40

Hauptmann von Köpenick

2 Köpenicker Schloss

The Köpenick palace, which is situated on Schlossinsel (palace island) in the south of the district, was built in 1677–81 to plans by the Dutch architect Rutger van Langervelt for Frederick, heir to the throne and future King Frederick I. In the 17th century, the charming Baroque palace was extended by Johann Arnold Nering and others. Today it houses part of the collections of the Berliner Kunstgewerbemuseum (arts and crafts museum). ◈ Schlossinsel
• closed for renovation until sometime in 2002 • (030) 20 90 55 66

3 Gedenkstätte Normannenstraße

The former headquarters of the much-feared "Stasi", East Germany's secret police, is now a memorial, commemorating the thousands of victims of the East German regime and of Erich Mielke, the minister in charge of the secret police. Visitors can see his offices, the canteen and various pieces of spying equipment, revealing the methods used by the Socialist big-brother regime.
◈ Ruschestr. 59, Haus 1
• 11am–6pm Mon–Fri; 2–6pm Sat, Sun
• (030) 553 68 54 • Admission charge

4 Deutsch-Russisches Museum

World War II ended here on 8 May 1945, when Germany signed its unconditional surrender. Documents, uniforms and photographs, displayed in the former officers' casino, relate the story of the war.
◈ Zwieseler Str. 4 • 10am–6pm Tue–Sun
• (030) 509 86 09 • Admission charge

Left **East Side Gallery** Centre **Inside Köpenicker Schloss** Right **Volkspark Friedrichshain**

5 East Side Gallery

A fragment of the Berlin Wall, 1.3 km (1,422 yards) long, was left standing next to the Spree River. In 1990, 118 artists from around the world painted colourful images onto the grey concrete wall, making it a unique work of art. Particularly famous is a picture by the Russian artist Dmitri Vrubel, showing Leonid Brezhnev and the East German leader Erich Honecker, exchanging fraternal Socialist kisses. Much has faded due to exhaust fumes, but it is now being restored. ⊛ At Mühlenstr./ Oberbaumbrücke • Map H4

6 Großer Müggelsee

Großer Müggelsee, known as Berlin's "bathtub", is the largest of the city's lakes, covering an area of 766 hectares (1,892 acres). Müggelsee is not as popular as Großer Wannsee, its West Berlin counterpart, mainly because it is so far from the centre, in the southeast corner of the city. The lake is known for the beer gardens on its south side, which can be reached by boat from Friedrichshagen. Further south, Müggelturm (tower) offers magnificent views over Berlin and the surrounding Brandenburg province. All around the lake there are excellent paths for walking and cycling. You can also swim in the lake,

for example at the beach resort of Rahnsdorf. ⊛ Friedrichshagen: Müggelturm: Straße zum Müggelturm 1 • Apr–mid-Nov 10am–7pm daily; mid-Nov–Mar 10am–7pm Sat, Sun • (030) 651 65 12

7 Treptower Park

Treptower Park, established in the 19th century as a recreation area for Berlin's working-class communities, is today best known for the giant Sowjetisches Ehrenmal (Soviet Memorial). In April 1945, 5,000 Red Army soldiers, who died during the liberation of Berlin, were buried here. Beyond the mass graves rises a 12-m (39-ft) bronze statue of a Russian soldier, holding a child in one arm and a sword in the other, which he has used to destroy a swastika. ⊛ Alt-Treptow

Memorial in Treptower Park

8 Volkspark Friedrichshain

Berlin's oldest landscaped gardens, the people's park, was designed by Joseph Peter Lenné in 1840. Today it provides an oasis of tranquillity in the middle of the densely built-up district of Friedrichshain. World War II has left its traces here, too. Kleiner and Großer Bunkerberg – two heaps of rubble (the latter nicknamed "Mount Rubble") reaching a height of 78 m (256 ft) – were piled up here after the war. Less traumatic is the Märchenbrunnen, a charming Neo-Baroque fairy-tale fountain created by Ludwig

Aviary in Tierpark Friedrichsfelde

Hoffmann. It is decorated with 106 richly ornamented figures from popular fairy tales.
🔗 *Am Friedrichshain • Map H2*

9 Tierpark Friedrichsfelde

This small zoological garden is situated in the middle of a beautiful park next to Friedrichsfelde Palace. The animal park is particularly worth visiting for the lions and Siberian tigers, which are kept in rocky outdoor enclosures. The elephant house, too, attracts many visitors. Matibi, a baby elephant, is the star among the pachyderms.
🔗 *Am Tierpark 125 • Apr–Oct: 9am–7pm daily, Nov–Mar: 9am till sunset daily • (030) 51 53 10 • Admission charge*

10 Gedenkstätte Hohenschönhausen

This former secret police prison for "political" prisoners was in use until 1990. Before 1951, it served as a reception centre for the Red Army. On a guided tour, you can visit the watchtowers and the cells – particularly horrifying are the so-called "submarine cells", rooms without windows used for solitary confinement, where inmates were interrogated and tortured.
🔗 *Genslerstr. 66 • Guided tours 11am and 1pm daily and by prior arrangement • (030) 98 60 82 30*

A Day in Berlin's Green Southeast

Morning

Begin your tour of Berlin's Southeast at Alexanderplatz, from where you can take the S-Bahn to the various sights, which are not always near each other.

First, take S-Bahn line S3 to Karlshorst, where you can visit the **Deutsch-Russisches Museum** *(see p145)*. From here it is not far to the **Stasi-Museum Normannenstraße** *(see p145)* – return to S-Bahn station Ostkreuz, then take S-Bahn line S4 and U-Bahn line U5 to Magdalenenstraße. After visiting all these museums you could recover outdoors. Take U-Bahn line U5 to **Tierpark Friedrichsfelde**, where you can visit both the zoological garden and Friedrichsfelde Palace.

Afternoon

For the afternoon make an excursion to Köpenick. Take S-Bahn line S3 to Köpenick, and enjoy a typically German meal in the **Ratskeller** *(see p149)*, the town hall cellar. Afterwards explore **Köpenick Old Town**. The centre of the old fishing village is especially worth a visit. There are many cafés near **Köpenicker Schloss** *(see p145)*, where you could stop for a coffee and a piece of cake, for example **Café Kietz** *(see p148)*. Continue your journey by S-Bahn to Friedrichshagen, the access point for **Großer Müggelsee**. From here take one of the tourist boats to the restaurant **Müggelseeperle**, where you can round off the day with a tasty evening meal.

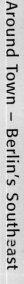

Left **Eierschale Haus Zenner** Centre **Altstadtcafé Cöpenick** Right **Kietz Café and Restaurant**

TOP 10 Cafés & Snack Bars

1 Altstadtcafé Cöpenick
This tiny café in Köpenick's Old Town serves coffee and cakes, outdoors, in summer, on a small veranda. ◈ *Alt Köpenick 16 • 10am–6:30pm daily • (030) 65 47 40 69 • no credit cards*

2 Eierschale Haus Zenner
One of the classic day-trip destinations, families once used to "bring and brew their own coffee". Today it is a popular outdoor café, often offering live music and dancing. ◈ *Alt-Treptow 14–17 • noon–midnight daily • (030) 533 73 70 • no credit cards*

3 Café L & B
Not far from the swimming baths, this café serves local fish dishes, as well as afternoon coffee and cakes. ◈ *Am Kleinen Müggelsee 1 • 11am–9pm Wed–Sun • (030) 659 82 24 • no credit cards*

4 Neu-Helgoland
A favourite day-trippers' restaurant on the lake, where locals and visitors alike enjoy the game and fish dishes. ◈ *Odernheimer Str., Kleiner Müggelsee • 11am–10pm daily • (030) 659 82 47 • no credit cards*

5 Seerestaurant Rübezahl
This beer garden, on the piers of Müggelsee, is a great place to aim for on a day out. You can reach the outdoor restaurant by ferry. Both sweet and savoury snacks are served here. ◈ *Am Großen Müggelsee • 11am–11pm daily • (030) 65 88 24 70 • no credit cards*

6 Schloss-Café
An oasis of tranquillity where you can chill out after a visit to Kunstgewerbemuseum (arts and crafts museum) on Schlossinsel. Enjoy coffee and cakes, overlooking the Dahme River. ◈ *Köpenicker Schloss, Schlossinsel • (030) 20 90 55 66 • no credit cards*

7 Kietz Café and Restaurant
A pleasant café, serving superb home-made cakes and snacks. A great draw in summer is the waterside terrace. ◈ *Müggelheimer Str. 1 • noon–midnight daily • (030) 651 71 09 • no credit cards*

8 Café Liebig
Charming, richly ornamented Art-Nouveau café in a historic building, dating back more than 130 years. The summer terrace overlooks Grünau regatta course. ◈ *Regattastr. 158 • 11am–11pm daily • (030) 674 33 33 • no credit cards*

9 Restaurantschiff Hoppetosse
A picture-book ship restaurant, serving everything including fish dishes. Light snacks – and the cakes are particularly tempting. ◈ *Eichenstr. 4 • from 11am daily • (030) 53 32 03 40 • no credit cards*

10 Hanff's Ruh
Sticking to an old tradition, guests can brew their own coffee here. The mushroom dishes are highly recommended. ◈ *Rabindranath-Tagore-Str. 25 • 11am–9pm Wed–Mon • (030) 674 33 68 • no credit cards*

Price Categories

For a three-course		
meal for one with half	€	under € 20
a bottle of wine (or	€€	€ 20–30
equivalent meal), taxes	€€€	€ 30–45
and charges included	€€€€	€ 45–60
	€€€€€	over € 60

Left **Restaurant freiheit fünfzehn** Right **The Ratskeller in Köpenick's Old Town**

🔟 Restaurants

1 freiheit fünfzehn

German and French cuisine are served aboard a schooner, which is moored at the pier. There are also occasional cabaret and live music performances. If you prefer dry land, you can enjoy your meals in the beer garden. ⊗ *Freiheit 15 • 6pm–midnight daily • (030) 65 88 78 25 • €€*

2 Ratskeller Köpenick

Traditional Berlin fare is served in the vast vaulted cellars where Wilhelm Voigt once famously took advantage of gullible local civil servants (see p145). ⊗ *Alt-Köpenick 21 • 11am–11pm daily • (030) 655 56 52 • €€*

3 Klipper Schiffsrestaurant

This two-master, dating back to 1890, has been turned into a cosy restaurant; the menu features French-inspired international dishes. ⊗ *banks of the Spree River, close to Insel der Jugend • 10am–1am daily • no credit cards • €€*

4 Schrörs am Müggelsee

Popular, informal beer garden near the lake, specializing in hearty food from the grill. ⊗ *Josef-Nawrocki-Str. 16 • 11am–10m pm daily • (030) 64 09 58 80 • no credit cards • €*

5 Die Spindel

This rustic restaurant serves traditional German food as well as a large selection of fondues, which need to be ordered in advance. ⊗ *Bölschestr. 51 • 11:30am–10pm daily • (030) 645 29 37 • €*

6 Ellis

One of the few American-style restaurants in Berlin, with authentic decor and American regional dishes. ⊗ *Fürstenwalder Allee 17 • 6–11pm Mon–Fri, noon–11pm Sat, Sun • (030) 648 91 81 • €€*

7 Krokodil

Situated in the Old Town, near the river baths in Gartenstraße, this is one of the nicest garden venues, especially in summer. ⊗ *Gartenstr. 46–48 • 6pm–midnight Mon–Fri, 11am–midnight Sat, Sun • (030) 65 88 00 94 • no credit cards • €€*

8 Bräustübl

A typical Berlin beer garden and restaurant, belonging to the Berliner Bürger-Brau brewery. Bürger-Brau beer and game dishes are served; occasional live concerts at weekends. ⊗ *Müggelseedamm 164 • noon–midnight daily • (030) 645 57 16 • €€*

9 Lehmofen

Meat and vegetarian dishes, freshly cooked in an antiquated clay oven, are the top attractions in this restaurant with summer terrace. ⊗ *Freiheit 12 • noon–midnight Mon–Thu • (030) 655 70 44 • €€*

10 Kiboko

African restaurant in a 19th-century fisherman's hut, serving ostrich and crocodile: one of the more exotic venues. ⊗ *Bölschestr. 10 • noon–1am Mon–Fri, 10am–1am Sat, Sun • (030) 64 19 73 24 • no credit cards • €€*

Note: All restaurants accept credit cards and offer vegetarian dishes unless stated otherwise.

Left **Inside Schloss Charlottenhof** Centre **Chinese tea-house** Right **Vestibül in Neues Palais**

Potsdam & Sanssouci

POTSDAM IS AN IMPORTANT PART OF EUROPEAN *cultural history – a splendid centre of European Enlightenment, which reached its climax in the 18th century in the architectural and artistic design of Frederick the Great's palace. The palace complex of Sanssouci, with its beautiful, extensive park, is both magnificent and playful and has been designated a World Heritage Centre of Culture by UNESCO. Every year, it enchants millions of visitors from around the world. The town of Potsdam, numbering some 300,000 inhabitants, is the capital of the federal province of Brandenburg. This former garrison town has much to delight its visitors, including small palaces and old churches, idyllic parks and historic immigrant settlements.*

Frederick the Great playing the flute in Sanssouci

🔟 Sights

1. Schloss Sanssouci
2. Neues Palais
3. Schlosspark Sanssouci
4. Schloss Cecilienhof
5. Schloss Charlottenhof
6. Marmorpalais
7. Holländisches Viertel
8. Nikolaikirche
9. Marstall (Filmmuseum)
10. Filmpark Babelsberg

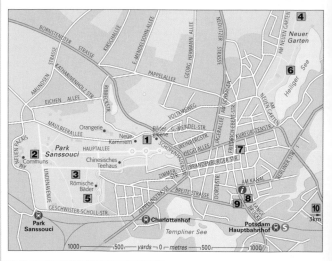

Preceding pages **The stairs leading up to Schloss Sanssouci**

1 Schloss Sanssouci

The Prussian King Frederick the Great wished to live "sans souci", in a palace outside the boundaries of the hated city – the French phrase means "without worries". In 1745, Frederick commissioned his favourite architect Georg Wenzeslaus von knobelsdorff to plan and construct this magnificent Rococo palace according to his own designs.

The main building with its yellow façade rises proudly above the former terraced vineyards, leading up to the domed building and its elegant marble hall at the centre of the palace complex. In both its design and shape, the marble hall pays homage to the Pantheon in Rome. To its left and right are some very attractive rooms designed by von Knobelsdorff and Johann August Nahl; these include the famous concert room, adorned with paintings by Antoine Pesne, and Frederick's library. In this wing, the monarch liked to play the flute or to philosophize with Voltaire. Valuable paintings by Frederick the Great's favourite painter, the French artist Antoine Watteau, adorn the palace walls. ⊗ Zur historischen Mühle
• Apr–Oct: 8:30am–5pm daily, Nov–Mar: 9am–4pm daily • (0331) 969 42 02
• Admission charge

Vase in Park Sanssouci

2 Neues Palais

To the north of Sanssouci palace park rises the Baroque Neues Palais, one of Germany's most beautiful palaces, built in 1763 for Frederick the Great according to designs by Johann Gottfried Büring, Jean Laurent Le Geay and Carl von Gontard. The vast, two-storey structure comprises 200 rooms, including the Marmorsaal (marble hall), a lavishly furnished ballroom, and the Schlosstheater, where plays are once more performed today. Frederick's private chambers are equally splendid, especially his study furnished in Rococo style, the upper gallery with valuable parquet flooring and the Oberes Vootibül, a room clad entirely in marble. ⊗ Am Neuen Palais
• Feb–Mar, Oct: 9am–12:30pm & 1–4pm Sat–Wed; Apr–Sep: 9am–12:30pm & 1–5pm Sat–Wed; Nov–Jan: 9am–12:30pm & 1–3pm Sat–Wed • (0331) 969 42 55
• Admission charge

3 Schlosspark Sanssouci

It is easy to while away an entire day in the palace park, which covers 287 hectares (709 acres). Of the charming buildings, hidden in the lavishly designed landscape garden, the Rococo-style Chinesisches Teehaus, built in 1754–6 by Johann Gottfried Büring, is especially worth seeing.

Left **Neues Palais** Right **Concert Hall in Schloss Sanssouci**

S-Bahn S7 goes to Potsdam from Berlin. The journey takes about 45 minutes.

Left **A street in Holländisches Viertel** Centre **Marmorpalais** Right **Marstall (Filmmuseum)**

Originally it served as a tea-house and dining room, and it now houses an exhibition of porcelain pieces from East Asia.

The Römische Bäder (Roman Baths), a group of pavilions next to the lake, are also inspired by historic models. Modelled on an Italian Renaissance villa, they were built between 1829 and 1840 by Friedrich Karl Schinkel as guest and bathing houses.

The Orangerie, constructed in 1851–60 by Friedrich August Stüler, was also originally intended to accommodate the king's guests. Today it houses a small gallery of paintings. ◈ *Teehaus: Ökonomieweg • Apr–Sep: 8am–6pm daily; mid-May–mid-Oct: 10am–12:30pm, 1–5pm Tue–Sun • (0331) 969 42 02*

◈ *Römische Bäder: Lennéstr.*
• mid-May–mid-Oct: 10am–5pm Tue–Sun
• (0331) 969 42 02

◈ *Orangerie: Maulbeerallee • mid-May–mid-Oct: 10am–12:30pm, 1–5pm Tue–Sun*
• (0331) 29 61 89

The Potsdam Conference

In July and August 1945, the heads of government of the United States (Harry Truman), the USSR (Joseph Stalin) and Great Britain (Winston Churchill) met in Schloss Cecilienhof, in order to seal the future of Germany in a treaty. Vitally important points such as the demilitarization of Germany, the level of reparations to be paid, the punishment of war criminals, the resettlement of Germans from Poland and the new borders of Germany were decided here.

4 Schloss Cecilienhof

This little palace, built in the style of an English country manor house, entered the history books in 1945, when Germany's fate was sealed by the Potsdam Conference. Built in 1914–7, the palace is now used as a hotel. It also houses a small exhibition documenting the Conference and the palace's furnishings.
◈ *Am Neuen Garten • Apr–Oct: 9am–5pm Tue–Sun; Nov–Mar: 9am–4pm Tue–Sun • (0331) 969 42 44*

5 Schloss Charlottenhof

A small Neo-Classical palace in Park Sanssouci, built in 1829 by Schinkel for the heir to the throne, Friedrich Wilhelm IV. Particularly worth seeing is the tent-like Humboldtsaal.
◈ *Geschwister-Scholl-Str. • mid-May–mid-Oct: 10am–12:30pm, 1–5pm Tue–Sun • (0331) 969 42 02*

6 Marmorpalais

This small, early Neo-Classical palace at the side of the lake was built in 1791–7 by Carl Gotthard Langhans and others. It features an elegant concert hall as well as contemporary furniture and porcelain.
◈ *Heiliger See (Neuer Garten) • mid-May–mid-Oct: 10am–12:30pm, 1–5pm Tue–Sun • (0331) 969 42 46*

7 Holländisches Viertel

A pleasant way to explore the district of Potsdam is a walk through the historic Old Town, with its art galleries, cafés and restaurants. Built between 1733

Nikolaikirche on Alter Markt

and 1742, the area originally served as a settlement for Dutch workers after whom it is now named. The small red-brick buildings are decorated with attractive stucco ornaments.

🔊 *Friedrich-Ebert-, Kurfürsten-, Hebbel-, Gutenbergstr.*

8 Nikolaikirche

Potsdam's most attractive church was designed by Schinkel in 1830 in an early Neo-Classical style. Its giant dome is particularly striking. 🔊 *Am Alten Markt • 2–5pm Mon, 10am–5pm Tue–Sat, 11:30am–5pm Sun • (0331) 50 14 43*

9 Marstall (Filmmuseum)

The small museum, based in the Baroque former stable buildings of the king's town residence, uses old cameras, props and projectors to document the history of German film.

🔊 *Am Alten Markt • 10am–6pm Tue–Sun • (0331) 27 18 10*

10 Filmpark Babelsberg

The Filmpark offers visitors a tour of the legendary UFA-Studios, which were among the world's most important when they operated here in Babelsberg from 1917 to 1945. Exciting U-boat trips, stunt performances and special effects are shown.

🔊 *Am Alten Markt • Mar–Jun & Sep–Nov: 10am–6pm daily, Jul–Aug: 10am–8pm daily • (018 05) 34 66 66*

A Day in Potsdam

Morning

🕐 Begin your exploration in the **Schlosspark Sanssouci** *(see pp153–4)* as early as possible in order to get ahead of the daily influx of visitors. Start with **Schloss Sanssouci** and **Neues Palais** *(see p153)*, then visit Chinesisches Teehaus, Römische Bäder and Orangerie. From the orangery's viewing terrace you will have magnificent views over the entire palace complex. If you are up for it, you could also climb up to Schloss Belvedere on top of the hill. From Schlosspark walk along Voltaireweg to Neuer Garten in the northeast of Potsdam, where you can rest and recover over a tasty lunch at **Schloss Cecilienhof** *(see p157)*.

Afternoon

Start the afternoon with a stroll through Neuer Garten. Visit **Schloss Cecilienhof** and, if you like, stop for a break at Heiliger See. Afterwards walk or drive into the centre of Potsdam, starting with the **Holländisches Viertel** (Dutch quarter) where you could pop into one of the numerous cafés. Then continue on a circular walk, strolling past Peter-und Paul-Kirche, the French church, **Nikolaikirche** and the town hall. Finish your day of sightseeing with a visit to the **Marstall** and the film museums in Potsdam and Babelsberg. Take a look at the palace and the telegraph hill. A delicious evening meal awaits you at **Villa Kellermann** *(see p157)* to round off your day in Potsdam.

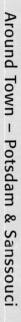

Left **Schloss Babelsberg** Centre **Alexandrowka-Haus** Right **Wasserwerk Sanssouci**

TOP10 Best of the Rest

1 Alexandrowka
A detour to the Russian colony in Potsdam feels like a journey to Russia itself. Decorated log cabins with picturesque gardens were built here in 1826 for a Russian military choir. ◈ *Russische Kolonie/Puschkinallee*

2 Wasserwerk Sanssouci
This building, resembling a mosque with minarets, houses the water pumping station for Schlosspark Sanssouci. The ancient pump, dating from 1842, can be inspected in the building. ◈ *Breite Str. • mid-May–mid-Oct: 10am–5pm Sat, Sun • (0331) 969 42 48*

3 Telegrafenberg
If you're prepared to climb telegraph hill, you could visit the elegant Einstein tower at the top. It was designed in 1920 by Erich Mendelsohn for the observation of the sun. ◈ *Albert-Einstein-Str. • Guided tours Einsteinturm: (0331) 29 17 41 • Admission charge*

4 Schloss Babelsberg
Built by Schinkel in 1833–5, this Gothic palace is situated in an idyllic park on the banks of the Havel River. ◈ *Park Babelsberg • Apr–Oct: 10am–12:30pm, 1–5pm Tue–Sun; Nov–Mar: 10am–4pm Sat • (0331) 969 42 50 • Admission charge*

5 Potsdam-Museum
A small museum presenting the history of the town of Potsdam, from prehistoric times to the present day. The museum is based in the historic Hiller-Brandtsche Häuser. ◈ *Breite Str. 8–12 • 9am–5pm Tue–Sun • (0331) 289 66 00 • Admission charge*

6 Altes Rathaus
The old town hall, built in 1753, is decorated with sculptures and Potsdam's coat of arms – two gilded Atlas figures, each carrying a globe. ◈ *Am Alten Markt*

7 Luisenplatz
This small square with its plain, restored buildings gives a good impression of Potsdam in the early 19th century. ◈ *Luisenplatz*

8 Französische Kirche
In 1752, Johann Boumann built this elliptical Huguenot church with its giant columned portico, while Schinkel designed the beautiful interior in the 1830s. ◈ *Am Bassinplatz • 11am–5pm Tue–Sun • (0331) 29 12 19*

9 Peter- und Paul-Kirche
The Catholic church of Saints Peter and Paul, modelled on Haghia Sophia in Istanbul, was built in 1867–70 by Stüler. ◈ *Am Bassinplatz • by prior arrangement • (0331) 280 49 42*

10 Brandenburger Tor
The most attractive of five former town gates was built by Gontard and Unger in 1770 in the Neo-Classical style to celebrate Prussian victory in the Seven Years' War. ◈ *Luisenplatz*

Left **Schloss Cecilienhof serves delicious food**

Price Categories

For a three-course	€	under € 20
meal for one with half	€€	€ 20–30
a bottle of wine (or	€€€	€ 30–45
equivalent meal), taxes	€€€€	€ 45–60
and charges included	€€€€€	over € 60

🔟 Restaurants & Cafés

1 Speckers Zur Ratswaage
The combination of Prussian interior, friendly service and a light, international cuisine make Ratswaage one of Potsdam's best restaurants. ◈ *Am Neuen Markt 10 • noon–3pm, 6–10pm daily • (0331) 280 43 11 • no credit cards • €€*

2 Cecilienhof
The historic palace is now the home of a luxury hotel. Its restaurant serves top-quality German food. ◈ *Am Neuen Garten • 11am–11pm daily • (0331) 370 50 • €€€*

3 Villa Kellermann
You can enjoy an excellent meal in this town house directly on Heiliger See, with great views of the Marmorpalais and Schloss Cecilienhof. The menu is dominated by Italian dishes.
◈ *Mangerstr. 34–36 • noon–midnight Tue–Sun • (0331) 29 15 72 • €€€*

4 Restaurant Juliette
A former manor house has been taken over by this French restaurant, one of the most charming eateries in the entire region, serving French classics. ◈ *Jägerstr. 39 • noon–midnight daily • (0331) 270 17 91 • no credit cards • €€*

5 Preußischer Hof
Pickled pork knuckle and other specialities from Berlin and Brandenburg province feature on the menu of this solid middle-class restaurant. ◈ *Charlottenstr. 11 • 11am–11pm daily • (0331) 270 07 62 • no credit cards • €€*

6 Maison Charlotte
Olde-worlde wine bar in a vaulted cellar, specializing in German and French country fare and boasting an excellent selection of wines. ◈ *Charlottenstr. 13 • 10am–7pm Mon–Fri • (0331) 280 54 50 • no credit cards • €€*

7 Barokoko
Fashion designer Wolfang Joop is a regular at this venue, which is based in an historic building and serves fresh Italian food, with particularly delicious pasta dishes. ◈ *Friedrich-Ebert-Str. 30 • noon–1am daily • (0331) 280 14 38 • €€*

8 Waage
Attractive historic restaurant in a central location. Regional game and fish dishes in often unusual new variations are particularly worth trying. ◈ *Am Neuen Markt • noon–midnight daily • (0331) 270 96 75 • no credit cards • €€*

9 Café Heider
A lovely old café in the middle of Potsdam's Old Town. Fantastic breakfast selection, which you can enjoy outside on the terrace in summer. ◈ *Friedrich-Ebert-Str. 29 • 9am–1am daily • (0331) 270 55 96 • €*

10 La Madeleine
A little bistro, serving all sorts of crêpes, such as sweet with jam or savoury with ham, but all ideal for a quick snack. ◈ *Lindenstr. 9 • 11am–10:30pm daily • (0331) 27 05 400 • no credit cards • €*

Note: *All restaurants accept credit cards and offer vegetarian dishes unless stated otherwise.*

STREETSMART

BERLIN'S TOP 10

Left **In Kurfürstendamm** Right **The Love Parade in July**

🔟 Planning your Trip

1 When to Go and Climate

The weather in Berlin is better than its reputation. The continental climate, which characterizes the entire region, guarantees mild and dry weather for the main holiday period from May to September. In spring and autumn it can be cold and wet, and it may be advisable not to travel to Berlin between November and February, when it is often cloudy, and a bitingly cold, easterly wind whistles through the city.

2 What to Wear

In the summer months you'll need only lightweight clothing. In spring and autumn you should definitely pack a rain- and windproof jacket as well as an umbrella. Locals dress informally and more flamboyantly than other German urbanites – anything you like goes. The capital has, however, gone more upmarket and you may feel out of place in many restaurants or theatres without a jacket and tie or evening dress.

3 Money

If you're arriving from abroad, you'll be able to buy euros at all banks and bureaux de change (many are based around Bahnhof Zoo). Credit cards, traveller's cheques and EC-cards are accepted everywhere in the centre of town.

4 Insurance

All travellers are well advised to buy insurance cover for accidents, illness and theft. Cancellation insurance may also be worth taking out.

5 Driving Licence

UK, US, Canadian and Australian driving licences are recognized in Germany.

6 Visa and Customs

All visitors to Berlin need valid passports. If you're staying in Berlin for 90 days or less, you will not normally need a visa. Ask your German Embassy for details. Non-EU citizens may import 200 cigarettes and one litre of spirits per adult.

7 Electrical Appliances

The electric current is 220 volt; but remember to bring an adaptor with two round pins.

8 Time Difference

Berlin is in the Central European time zone, which means that it is one hour ahead of Greenwich Mean Time, six hours ahead of US Eastern Standard Time and 11 hours behind Australian Eastern Standard Time.

9 Children's Needs

If you are travelling with children, book into child-friendly accommodation. Always look out for family reductions. It can be a lot of fun to explore the city together with children, but you are advised to avoid the rush hours on U-Bahn and buses, especially if you are travelling with babies or very young children.

10 Pupils and Students

Many museums, theatres and other cultural establishments offer up to 50 per cent reductions for pupils and students on production of a valid student card.

Embassies

Australian Embassy
Friedrichstr. 200 • Map L4 • (030) 88 00 88 0

British Embassy
Wilhelmstr. 70–71 • Map K3 • (030) 20 45 70

Canadian Embassy
Friedrichstr. 95 • Map L4 • (030) 20 31 20

New Zealand Embassy
Friedrichstr. 60 • Map L4 • (030) 20 62 10

South African Embassy
Friedrichstr. 60 • Map L4 • (030) 22 07 30

US Embassy
Neustädtische Kirchstr. 4–5 • Map K3 • (030) 832 92 33

Online map of Berlin: www.stadtplandienst.de

Left **Flughafen Tegel** Centre **The ICE to Berlin** Right **Three typical road signs**

🔟 Arriving in Berlin

1 Flughafen Tegel
Berlin's largest airport is situated a mere 8 km (5 miles) to the north-west of the city centre. Though it is a relatively small airport, Lufthansa, Deutsche BA, British Airways, KLM, Air France, Iberia and Alitalia and others all operate direct flights here There are no intercontinental flights to Berlin. A taxi from the airport to Ku'damm costs around € 13 and takes about 20–30 minutes (depending on traffic). Less expensive and nearly as fast is the journey by bus – Nos X09 or 109 (about € 2.10) stop everywhere in central Berlin. Ⓢ Airport information: 01805 00 01 86

2 Flughafen Schönefeld
Located approximately 20 km (12 miles) south-east of Berlin, in Brandenburg province, this airport is served by charter and Fast European airlines. S-Bahn lines 39 or 845 will take you directly to the city centre. A taxi trip from Schönefeld is not recommended because it is too far out of town. Ⓢ Airport information: Tel. 01805 00 01 86

3 Flughafen Tempelhof
The small historic city airport south of Kreuzberg provides regional connections to medium-sized German towns and to Scandinavia. From Flughafen Tempelhof take U-Bahn line U6 from Platz der Luftbrücke station or bus No. 119 to Ku'damm. Ⓢ Airport information: 01805 00 01 86

4 Airlines
Both Lufthansa and Deutsche BA have offices in the western part of the city. Ⓢ Lufthansa: Kurfürstendamm 21 (Neues Kranzler-Eck) • Map P4 • 10am–8pm Mon–Fri, 10am–4pm Sat • (030) 88 75 38 00 Ⓢ Deutsche BA: Budapester Str. 18b • Map N5 • 9am–6pm Mon–Fri • (030) 254 00 00

5 Bahnhof Zoologischer Garten
Most long-distance trains from Germany and Western Europe arrive at Bahnhof Zoo in the western part of the centre. There are excellent connections from this station to other parts of town by S- and U-Bahn, and taxis are always waiting at the taxi ranks outside the station. Ⓢ Hardenbergplatz • Map N4 • (030) 29 74 93 50

6 Ostbahnhof
Ostbahnhof is the point of arrival for travellers from Eastern Germany or Eastern Europe. S-Bahn lines S5 and S7 will take visitors straight to the main Bahnhof Zoo station. Ⓢ Straße der Pariser Kommune • (030) 29 72 00 75

7 Bahnhof Lichtenberg
Trains from Southern and Eastern Europe arrive at this station, and many through trains from the West stop here, too. This is the best place to arrive if your final destination is in the eastern part of the city. Ⓢ Weitlingstr. 22 • (030) 29 /1 29 49

8 Zentraler Omni-busbahnhof (ZOB)
The coach station near Funkturm in Charlottenburg offers fast and inexpensive coach connections to all German and European cities. Ⓢ Masurenallee 4–6 • Map A4 • (030) 301 80 28

9 Motorways
If you're travelling to Berlin by car, you will have to get there via Berliner Stadtring, an orbital motorway around the city. From the north you will reach the city motorway on the A111 motorway via Stolpe in the direction of Autobahndreieck Funkturm; from the south you will reach the centre on the A115 – the famous Avus motorway.

10 By Car
The speed limit on the orbital Berliner Ring is mostly 100 km/h (62.5 miles per hour); on the urban motorways in Berlin you are limited to 80–100 km/h (50–62.5 miles per hour). There are frequent radar checks.

Left **S-Bahn** Centre **At a bus stop** Right **Exploring Berlin by Velotaxi**

🔟 Getting Around Berlin

1 U-Bahn
The Berlin U-Bahn, or underground railway, has one of the largest networks in Europe, providing the fastest and most convenient means of getting around the city. There are ten U-Bahn lines each sporting their own colour. The U-Bahn runs from 5am to 1am; at weekends lines U1 and U9 run throughout the night. The station indicated on the platform is the final destination of the train. ◈ *BVG customer service (030) 194 49*

2 S-Bahn
The S-Bahn or Stadtbahn (city railway) has 15 lines, connecting the centre with the suburbs, They run at 10- to 20-minute intervals. Many lines share tracks so you will need to pay attention to indicator boards. ◈ *Information S-Bahn • Bhf. Alexanderplatz • 8am–9pm Mon–Fri, 9am–3:30pm Sat, Sun • (030) 29 72 06 48*

3 Buses
Berlin has a dense network of bus routes. The famous yellow, double-decker buses operate mostly in the centre. Bus lines have three-digit numbers, except for express services, which have two-digits or a preceding "X". After midnight, many routes provide night services. When boarding the bus, you may use the back door (which opens when a button is pushed) until 8pm. Afterwards you may board the bus only at the front, and you will have to present your ticket to the driver. ◈ *BVG customer service (030) 194 49*

4 Tickets
Tickets for U- and S-Bahn trains and for buses in Berlin are available at all stations and bus stops as well as from bus drivers. Berlin is divided into three zones, A, B and C. The best value for money is a day ticket at € 6.10, which is valid until 3am the following day and covers all three zones. A single journey, costing € 2.10, is valid for unlimited travel for two hours. A "Kurzstrecke" (short distance) counts as up to three railway stations or six bus stops, and costs € 1.20. Children under 14 years pay a reduced rate, children under six travel free. You have to stamp your ticket in a red machine in the station or on the bus before starting the journey. ◈ *BVG customer service (030) 194 49*

5 Trams
Trams – operating only in the eastern part of the city – are part of the same network (BVG).

6 Taxis
There are taxi stands all over Berlin. It is not always easy to hail a passing taxi. The basic starting price is € 2.30, and a further € 0.10 is charged per km (⅔ of a mile). A short-distance tariff also exists: if you hail a taxi in the street, you can travel for up to 2 km (1 mile) for € 3.10. ◈ *Taxi: (030) 26 10 26, (030) 55 12, (030) 21 01 01.*

7 Car Hire
You can hire a car from any of the large operators on production of a valid driving licence, passport and credit card; some only accept customers aged 21 years or over. There are car hire places at all airports and in central Berlin. ◈ *Avis: (06171) 68 18 00; Europcar: (0180) 580 00; Hertz: (01805) 33 35 35; Sixt: (030) 212 98 80*

8 Velotaxis
An unusual way to explore Berlin is by velotaxi – a bicycle rickshaw. These can be found in the city centre (from April to October only).

9 Bicycle Hire
There are several bike hire places in town. ◈ *Bicycle station Bhf. Friedrichstr. • Map K4 • 10am–7pm Mon–Fri, 10am–4pm Sat, Sun • (030) 20 45 45 00*

10 Berlin on Foot
It can be rewarding but exhausting to explore Berlin on foot. You should, however, make sure you stroll along Ku'damm and Unter den Linden. Take particular care when crossing the cycle paths, which are marked in red.

Left **Berlin city guides** Centre **A newspaper kiosk** Right **The logo of tourist information offices**

🔟 Information & Advice

1 Berlin Tourismus Marketing GmbH

The municipal tourist information service BTM has offices in the Europa-Center, near Brandenburg Gate and in Tegel airport. There you can obtain leaflets and up-to-date information as well as souvenirs and general brochures on Berlin. A telephone hotline gives information about all current events.

🔘 *Berlin Tourismus Marketing GmbH, Am Karlsbad 11 • Map E4 • (030) 25 00 25, Fax (030) 25 00 24 24 • www.berlin.de*

🔘 *Europa-Center, Budapester Str. • Map K3 • 8:30am–8:30pm Mon–Sat, 10am–6:30pm Sun.*

🔘 *Brandenburger Tor • 9:30am–6pm daily.*

🔘 *Flughafen Tegel • 5am–10:30pm daily.*

2 Berlin's Municipal Museums

Detailed up-to-date information on the municipal museums and all the establishments on Museumsinsel can be obtained from a bilingual phoneline. Here you will also find out about the current programme of events – for example about the "long night of the museums".

🔘 *(030) 20 90 55 55*

3 Sanssouci

The visitors' advice service for the palaces and gardens of Potsdam and Sanssouci supplies accurate information and tips as well as guided tours and more via their own telephone service.

🔘 *(0331) 969 42 02*

4 Potsdam Information

Potsdam city council has its own tourist information service, offering brochures as well as an accommodation service and guided tours.

🔘 *Friedrich-Ebert-Str. 5 • Apr–Oct: 9am–8pm Mon–Fri, 9am–6pm Sat, Sun, Nov–Mar: 10am–6pm Mon–Fri, 10am–2pm Sat, Sun • Tel (0331) 275 580, Fax (0331) 275 58 99*

5 Where to Stay

The Berlin Tourismus Marketing GmbH (BTM) has a telephone hotline which will help reserve a room (for a fee). Several offices also arrange private accommodation, where visitors book into shared apartments for a period of several days or weeks. 🔘 *Tel (030) 25 00 25, Fax (030) 25 00 24 24*

6 What's On

There are two fortnightly city magazines with detailed information on all kinds of events – *tip* and *zitty*. The monthly *Berlin-Programm* with detailed events listings is also worth consulting. For younger readers, the magazines *prinz*, *flyer* and *030* contain information on nightclubs and bars. Daily newspapers such as *Tagesspiegel*, *Berliner Zeitung* and *Berliner Morgenpost* usually publish listings of cultural events on Wednesdays and Thursdays respectively, while tips and reviews can be found in the papers every day.

7 Radio Stations

For radio news in English, you can tune into Inforadio (93.1 MHz), the BBC World Service (90.2 MHz) or the multilingual SFB 4 Multikulti (106.8 MHz).

8 Television

In addition to the national TV stations, the SFB offers a regional programme; tv berlin, a private TV station, also broadcasts information on what's on. Thanks to cable and satellite you can easily tune into English programmes.

9 Advice for Foreign Nationals

This Senate Office, which deals with the concerns of foreign nationals who live in Berlin, is also a good point of advice for foreign visitors.

🔘 *Potsdamer Str. 65 • Map E5 • 9am–1pm Mon–Fri except Wed, plus 3–6pm Thu • (030) 901 72 39*

10 Advice for Gay Visitors

Advice and information for gay and lesbian visitors is always available at Mann-o-Meter *(see p58)*.

🔘 *Bülowstr. 106 • 5–10pm Mon–Fri, 4–10pm Sat, Sun • (030) 216 80 08*

➡ *Find out what's happening this week on* **www.berlinonline.de** *(German language only)*

Left **Parking for the Disabled** Centre **Adapted bus door** Right **Lift to the U-Bahn station**

Berlin for Disabled Visitors

1 Streets and Pavements

Nearly all pavements in Berlin are sloped at junctions to make them suitable for wheelchair users. However visitors in wheelchairs will need to watch out for cyclists using the red cycle tracks, often in both directions.

2 Stations

Most underground stations in the centre, including those that are actually above ground in high-level stations on viaducts, are equipped with lifts, giving wheelchair users easy access from the road to the platform.
- BVG service for disabled access to stations
- (030) 25 62 20 96
- S-Bahn service for disabled access to stations
- (030) 29 74 33 33

3 U- and S-Bahn

Underground trains are accessible to wheelchair users although they are a little narrow. If you wish to travel by U-Bahn, wait at the head of the platform. After the train has stopped, the driver will put up a ramp to bridge the difference in height between platform and train. If you wish to travel by S-Bahn, speak to the station manager before the arrival of the train; he or she will install the ramp you need to board the train.
- Berliner Verkehrsbetriebe
- around the clock
- (030) 194 49.
- Deutsche Bahn Berlin
- around the clock
- (01805) 99 66 33

4 Buses

All buses displaying a wheelchair symbol are specially equipped for disabled access; most buses in the centre have one door with a ramp that can be lowered down to the pavement. At certain times, however, these buses run only at 20-minute intervals.

5 Cars Services and Guided Tours

Disabled visitors wishing to explore Berlin and Brandenburg province on their own by car, or to share a car with driver with other disabled visitors, can contact several specialist travel agents.
- BBV Tours Behinderten-fahrdienst, Bizetstr. 51–55
- (030) 92 70 36 30
- Micky Tours, Sewanstr. 2
- (030) 515 33 36
- Berlin Erkundungen Gangart Berlin, Hainbuchen-str. 2 • (030) 32 70 37 83
- Spuren Suche E. Schiel-zeth, Parchimer Allee 55c
- (030) 601 01 07

6 Movado.de

The internet website www.movado.de gives information on wheel-chair access to restaurants, hotels and shops in Berlin. This association also offers interactive guided tours of the city, covering the areas that are most popular with tourists, and it provides information on disabled access to sights.
- www.movado.de

7 Berliner Behinder-tenverband e.V.

This charitable association gives advice and support on all issues concerning disabled people in Berlin.
- Information hotline (030) 204 38 47
- Call times Wed, Fri

8 Landesamt

Berlin's Regional Office for Health and Social Security runs a citizen's advice bureau with a telephone helpline.
- Albrecht-Archilles-Str. 62
- Map B5
- (030) 90 12 61 14
- Information for young disabled people
- (030) 26 54 24 03
- Service for the disabled and senior citizens
- (030) 859 40 10

9 Wheelchair Hire

The Regional Office (see above) also rents out wheelchairs for a fee. Order one in advance by telephone.
- (030) 341 17 97

10 Sight-impaired Visitors

Berlin's charitable association for the blind and sight-impaired advises on facilities that are available for blind visitors.
- Allgemeiner Blinden-und Sehbehindertenverein, Auerbacherstr. 7
- (030) 89 58 80

Left **Historic letter box** Centre **Modern card telephone** Right **Bureau de change**

Banking & Communications

1 Banks

All the large German banks have branches in the centre of town. Most banks open 9am–5pm Mon–Fri; many open for shorter periods on Fridays and Wednesdays.
◈ Commerzbank, Europa-Center, Tauentzienstr. 9 and Uhlandstr 181–183 • Map N/P5 and P3 • 9am–4pm Mon, 9am–6.30pm Tue, Thu, 9am–3pm Wed, 9am–1:30pm Fri. ◈ Deutsche Bank, Otto-Suhr-Allee 6–16 • Map M3 • 9am–3:30pm Mon, Wed, 9am–4pm Tue, Thu, 9am–6pm Fri. ◈ Berliner Sparkasse, Rankestr. 33–34 • Map P4 • 9am–6pm Mon–Fri

2 Changing Money

Money is changed at a Wechselstube (bureau de change); you can find these near Bahnhof Zoo, at the airports or at a bank. Make sure you ask about commission and charges. Hotels will also change money, but may charge higher fees.
◈ American Express, Bayreuther Str. 37 • Map P5 • 9am–7pm Mon–Fri, 9am–2pm Sat • (030) 21 47 62 92. ◈ Reisebank Bahnhof Zoo • Map N4 • 7am–10pm Mon–Sat, 8am–9pm Sun • (030) 881 71 17. ◈ Thomas Cook, Friedrichstr. 56 • Map L4 • 9am–8pm Mon–Fri, 9am–4pm Sat • (030) 20 16 59 16

3 Credit Cards

Everywhere in the centre of Berlin you'll be able to use a standard credit card, such as Visa or Euro/MasterCard, to pay at most restaurants, cafés and shops. American Express and Diner's Club are less commonly accepted. You can also use your credit or EC card (plus PIN number) to withdraw money from a machine. Should you lose your card, tell your bank or provider immediately.
◈ American Express • (069) 97 97 10 00
◈ EuroCard • (069) 74 09 87
◈ MasterCard • (069) 33 19 10 ◈ Diner's Club • (05921) 06 12 34
◈ Visa • (0800) 814 91 00

4 Telephones

There are public phones (both enclosed cells and open phones) all over the centre of town. These are almost exclusively card phones. Telephone cards can be bought from post offices, in department stores and at kiosks.

5 Post Offices and Letter Boxes

Post offices are hard to miss – they are painted a bright yellow. Like elsewhere in Germany, Berlin letter boxes are also yellow, but there are some blue "historic" boxes.
◈ Center-Filiale, Joachimstaler Str. 7 • Map P4 • 8am–midnight Mon–Sat, 10am–midnight Sun and holidays.
◈ Bahnhof Friedrichstr., Georgenstr. 12 • Map K4 • 6am–10pm Mon–Fri, 8am–10pm Sat, Sun.

6 Postage

A standard letter (up to 20 g) to anywhere in the EU costs € 0.56; a compact letter (up to 50 g) € 1.12; a postcard € 0.51. Stamps can be bought at the post office, from card shops and machines.

7 Internet Cafés

You can surf the internet and pick up your e-mails anywhere. Easy-everything is one of the largest internet cafés.
◈ easy-everything, Kurfürstendamm 224 • Map P4 • around the clock • (030) 88 70 79 70

8 Secretarial Services

If your hotel does not offer secretarial services, you could use an independent service. Details of such services are listed in the "Yellow Pages" of the telephone directory.

9 Travellers' Cheques

Travellers' cheques made out in euros or any other currency can be exchanged at all larger banks or at branches of the issuers. Most banks charge a fee.

10 Important Numbers

Important Deutsche Telekom helpline numbers are as follows:
• national directory enquiries 118 33
• international directory enquiries 118 34
• operator (0180) 200 10 33

Left **Ambulance Centre** **A pharmacy in the centre of Berlin** Right **A police van**

TOP 10 Security & Health Tips

1 Emergencies
As elsewhere in Germany, the emergency phone numbers are 112 for ambulance and fire brigade, and 110 for the police. These can be dialled free of charge from public phone boxes.

2 Safety
Berlin is a fairly safe city. Like in any other metropolis, however, you are advised to follow a few golden rules. Keep an eye on your valuables, such as your wallet or handbag, at all times, especially on U- and S-Bahn trains and on buses. At night, the following areas are best avoided: the area behind the Gedächtniskirche, U-Bahn line U9 north of the Zoo, the districts Lichtenberg (especially the station) and Friedrichshain. Eastern areas can be less safe; black or openly homosexual visitors are also advised not to take the S-Bahn at night east of Alexanderplatz or to Brandenburg.

3 Theft
Ask the hotel to place your documents and valuables in a safe if possible, or carry them close to your body. Even if you are making a short visit, it is worth taking out insurance unless you are already covered by your household insurance. Be sure to inform the police immediately of any theft; you'll usually easily find

police officers patrolling the streets in the centre.
◈ *Polizeipräsidium, Platz der Luftbrücke 6*
• *(030) 69 95*

4 Lost Property
The Zentrales Fundbüro (central lost-property office) keeps anything that has been lost and found anywhere in Berlin. If you have lost an item on public transport, enquire with the Fundbüro der BVG. The Fundbüro der Deutschen Bahn AG is responsible for all items lost on the S-Bahn or the railways.
◈ *Zentrales Fundbüro, Platz der Luftbrücke 6*
• *(030) 69 95*
◈ *Fundbüro der BVG, Potsdamer Str. 182*
• *(030) 25 62 30 40*
◈ *Fundbüro der DB*
• *(01805) 99 05 99*

5 Hospitals
Visitors from EU countries are covered for emergency treatment, but British visitors should obtain form E111 from a post office before leaving home. Non-EU visitors should buy special travel insurance to cover medical emergencies.

6 Chemists
There are numerous *Apotheken* (chemists or pharmacies) all over town. After 8pm, an emergency phone line will give you information on where to find the nearest open chemist.
◈ *(030) 31 00 31*

7 Dentists
The dental emergency phone line will refer you to the nearest dentist for treatment.
◈ *(030) 89 00 43 33*

8 Emergency Services
There are several other important numbers for emergencies, which usually operate throughout the night. These will provide telephone advice or inform you of other emergency services if necessary.
◈ *Doctors on call*
• *(030) 310 031*
◈ *German Red Cross Rescue Service*
• *(030) 85 00 55*
◈ *Emergency Poison Helpline*
• *(030) 192 40*
◈ *Narcotics Emergencies*
• *(030) 192 37*
◈ *Telephone helpline for emotional problems*
• *0800 111 0 111* • *0800 111 0 222 (spiritual help)*

9 Embassies
Foreign visitors who have lost their passport or need legal advice or help with their visa should contact their embassy *(see p160)*.

10 Women travelling on their own
Berlin is quite safe for women on their own, but avoid parks and dark, quiet streets at night, as well as the outer districts of East Berlin. ◈ *Confidential helpline for women* • *(030) 615 42 43*

Online list of pharmacies:
www.berlinonline.de/service/apotheken/

Left **By S-Bahn to the outer districts** Centre **Travelling on Havel and Spree** Right **In Spreewald**

⑩ Excursions & Days Out

1 Spreewald
The river landscape around the little towns of Lübben and Lübbenau, southwest of Berlin, is a unique and unspoilt area of natural beauty. From here you can explore by boat the old settlements of the Sorbs, a Slavic people. Make sure you also enjoy the specialities of the region – fresh fish and vegetables, but most of all the famous pickled Spreewald gherkins. ⊗ *Tourismusverband Spreewald e. V., Lindenstr. 1, Raddusch • (035433) 5010*

2 Sachsenhausen concentration camp
A visit to Sachsenhausen, Germany's first Nazi concentration camp, is a haunting experience. It was opened in 1933 as a "wild camp" for political prisoners. From 1936 to 1945, some 100,000 people were murdered here. Next to the camp is an exhibition. ⊗ *Gedenkstätte und Museum Sachsenhausen, Straße der Nationen 22 • Apr–Sep: 8:30am–6pm Tue–Sun; Oct–Mar: 8:30am–4:30pm Tue–Sun • (03301) 20 00*

3 Schloss Rheinsberg
This small palace is an excellent destination for a day-trip. The palace was made famous by the love story of Kurt Tucholsky. Today the palace is a home for senior citizens and can be seen only from the outside. ⊗ *Fremdenverkehrsamt Rheinsberg, Markt-Kavaliershaus • (033931) 20 59*

4 Werder
Surrounded by the Havelland fruit orchards, this small village celebrates Baumblütenfest, the blossoming of the fruit trees in April and May. ⊗ *Potsdam-Information, Friedrich-Ebert-Str. 5 • (0331) 27 55 80*

5 Caputh
This picturesque small village near Potsdam, surrounded by numerous lakes, boasts a charming Baroque palace as well as Albert Einstein's summer residence at No 7 Waldstraße. ⊗ *Potsdam-Information, Friedrich-Ebert-Str. 5 • (0331) 275 580*

6 Frankfurt/Oder
The other Frankfurt, on the Oder River, about 70 km (43 miles) east of Berlin, is well worth visiting, if only for its superb museum devoted to the playwright Heinrich-von-Kleist. ⊗ *Faberstr. 7 • 10am–5pm Tue–Sun • (0335) 53 11 55*

7 Bad Saarow
An old spa town and once a celebrity haunt, Bad Saarow's thermal springs and hotel invite you for a relaxing weekend. ⊗ *Kur- und Fremdenverkehrs-GmbH, Seestr. 36 • (033631) 8680 and 2142 (tourist information)*

8 Buckow
The small village of Buckow is the centre of the so-called Märkische Schweiz (the Swiss Mark). A landscape of lakes and hills, which seems almost untouched, it is a good place for walking, swimming and boating. The best area is around Schermützelsee. Also at Buckow, the summer residence of Bertolt Brecht can be visited. ⊗ *Umwelt- und Fremdenverkehrsamt Märkische Schweiz, Wriezener Str. 1a • (033433) 57 500*

9 Sacrow
North of Potsdam is the tiny village of Sacrow. It has become a favourite tourist spot because of its dreamy Saviour's Church, on the lake of the same name. ⊗ *Potsdam-Information, Friedrich-Ebert-Str. 5 • (0331) 27 55 80*

10 Königs Wusterhausen
A beautiful landscape of lakes stretches all around Königs Wusterhausen, 27 km (17 miles) south east of Berlin. There are numerous romantic villages such as Grünau and Zeuthen, and one of its most attractive spots is the village of Teupitz, on Teupitz lake. The Schlosshotel is an ideal place to relax. ⊗ *Kultur- und Tourismusverband Dahmeland, Am Bahnhof, Königs Wusterhausen • (03375) 25 200*

Left **A historic double-decker bus** Centre **Sightseeing by bus** Right **Visiting the city by velotaxi**

TOP 10 Guided Tours

1 Sightseeing by double-decker bus

Nothing is more fun than a sightseeing tour of the city on the double-decker nostalgia bus, which is open-top in summer. Buses depart from the corner of Ku'damm and Rankestraße. English and German commentary is available. ◈ *Stadtrund-fahrtbüro Berlin, Kurfürsten-damm 236 • (030) 261 20 01*

2 Buses 100 and 200

The cheapest and fastest way to see the city is a journey on buses Nos 100 or 200. These double-deckers go from Bahnhof Zoo and Alexanderplatz right into Prenzlauer Berg, passing all the important sights between West and East *en route*. A Berlin tour for only € 2.10.

3 StattReisen

StattReisen was one of the first agencies in Germany to offer inform-ative themed walks through the city. Among the most popular themes for guided tours are "Jewish Berlin" and a guided overview tour of the centre (lasting up to three hours). ◈ *Malplaquetstr. 5 • (030) 455 30 28*

4 Sightseeing Bus Tours

Traditional sightseeing tours by bus, with com-mentary in up to eight different languages, are good for getting a quick overview. The tours

depart from Kurfürsten-damm (corner of Meine-kestr. or Rankestr.), and in summer they leave every hour. These bus tours usually last between two and four hours, and take in all the most im-portant sights of Berlin. There are special tours to Potsdam. Departure points: ◈ *Berolina Berlin-Service, Kurfürstendamm 220 • (030) 88 56 80 30* ◈ *Severin & Kühn, Kurfürs-tendamm 216 u. Alexan-derplatz• (030) 880 41 90* ◈ *Bus Verkehr Berlin (BVB), Kurfürstendamm 225 • (030) 88 68 37 11*

5 art:berlin

This agency cuts a swathe through Berlin's artistic jungle. Small, well-conducted tours lead visitors through the museums, galleries, cultural events and – of course – to the city's most exciting architec-tural treasures. ◈ *Oranienburger Str. 32 • (030) 28 09 63 90*

6 Boat Tours

Berlin's waterways – Havel and Spree Rivers, Landwehrkanal and the lakes Wannsee and Müg-gelsee – can all be explored by boat. Many tours allow you to take in Berlin's historic sights between Charlottenburg and the centre from the water. Tours last two or three hours, and there are piers at Schloss Charlot-tenburg, next to the Haus der Kulturen der Welt in

Tiergarten, next to the Schlossbrücke bridge as well as in Treptow. ◈ *Stern- und Kreis-Schiff-fahrt, Puschkinallee 15 • (030) 536 36 00.* ◈ *Weiße Flotte Potsdam, Lange Brücke • (0331) 275 92 10*

7 Berlin from the Air

Several enterprises offer sightseeing trips over Berlin and Brandenburg province by helicopter and in historic planes. ◈ *Kanzler International Executive Services, Kommandantenstr. 14 • (030) 694 94 90* ◈ *Air Service Berlin, Flughafen Schönefeld • (030) 60 91 84 00*

8 Berlin Walks

This small agency personally conducts themed English-language walks, which depart daily from the taxi rank outside Zoologischer Garten. ◈ *Bahnhof Zoo • 10am daily and by prior arrangement • (030) 301 91 94*

9 Velotaxis

An inexpensive, relaxing and personalized way to see the town is by velotaxi *(see p162)*.

10 Berlin Underground

A very special sort of tour are these guided walks through the spooky underbelly of the metropolis, making your way through bunkers and ancient tunnels. ◈ *(030) 31 50 98 65*

Official guided tours: www.stattreisen.berlin.de
or: www.severin-kuehn-berlin.de

Left **Relaxation can be found in one of the city's many parks** Right **Exploring Berlin on foot**

🔟 Ways to Escape the Crowds

1 Rush Hours
If you're driving around Berlin, try to avoid the main rush hours – between 7am and 9am in the morning, and between 4:30pm and 7pm in the evening. Buses, U- and S-Bahn, too, are very crowded at these times.

2 Lunchtime
At restaurants, cafés and snack bars in the centre, you will often have to stand in line or wait to be seated if you arrive between 12:30pm and 2pm. Most venues in Berlin, though, will continue to serve the same dishes. So, if you wish to enjoy your meal in peace and quiet, set off after 1:30pm.

3 Evenings Out
Popular restaurants, particularly those around Savignyplatz, Gendarmenmarkt and Kollwitzplatz are often booked up between 7pm and 8pm, especially in summer, even during the week. You are therefore best advised to reserve a table in advance, or to arrive a little later, after about 9pm.

4 Early Risers
Many of the popular sights get very crowded, especially from Thursdays to Sundays. It's a good idea to arrive early, and to start your visit as soon as a place opens – especially the Reichstag.

5 Weekends
Most tourists come to Berlin for weekends, and so Ku'damm and Friedrichstraße are completely overrun by visitors on a Saturday morning. In the evening, many events, especially concerts by the Berlin Philharmonic Orchestra and performances in the best theatres, will be sold out. If possible arrange for your visit to start on a Sunday and take in the first few days of the week.

6 Holidays
High season for Berlin visitors is the period from May to July. From the end of July or the beginning of the school holidays, however, the town gets noticeably quieter, as many locals go on holiday then. You'll easily find parking spaces and many restaurants are much emptier than usual – especially in August. The only disadvantage is that theatres and concert halls close then for a summer break.

7 Berlin Parks
If, after a couple of days, you're tired of the hustle and bustle of the big city, go to one of the parks to chill out – Viktoriapark in Kreuzberg, Jungfernheide in Charlottenburg and the area around Tegeler See are picturesque places where you can relax in peace and quiet.

8 Sunday Morning
Even the central areas in Berlin are often completely deserted early on Sunday mornings – the ideal time for a quiet stroll down Kurfürstendamm or Unter den Linden. Most cafés and museums open at 10am, so you won't miss out on either cultural discoveries or refreshment.

9 Reservations
Whether you wish to visit the theatre, the opera, the Philharmonie concert hall, a multiplex cinema or a special event, it is almost always worth trying to book tickets as early as possible by phone or at one of the agencies – you'll rarely be lucky enough to buy tickets for the most popular events on the day.

10 Nights
Berlin is a city that never sleeps – it is "open" 24 hours a day. If you don't have to stick to particular times, for example, make the most of your freedom – in most restaurants you can still enjoy a good meal after 11pm. The same is true of pubs and bars – many close at 3am or 4am, or not at all. Nightclubs and discos don't get going until midnight or later, even during the week. And some museums stay open late, until 10pm, on Thursdays.

Left **In the Europa-Center** Centre **Inside Galeries Lafayette** Right **A stand selling souvenirs**

Shopping

1 Shopping Streets

Kurfürstendamm, Tauentzienstraße and Friedrichstraße are the main three shopping streets in Berlin. You'll find inexpensive shops around Tauentzienstraße and Alexanderplatz. Friedrichstraße with the "Friedrichstadtpassagen" shopping centre and the Galeries Lafayette department store as well as the west side of Ku'damm are decidedly upmarket – which is reflected in the prices. A good mix of shops can be found in the arcades at Potsdamer Platz, Schlossstraße in the south of Berlin and the Gesundbrunnen-center in the north.

2 Opening Hours

Normally, all shops are open between 10am and 8pm on Mondays to Fridays; on Saturdays many open at 9am, but close at 4pm. In the four weeks before Christmas, shops are allowed to stay open until 6pm. During special events (for example during the IFA International Broadcasting Exhibition or the Berlinale Film Festival) special opening hours may be in force.

3 How to Pay

Most shops in the city centre accept credit cards such as Visa, Euro-/Mastercard and American Express, less commonly Diner's Club. Almost all shops take EC-cards.

4 Consumer Protection

If you feel that you are not being treated fairly or if a product you have bought proves to be faulty (and an exchange is refused), you can contact the consumer protection association.
🗞 *Verbraucherzentrale Berlin, Bayreuther Str. 40 • 9am–12:30pm Mon, 9am–4:30 Tue, Fri, 9am–8pm Wed • (030) 21 48 50*

5 Sales

End-of-season sales take place at the end of January and the end of July. But you'll be able to find bargains throughout the year in the department stores and shops, often laid out on special stands right next to the main entrance.

6 Fashion

The best fashion and designer stores, selling coveted labels such as Gucci, Versace, Jil Sander, DKNY or Prada, can be found on the west side of Ku'damm and in Friedrichstraße. Kaufhaus des Westens has a good large range of ladies' and gentlemen's fashions *(see p60)*.

7 Music

Apart from large multi-media and CD-store chains such as WOM (Karstadt, Wertheim), Saturn, MediaMarkt, Promarkt and Kaufhof, you will find a vast selection of CDs at Kulturkaufhaus Dussmann *(see p119)*, at Kiepert as well as in the Kaufhaus des Westens or KaDeWe *(see p60)*.

8 Gifts and Souvenirs

If you're looking for gifts and souvenirs to take home, try the Europa-Center *(see p24)* and the KaDeWe *(see p60)*. There are also souvenir shops in Unter den Linden (near Pariser Platz), on Potsdamer Platz as well as at Checkpoint Charlie.

9 Art and Antiques

Most antiques shops are clustered south of Nollendorfplatz *(see p104)* and in the smaller streets off Kurfürstendamm. However, the flea and art fair on the Straße des 17 Juni *(see p60)* and the antiques shops in the S-Bahn arches between Friedrichstraße and Museumsinsel are often much better value and offer a wider range of goods and antiques.

10 Around Berlin

In Potsdam as in other small towns, there are many excellent places to shop for arts and crafts items or clothes. A good place for bargain hunters is the "B96" shopping centre, situated on the national road with the same number. Here many fashionable items are sold at heavily discounted prices. 🗞 *B96, exit Elstal • 10am–8pm Mon–Fri, 9am–4pm Sat*

Left **Theatre ticket office** Right **Enjoy Berlin's parks for free**

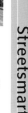

⁵⁰10 Berlin on a Budget

1 Accommodation

For low-cost accommodation you can check into inexpensive youth hostels, hostels run by the YMCA, or a backpacker hostel. Or try a Mitwohnzentralen, an agency arranging shared accommodation in private homes at a low cost *(see also p163)*.

2 Restaurants

As in Britain, Indian and Turkish restaurants are often particularly good value. Another cheap alternative are Turkish doner kebab snack bars and German curry sausage stands – these often also sell other snacks at low prices.

3 Museums

Berlin's municipal museums, especially those on Museumsinsel, can all be visited on a day ticket costing only € 6. Admission is also free on the first Sunday in every month.

4 WelcomeCard

The BVG Welcome-Card offers the best and cheapest way of visiting exhibitions and museums in Berlin and using public transport throughout the city. The card is available at € 8 from S- and U-Bahn stations as well as from tourist information centres. Valid for two adults and up to three children, it allows you to travel in zones A and B with all BVG vehicles for

three days. The card also gives you a reduction of up to 50 per cent of the admission price in many museums. You'll even get a useful information pack with your card.

5 Reduced Tickets

Theatres and the opera house sell reduced tickets at the door on the day of the performance, mainly for pupils and students who can show a valid student card. Alternatively, tickets can be bought cheaply in advance by anyone from ticketing agencies such as Hekticket. ✆ *Hekticket (030) 230 99 30*

6 Street Artists

Berlin has always been a good place for street artists, especially on Breitscheidplatz and along Ku'damm. There is a legendary mime artist, dressed as a clown, who mimics passers by outside the cafés on the eastern side of Ku'damm. In summer, in Charlottenburg and Prenzlauer Berg, you can often listen to street musicians and singers directly at your table or outside the restaurant or café.

7 Day of the Open Door

Since Berlin is Germany's political and cultural capital, many public and private institutions regularly offer the chance to take a look behind the scenes, free of charge. A

visit to one of the federal ministries is particularly interesting. Daily newspapers will list these events. Every year in summer, "Schaustelle Berlin" (a pun on "Baustelle", meaning building site) conducts guided tours to Berlin's major building sites and other projects *(see also www. berlin.de)*.

8 Free Concerts

Churches and smaller concert halls in the outer districts often put on classical concerts for a low admission fee or even free of charge. The city magazines and daily newspapers list such events in the appropriate columns. All Berlin daily newspapers also give away free tickets for current exhibitions and events. Look at the Berlin pages in the papers for what is currently on offer.

9 Markets

Berlin's weekly flea markets always have a vast range of special offers for sale, besides which they'll offer you the opportunity to try out your haggling skills *(see also pp60–1)*.

10 Parks

Admission to all of Berlin's parks and green spaces is free. You can enjoy their sports facilities, and often also open-air-concerts, without having to fork out for a ticket *(see also pp68–9)*.

Left **Hotel Charlot** Centre **Reception in the Econtel** Right **Hotel Künstlerheim Luise**

🔟 Modest Hotels & Hostels

1 die fabrik
This hotel, its name meaning "the factory", is a guesthouse cum youth hostel. An alternative youth and arts centre in the middle of deepest Kreuzberg, it attracts backpackers from around the world, hoping to meet locals and others. ✆ *Schlesische Str. 18 • (030) 611 7116 • www. diefabrik.com • no credit cards • €*

2 Hotel Künstlerheim Luise
The 30 rooms in this small, pleasant hotel were all individually and imaginatively designed by different local artists, with themes ranging from loud pop art to classic Modernism. The hotel is centrally located, close to lively Scheunenviertel and Unter den Linden. ✆ *Luisenstr. 19 • Map J/K3 • (030) 28 44 80 • www. kuenstlerheim-luise. de • €€*

3 Boardinghouse Mitte
A well-run apartment hotel, offering good-value accommodation, especially suited to those wishing to stay for longer periods of time. The rooms are large and brightly furnished, and the hotel is in a central location, making it an ideal base for exploring Scheunenviertel. ✆ *Mulackstr. 1 • Map H3 • (030) 28 38 84 88 • www.boarding-house-berlin.de • €–€€€*

4 Econtel
This small hotel, near Schloss Charlottenburg, is well suited so families, as some of its rooms have been specially designed for children's play. A buffet breakfast is included in the price. ✆ *Sömmeringstr. 24–26 • Map B3 • (030) 34 68 10 • €*

5 Pension Niebuhr
A typical Berlin guesthouse, with a great atmosphere, situated in the most attractive part of Charlottenburg. Breakfast can be served in the rooms. ✆ *Niebuhrst. 74 • Map P2 • 0800 324 95 95 • www.pensio–niebuhr.de • €*

6 Hotel–Pension Funk
Slightly antiquated, venerable guesthouse close to Ku'damm, based in the apartment of the silent-film star Asta Nielsen. The rates are unbeatable while furnishings and service are personal and friendly. There are only 15 rooms. ✆ *Fasanenstr. 69 • Map N/P4 • (030) 882 71 93 • €*

7 Pension Kreuzberg
Clean and friendly, this hotel-guesthouse in Kreuzberg boasts an excellent atmosphere – but unfortunately no en-suite bathrooms. The landlady takes great care of her guests and is happy to pass on her personal tips for nightlife and culture in Berlin. ✆ *Großbeerenstr. 64 • Map F5/6 • (030) 251 13 62 • (no credit cards • €*

8 Hotel Transit
Housed on two floors of a former industrial building, this international youth hostel is located in a lively area close to the town centre. It has large rooms, sleeping up to six people. ✆ *Hagelberger Str. 53–54 • Map F6 • (030) 789 04 70 • www.hotel-transit.de • €€*

9 Hotel Charlot
A small hotel, popular with student and school groups, and therefore a little noisy at times. It is situated in a quiet square close to Ku'damm, where you will find several pubs and the UFA-Arthouse-Kino, which screens English-language films currently on release. ✆ *Giesebrechtstr. 17 • Map P2 • (030) 327 96 60 • €€*

10 mitArt Pension
Tucked away opposite the Tacheles art centre is this small guesthouse, based in an old building dating from the 19th century. The rooms are plain, with modern furnishings, and the walls are decorated with avant-garde paintings. There are only nine rooms, which get booked up quickly, so you are advised to reserve early ✆ *Friedrichstr. 127 • Map J4 • (030) 28 39 04 80 • no credit cards • €*

Note: *Unless otherwise stated, all hotels accept credit cards, and have en-suite bathrooms.*

Price Categories

Price for a standard	€	under € 60
double room per	€€	€ 60–100
night, with breakfast,	€€€	€ 100–150
taxes and other	€€€€	€ 150–200
charges included	€€€€€	over € 200

Left **A small room in Bleibtreu-Hotel** Right **Courtyard of Hackescher Markt**

TOP 10 Medium-Priced Hotels

1 Bleibtreu-Hotel
Here, you'll fancy yourself in Tuscany – the hotel's stylish interior courtyard and bright, tastefully furnished rooms are an oasis of tranquillity in the bustle of the western half of the city. The international clientele is equally stylish. The hotel has its own restaurant, pool, sauna, massage and much more on offer, and there are shops right outside. ✪ *Bleibtreustr. 31* • *Map P3* • *(030) 88 474 0* • *www.bleibtreu.com* • *€€€*

2 Hackescher Markt
A charming hotel in an unbeatable location right opposite Hackesche Höfe – few places in this price range can compete. Large, bright rooms with elegant furnishings, friendly service, an excellent restaurant and many pleasant extras, such as an attractive patio, guarantee a pleasant stay. ✪ *Große Präsidentenstr. 8* • *Map J5* • *(030) 28 00 30* • *www.hackescher-markt. com* • *€€€*

3 Alsterhof
A quiet classic, this hotel boasts attentive staff, rustic rooms and its own small beer garden in summer, all in an excellent location near the KaDeWe. Ask about special weekend rates. Non-smoking rooms available. ✪ *Augsburger Str. 5* • *Map P5* • *(030) 21 24 20* • *www.alsterhof.de* • *€€€*

4 Hotel am Scheunenviertel
Well-run establishment with an intimate atmosphere (there are only 18 rooms), popular with tourists on cultural visits. Rooms and lobby have been kept deliberately plain, which creates a slightly spartan impression, but all needs are catered for. ✪ *Oranienburger Str. 38* • *Map J4/5* • *(030) 282 21 25* • *€€*

5 Hotel-Pension Augusta
This small hotel is a little old-fashioned, and some rooms could do with refurbishing, but that's more than made up for by its surplus of old Berlin charm, central location and low prices ✪ *Fasanenstr. 22* • *Map P4* • *(030) 883 50 28* • *www.hotel-augusta.de* • *€€*

6 Hotel am Zoo
A trendy hotel in a uniquely central location, on Ku'damm. The rooms are all surprisingly large, and the windows have been sound-proofed. ✪ *Kurfürstendamm 25* • *Map P4* • *(030) 88 43 70* • *www.hotel-am-zoo.de* • *€€*

7 Hotel-Pension Kastanienhof
A charming hotel in a building dating back to the turn of the 20th century. The rooms are basic but well equipped (with safe, minibar and hairdryer). An ideal base for exploring Prenzlauer Berg. ✪ *Kastanienallee 65* • *Map G2* • *(030) 44 30 50* • *www.hotel-kastanienhof-berlin.de* • *€€*

8 Riehmers Hofgarten
In Riehmers Hofgarten you can live the life of a Prussian officer. Old Kreuzberg apartments, with sombre rooms and elegant bathrooms, are the perfect setting for a 19th-century lifestyle. The hotel, part of a large complex of 19th-century Gothic red brick buildings, is certainly remarkable. ✪ *Yorckstr. 83* • *Map F6* • *(030) 78 09 88 00* • *www. hotel-riehmers-hofgarten.de* • *€€*

9 Hotel Berliner Hof
You can find a more attractive room in other hotels, but you'll be hard pushed to find one at such a low price and in such a central location, on Tauentzienstraße, opposite the KaDeWe department store. ✪ *Tauentzienstr. 8* • *Map P5* • *(030) 25 49 50* • *www. berliner-hof.com* • *€€*

10 Myer's Hotel
A family-run hotel in the centre of Prenzlauer Berg, ideal for families or young couples. The rooms are simple yet modern, and the hotel is located in an historic part of town; the service is attentive, the atmosphere relaxed. ✪ *Metzer Str. 26* • *Map H2* • *(030) 44 01 40* • *€€*

Left **In the art'otel berlin** Centre **Lobby and bar in Hecker's Hotel** Right **Soral Hotel Spreebogen**

TOP 10 Designer Hotels

1 art'otel berlin
Berlin's best designer hotel places emphasis on every little detail, and everything here has been styled, from the furniture to the soap you'll find in your bathroom. The walls of the historic building are decorated with paintings by Georg Baselitz. The hotel is in a central location, close to Nikolaiviertel. ✪ *Wallstr. 70–73 • Map L6 • (030) 24 06 20 • www.artotel.de • €€€*

2 Dorint Schweizerhof Berlin
The newest of Berlin's luxury hotels, Schweizerhof features beautifully clean lines, precious woods and a large, well-designed fitness area – all in the centre of the western city. Art plays a major part in the hotel – the brightly furnished, Scandinavian-style rooms are decorated with paintings by the artist Ter Hell. ✪ *Budapester Str. 25 • Map N5 • (030) 269 60 • www. dorint.de • €€€–€€€€*

3 Brandenburger Hof
The only hotel in Berlin to be influenced by the Bauhaus, the Brandenburger Hof has free-swinging leather seats and ball-shaped lamps, forming an exciting contrast to the historic building, near Ku'damm. ✪ *Eislebener Str. 14 • Map P4 • (030) 21 40 50 • www. brandenburger-hof. com • €€€–€€€€*

4 DeragHotel Großer Kurfürst
If you prefer modern designs, this hotel is not for you – the rooms here are all classically styled. The Großer Kurfürst has successfully incorporated modern facilities into an historic building. It also features many useful extras, such as free public transport and bicycle hire. ✪ *Neue Roßstr. 11–12 • Map L6 • (030) 24 60 00 • www.deraghotels.de • €€€–€€€€*

5 Hecker's Hotel
The plain façade of this modern business hotel, centrally situated in a side street just off Ku'damm, belies the much more sophisticated interior – you'll be greeted by modern art, cool minimalism, clever lighting and first-class service. ✪ *Grolmanstr. 35 • Map N3 • (030) 889 00 • www.heckers-hotel.com • €€€*

6 Sorat Hotel Spree-Bogen
Architect Wolfang Borchardt has succeeded in turning the old Bolle Dairy into a modern hotel with friendly rooms and a restaurant, both overlooking the Spree River. Next door are the semi-circular modern glass buildings of the Ministry of the Interior. ✪ *Alt-Moabit 99 • Map J1 • (030) 39 92 00 • www. sorat-hotels.de • €€€*

7 artemisia
Art and women rule at this small guesthouse – the hotel is run by and for women and all the rooms are beautifully colour-coordinated. Regular exhibitions by women artists from Berlin are held. ✪ *Brandenburgische Str. 18 • Map B5/6 • (030) 873 89 05 • €€*

8 Maritim proArte Hotel Berlin
Predominantly styled in tones of green and blue, this modern business hotel boasts almost 300 modern paintings, which decorate the rooms. Every piece of furniture has been carefully styled. ✪ *Friedrichstr. 151 • Map K/L4 • (030) 203 35 • www. maritim.de • €€€–€€€€*

9 SORAT art'otel Berlin
Works of art hang, stand and lie everywhere inside and outside this hotel, especially works by Wolf Vostell, and the interior is boldly designed in ultra-modern vibrant colours. ✪ *Joachimsthaler Str. 29 • Map P4 • (030) 88 44 70 • www.sorat-hotels.com • €€€–€€€€*

10 INN SIDE Residence Hotel
This small hotel is full of modern works of art – even the showers are art installations. The rooms also have kitchens. ✪ *Lange Str. 31 • Map H3/4 • (030) 29 30 30 • www.inside.de • €€*

Note: *Unless otherwise stated, all hotels accept credit cards, and have en-suite bathrooms.*

Price Categories

Price for a standard	€	under € 60
double room per	€€	€ 60–100
night, with breakfast,	€€€	€ 100–150
taxes and other	€€€€	€ 150–200
charges included	€€€€€	over € 200

Left **Dining at the Hilton Berlin** Right **The lobby of Estrel Residence Congress Hotel**

🏆10 Hotels for Business Travellers

1 Hilton Berlin

Top executives favour this luxury hotel because of its central location, the views across Gendarmenmarkt, an excellent breakfast and specially designed executive rooms. A full secretarial service is included. ◈ *Mohrenstr. 30 • Map L4 • (030) 20230 • www.hilton.com • €€€–€€€€*

2 Heinrich-Heine City Suites

This hotel is the best choice if your business requires a longer stay in town. Close to Nikolaiviertel, the apartments are equipped with desks and kitchens; and staff are specially trained to cater for the needs of business travellers. ◈ *Heinrich-Heine-Platz 11 • Map H4 • (030) 27 80 47 80 • www.astronhotels.com • €€–€€€*

3 Estrel Residence Congress Hotel

With over 1,000 rooms, this hotel is Europe's largest, offering a three-to four-star service at moderate prices. Its numerous conference rooms and the latest technological equipment make it the perfect venue for conferences or international business meetings. Yet the hotel is equally ready to cater for the needs of the individual business traveller. ◈ *Sonnenallee 225 • (030) 683 10 • www.estrel.com • €€–€€€*

4 Crowne Plaza Berlin City Centre

Part of an American hotel chain, the Crowne Plaza offers attentive service, tasteful rooms and all the creature comforts that business travellers expect, plus a central location, in the western part of the city. ◈ *Nürnberger Str. 65 • Map P5 • (030) 21 00 70 • www.cp-berlin.com • €€€*

5 Holiday Inn Garden Court

It may seem a little impersonal, but the Holiday Inn's excellent location makes it popular with business travellers from the US. One disadvantage: it has no restaurant. ◈ *Bleibtreustr. 25 • Map P3 • (030) 88 09 30 • www.holiday-inn.com • €€€*

6 Madison City Suites

A central boarding house with suites of 40–100 square metres (430 to 1,076 square feet), fully equipped as offices and offering a near-perfect secretarial service – just what today's business traveller needs. All the rooms are elegantly furnished using the very best materials. ◈ *Friedrichstr. 185–190 • Map K/L4 • (030) 20 29 20 • www.madison-berlin.de • €€€*

7 Dorint Budget Hotel Airport Tegel

Conveniently situated near the airport, this hotel is ideal for brief business trips. A good night's rest is guaranteed, and the service is efficient and friendly. ◈ *Gotthardstr. 96 • (030) 49 88 40 • www.dorint.de • €€*

8 Berlin Excelsior

Prestigious member of Berlin's Blue-Band-Hotels, the Excelsior is generally characterized more by sober efficiency than by friendliness. But this hotel hits the mark with moderate prices, excellent location and a vast range of business services. ◈ *Hardenbergstr. 14 • Map N4 • (030) 315 50 • www.hotel-excelsior.de • €€€*

9 Astron Berlin-Alexanderplatz

Slightly unfriendly but well-equipped four-star hotel near the centre of the eastern part of the city (only ten minutes away). You can work here in peace and quiet, without any disruptions. ◈ *Landsberger Allee 26–32 • Map H3 • (030) 422 61 30 • www.astron-hotels.de • €€*

10 Hotel Ambassador Berlin

A medium-priced hotel near KaDeWe, offering a full office service, quiet rooms, a lovely pool with good views and an excellent buffet dinner. ◈ *Bayreuther Str. 42–43 • Map P5 • (030) 21 90 20 • www.ambassador-berlin.de • €€€*

See also pp72–3.

Left **Schlossparkhotel** Centre **Pool in Hotel zur Bleiche** Right **Relaxa Schlosshotel Cecilienhof**

🔟 Hotels in Green Surroundings

1 Relexa Schloss-hotel Cecilienhof
Potsdam's best hotel, the Relaxa is based in an historic building in the middle of Neuer Garten *(see p154)*. At night, peace descends once the day trippers have gone. ⊗ *Am Neuen Garten Potsdam • (0331) 370 50 • www. castle-cecilienhof.de • €€€€*

2 Landhaus Schlachtensee
This villa, near Schlachtensee and Krumme Lanke, now a small boarding house, oozes the charm of bygone days in rural Berlin. The furnishings in its 20 rooms are a little old-fashioned, but the service making for very personable, making for a pleasant stay. ⊗ *Bogotastr. 9 • (030) 809 94 70 • €€*

3 Schlossparkhotel
Only a few minutes from the western part of the city, this is the only hotel near Schloss Charlottenburg, right next to Schlosspark. Attached to it is a health and fitness centre – the facilities and the service are surprisingly good for such a small place: the hotel has only 40 rooms. ⊗ *Heubnerweg 2a • Map A/B3 • (030) 326 90 30 • www.schloss parkhotel.de • €€*

4 Hotel Seehof am Lietzensee
A well-run hotel, centrally located in Charlottenburg, not far from Messegelände (exhibition grounds), in a picturesque spot on Lietzensee. Apart from a beautiful indoor pool, the hotel also has a delightful sun terrace, which overlooks the lake. ⊗ *Lietzenseeufer 11 • Map A4 • (030) 32 00 20 • www. hotel-seehof-berlin.de • €€€*

5 Dorint Hotel Berlin-Müggelsee
A luxury hotel on Müggelsee, combining Mediterranean and Asian features. There is a skittle alley, a fitness club, tennis courts, sauna and billiards as well as boat and bicycle hire and an extensive programme of leisure events. ⊗ *Am Großen Müggelsee • (030) 65 88 20 • www. dorint-berlin.de • €€€*

6 Haus La Garde
This tiny guesthouse with only four rooms is hidden in a romantic villa on the green Schlachtensee. If lakes aren't your thing, you can chill out in the villa's own gardens. ⊗ *Bergengrünstr. 16 • (030) 801 30 09 • €*

7 Spreeidyll-Hotel am Yachthafen
A small family-run house on the Müggelspree, not far from a bathing beach and a boat-hire booth – the ideal place to relax and forget all about the hustle and bustle of the big city, which is, however, only a few kilometres to the northwest. Come here to chill out. ⊗ *Müggelseedamm 70 • (030) 645 38 52 • www.spree-idyll.de • €*

8 Hotel Rheinsberg am See
You are guaranteed a relaxing stay at this rustic hotel in the north of Berlin, which offers a huge breakfast buffet. The hotel pool help you forget the stresses of life and improve your fitness. ⊗ *Finsterwalder Str. 64 • (030) 402 10 02 • www. hotel-rheinsberg.com • €€*

9 Courtyard Berlin-Köpenick
The slightly sterile and impersonal atmosphere of the Marriott is more than made up for by its perfect location. It is right in the centre of the southeastern district of Köpenick, on the banks of the Dahme River – and both Müggelsee and Schönefeld Airport are only a few minutes' drive away by car or S-Bahn. ⊗ *Grünauer Str. 1 • (030) 65 47 90 • www. courtyard.com • €€*

10 Hotel zur Bleiche
This country-house hotel, located in the middle of the Spreewald lake district, has great facilities including pool, steam rooms, saunas and a great restaurant – a veritable paradise for health and fitness fans. ⊗ *Bleichestr. 16, Burg • (035603) 620 • www.hotel-zur-bleiche.de • €€*

Note: Unless otherwise stated, all hotels accept credit cards, and have en-suite bathrooms.

Price Categories

Price for a standard double room per night, with breakfast, taxes and other charges included	**€** under € 60
	€€ € 60–100
	€€€ € 100–150
	€€€€ € 150–200
	€€€€€ over € 200

Left **The Backpacker Hostel** Right **At BaxPax, you'll sleep in a VW Beetle**

TOP 10 Budget Hotels & Hostels

1 BaxPax
Much better than a youth hostel yet much cheaper than a guest-house: in the BaxPax you'll be sleeping in beds in decommissioned VW beetles, at under € 20 per night. Plus you'll meet young, friendly people from around the world (great for making friends). This dive is in deepest Kreuzberg, and not suitable for those over 30. ✆ Skalitzerstr. 104 • Map H5 • (030) 69 51 83 22 • www.baxpax.de • no credit cards • €

2 Jugendgästehaus der DSJ
This vast youth guesthouse is situated in an excellent spot, in the heart of Kreuzberg, and close to the Jüdisches Museum. The showers are shared, but a bed in a multi-bedded room is not expensive. The hostel is favoured by a young and international crowd. ✆ Franz-Künstler-Str. 4–10 • Map G5 • (030) 615 10 07 • no credit cards • €

3 Jugendgästehaus Kluckstraße
One of Berlin's largest youth hostels offers slightly antiquated but comfortable multi-bedded rooms. The staff are very friendly for a hostel in a large city, but the hostel is often overrun by noisy hordes of school kids. ✆ Kluckstr. 3 • Map E5 • (030) 261 10 98 • no credit cards • €

4 acksel Haus
Basic apartment rooms in a small, slightly alternative guesthouse, based in an old tenement block. The "acksel haus" is near Kollwitzplatz, a popular area with young people. ✆ Belforter Str. 21 • Map H2 • (030) 44 33 76 33 • no credit cards • €

5 Jugendgästehaus am Wannsee
One of Berlin's oldest youth hostels, popular with groups of students and pupils and not the best place for visitors seeking peace and quiet. The picturesque location on Wannsee makes up for communal showers and dormitories, particularly in summer. ✆ Badeweg 1 • (030) 803 20 34 • no credit cards • €

6 Bed & Breakfast
Berliner Mitwohnzentrale, an agency, arranges shared accommodation in private homes all over town, at low prices. You'll normally have your own room with one or two beds. Quality varies considerably but the rooms are mostly priced at under € 25 per night. ✆ (030) 746 14 46 • no credit cards • €

7 Timmy's Bed and Breakfast
A private gay-and-lesbian-friendly guesthouse, offering basic rooms and many insider tips on culture and nightlife. The only disadvantage is its location in Moabit – not one of Berlin's most attractive areas. ✆ Perlebergerstr. • Map D/E2 • (030) 81 85 19 88 • www.gaybed.de • €

8 Backpacker Hostel Berlin
A typically charming Berlin guesthouse, in the most attractive part of Charlottenburg. You can even have your breakfast served in the room. ✆ Niebuhrstr. 74 • (030) 324 95 95 • www.pension-niebuhr.de • €

9 Hotel-Pension Korfu II
The name of this small hotel with only 19 rooms may seem over the top, but this venue is ideally suited for young people and families. The rooms are basic but well cared for, and the service is efficient. The house is in a central spot, opposite Kaiser-Wilhelm Gedächtniskirche. ✆ Rankestr. 35 • Map P4 • (030) 212 47 90 • www.hp-korfu.de • €

10 Hotel Christopherus-Haus
This hotel is a little more expensive than others in the same category, but the accommodation in green surroundings is perfect for families. The hotel is run by the Protestant church. ✆ Johannesstift, Schönwalder Allee 26 • (030) 33 60 60 • www.vch.de • €€

Left **In Villa Kastania** Centre **The pool in Alexander Plaza** Right **Propeller Island City**

🔟 Hotels & Guesthouses with Charm

1 Golden Tulip Residenz Hotel
Although this hotel is part of a US chain, it is based in one of the most beautiful old-Berlin town houses near Ku'damm, and guests enjoy the intimate, characterful atmosphere. The turn-of-the-century rooms are tastefully furnished, and the restaurant has outdoor seating in summer.
Ⓢ Meinekestr. 9 • Map P4 • (030) 88 44 30 • www.hotel-residenz.com • €€€

2 Hotel-Pension Dittberner
Berlin's best guesthouse, close to Ku'damm, consists of several rooms in an old building, connected by endless corridors with lots of nooks and crannies. Some of the furniture has seen better days, but breakfast and atmosphere are perfect.
Ⓢ Wielandstr. 26 • Map P2 • (030) 881 64 85 • €€

3 Alexander-Plaza
Based in an historic building from the late 19th century, this hotel perfectly combines old and new features. The elegant rooms are decorated with plaster ceiling mouldings and equipped with timelessly sophisticated furnishings. This is a very pleasant hotel indeed, both to look at and to stay in.
Ⓢ Rosenstr. 1 • Map J5 • (030) 24 00 10 00 • www.alexander-plaza.com • €€

4 DeragResidenz-hotel Henriette
A stylish hotel with classic decoration – oak-panelled walls and thick carpets and curtains adorn the rooms, which are arranged around an inner courtyard. Few hotels in town are better than this, and the service is very friendly.
Ⓢ Neue Roßstr. 13 • Map L6 • (030) 24 60 09 00 • www.deraghotels.de • €€

5 Hotel Gendarm
This small hotel on Gendarmenmarkt is based in a venerable town residence. The rooms, too, with their design and furnishings, seem to hark back to the 19th century, but in fact everything is brand-new. The hotel also boasts a sauna, pool and fitness facilities. Ⓢ Charlottenstr. 60 • Map L4 • (030) 206 06 60 • www.hotel-gerndarm-berlin.de • €€

6 Hotel-Pension Wittelsbach
The furnishings in this medium-sized hotel-guesthouse are hopelessly stuck in the 1970s – and this is what makes it so charming. The service is very friendly, children and pets are both welcome, and the breakfast buffet is so generous that you won't need to eat anything else for the rest of the day.
Ⓢ Wittelsbacherstr. 22 • Map B5 • (030) 864 98 40 • €-€€

7 Art Nouveau Hotel
An old-fashioned but well-run guesthouse, based in a beautiful Art-Nouveau building. The rooms are furnished in a discreet modern style, and the hotel is typical of Berlin's older buildings.
Ⓢ Leibnitzstr. 59 • Map P2 • (030) 327 74 40 • www.hotelartnouveau.de • €€

8 Artist Riverside Hotel Berlin-Mitte
A small hotel promising big things, and in terms of its furnishings at least it keeps these promises. The stylish 19th-century house, with sophisticated interior and excellent service, is popular with American visitors.
Ⓢ Friedrichstr. 106 • Map K/L4 • (030) 28 49 00 • www.tolles-hotel.de • €€

9 Villa Kastania
Service of a high standard, and beautiful rooms with kitchen and bathroom – well suited for self-catering and situated in the middle of Prenzlauer Berg.
Ⓢ Kastanienallee 20 • (030) 300 00 20 • €€

10 Propeller Island City Lodge
If you're staying at this lodge, you will share it with the artist Lars Stroschen, who designed the rooms himself. Ⓢ Paulsborner Str. 10 • Map B5 • (030) 891 90 16 • www.propeller-island.net4.com • no credit cards • €

Note: Unless otherwise stated, all hotels accept credit cards, and have en-suite bathrooms.

Price Categories

Price for a standard	€	under € 60
double room per	€€	€ 60–100
night, with breakfast,	€€€	€ 100–150
taxes and other	€€€€	€ 150–200
charges included	€€€€€	over € 200

Left **The Dorint am Gendarmenmarkt** Right **A suite in Hotel Palace**

Luxury Hotels

1 Hotel Palace

The expensively restored hotel on the second floor of the Europa-Center is a real find – all the rooms are exquisitely designed, two of the suites (Zackenbarsch and Panda) were styled by the director himself. The hotel staff are unobtrusive and very helpful.
◈ Budapester Str. 45 • Map N/P5 • (030) 250 20 • www.palace.de • €€€€

2 Dorint am Gendarmenmarkt

Relatively inexpensive and the smallest of the first-class hotels (70 rooms, 21 suites), the Dorint is probably also one of the most attractive, with excellent views of Gendarmenmarkt.
◈ Charlottenstr. 50–52 • Map L4 • (030) 203 750 • www.dorint.de • €€€€

3 Hotel Inter-continental Berlin

Luxury hotel in Tiergarten, recently renovated, with great views over the central park, this hotel is popular with business travellers. Although the building itself is not particularly attractive, the rooms are furnished in a timelessly elegant style. Its three restaurants offer first-class food, and the bars, pool and fitness area are also excellent.
◈ Budapester Str. 2 • Map N5/6 • (030) 260 20 • www.berlin.interconti.com • €€€€€

4 Westin Grand Hotel

Luxury accommodation in an historic spot, at the corner of Friedrichstraße and Unter den Linden, offering large, elegant rooms and US-style service. The lobby and the grand stairs are breathtaking. There's also a café and a bar.
◈ Friedrichstr. 158–164 • Map K4 • (030) 202 70 • www. westin-grand.com • €€€€€

5 Grand Hotel Esplanade

Glitzy, modern hotel, with furnishings somewhere between functional sobriety and Bauhaus-style. Service and facilities are first-class and Harry's New York Bar is very popular.
◈ Lützowufer 15 • Map N6 • (030) 25 47 80 • www.esplanade.de • €€€€€

6 Swissôtel Berlin

One of Berlin's new luxury hotels, the Swissôtel is located at the busy corner of Ku'damm and Joachimsthaler Straße. Great views of the city, especially at night.
◈ Augsburger Str. 44 • Map P4 • (030) 22 01 00 • www.swissotel.com • €€€€

7 Madison Potsdamer Platz

This apartment hotel, in a great spot in Potsdamer Platz, has suites of 35–100 sq m (375–1,100 sq ft) with kitchen, stereo, fitness area, sauna, daily papers and anything else you could possibly wish for. ◈ Potsdamer Str. 3 • Map K3 • (030) 590 05 00 00 • www.madison-berlin.de • €€€€

8 Steigenberger Berlin

A first-class hotel, hidden away in a quiet park-like square, yet close to Ku'damm. The deluxe rooms are a particularly good deal – a private lounge, daily newspapers and free drinks are included if you stay here.
◈ Los-Angeles-Platz 1 • Map P4 • (030) 212 70 • www.steigenberger.de • €€€€

9 Dorint Sanssouci Berlin-Potsdam

This new four-star hotel is located near Alexandrovka, the historic Russian colony, within walking distance of Schlosspark Sanssouci. Offering great facilities (fitness centre, pool, restaurant, bars), it is particularly well suited as a base for excursions into Brandenburg province.
◈ Jägerallee 20 • (030)) 27 40 • www.dorint.de • €€€€

10 Hotel Mondial

Modern and not very attractive from the outside, this hotel is situated in a perfect location and boasts a surprisingly stylish and elegant interior. It has been fully equipped for disabled visitors. ◈ Kurfürstendamm 47 • Map P3 • (030) 88 41 10 • €€€€

General Index

Acknowledgements

The Author
Historian Jürgen Scheunemann has published several documentary and photographic books on Berlin and other destinations. His award-winning articles are published in travel magazines and daily newspapers in Germany and the US, and have appeared in the Berlin daily *Tagesspiegel*, among others.

FOR DORLING KINDERSLEY VERLAG, MUNICH:
Publishing Director
Dr. Jörg Theilacker
Editors
Brigitte Maier, Gerhard Bruschke
Design & Layout
Ulrike Meyer
Proofreader
Linde Wiesner
Editorial Assistants
Jasmin Jouhar, Robert Kocom

Photography
Jürgen Scheunemann

Additional Photography
Dorota and MariuszJarymowicz

Artwork
Chris Orr & Assocaites

Cartography
Dominic Beddow, Simonetta Siori
(Draughtsman Ltd)

FOR DORLING KINDERSLEY, LONDON:
Translation & Editing
Sylvia Goulding/Silva Editions
Senior Publishing Manager
Louise Lang
Publishing Manager
Kate Poole
Senior Art Editor
Marisa Renzullo
Director of Publishing
Gillian Allan
Publisher
Douglas Amrine
Cartography Co-ordinator
Casper Morris

DTP
Jason Little, Conrad van Dyk
Production
Sarah Dodd

Picture Credits
t-top; tc-top centre; tr-top right; cla-centre left above; ca-centre above; cra-centre right above; cl-centre left; c-centre; cr-centre right; clb-centre right below; cb-centre below; crb-centre right below; bl-below left; bc-below centre; br below right.

The publishers would like to thank the following individuals, companies and picture libraries for permission to reproduce their photographs:

808 Lounge Bar: 128tl. Alexander Plaza: 178tc. Ars vitalis: 69br. Art'otel Berlin: 174tl. Backpacker Hostel/Axbax: 177tl, 177tr. Bar jeder Vernunft: 57cla. Berliner Bäder-Betriebe: 69tl. Berliner Film-festspiele: 62cl. Bleibtreu-Hotel: 173tl. Deutsche Guggenheim: 113clb. Dorint am Gendarmenmarkt: 179tl. Econtel Hotel: 172tc. Estrel Residence Congress Hotel: 175tr. Funpool: 68tr. Galeries Lafayette: 119tc. Heckers Hotel: 174tc. Hertha BSC: 68bl. Hotel Adlon: 8crb, 116cb. Hotel Hackescher Markt: 173tr. Hotel Künstlerheim Luise: 172tr. Hotel zur Bleiche: 176tc. Jüdisches Museum: 102tr. Margaux: 74b. Museum für Kommunikation: Herbert Schlemmer: 117b. Propeller City Island: 178tr. Quartier 206 Department Store: 60tl, 115tl. Relaxa Hotel Cecilienhof: 176tr. Schlossparkhotel: 176tl. Schneider, Günter: 95–5. Sorat Hotel Spreebogen: 174tl. Siegessäule: 58b. Tourismusverband Spreewald e. V.: Rainer Weisflog 167tr. Trabrennbahn Mariendorf: 68tc. Trenta sei: Benjamin Hüter 120tc;

Jens Gläser 121tr. Zoologischer Garten: 36-7c.

BILDARCHIV PREUSSISCHER KULTURBESITZ, BERLIN: 20tl, 31tr, 35c; Ägyptisches Museum/ Margarete Büsing 4c; Antikensammlung 7tl, 21tl, 21clb, 21br, 21–2c, 22b, 22t, 46tl, 114c; Antikensammlung/Ingrid Geske-Heiden 114b; Ethnologisches Museum 30br; Gemäldegalerie, *Madonna in Church* by Jan van Eyck (c1425) 32t, *Portrait of the Merchant Georg Gisze* by Hans Holbein (1532) 34tr, *Venus and the Organ Player* by Titian (1550–2) 34tc, *Portrait of Hieronymus Holzschuher* by Albrecht Dürer (1529) 34tr, *Madonna with the Child and Singing Angels* by Botticelli (c1477) 34c, *Victorious Eros* by Caravaggio (1602) 34bl, 48tc, *Adoration of the Shepherds* by Hugo van der Goes (1470) 48tl, *The Glass of Wine* by Jan Vermeer (c1658–61) 48bu; Kunstgewerbemuseum 7cb, 33t, 46tr, 47c; Kupferstichkabinett, *Portrait of Dürer's Mother* by Albrecht Dürer 114c; Museum für Vor- und Frühgeschichte 29br; Nationalgalerie, *Farm in Dangart* by Karl Schmidt-Rottluff (1910) 32b, *Mao* by Andy Warhol (1973) © The Andy Warhol Foundation for the Visual Arts Inc. / ARS, NY & DACS, London 2001 4cr; Nationalgalerie, Berggruen Collection, *Head of a Faun* by Pablo Picasso (1937) © Succession Picasso / DACS 49ol; Vorderasiatisches Museum 20c, 20cbr, 20b, 21cbr, 23c, 23b, 23t,

BRECHT-WEIGEL-GEDENKSTÄTTE, BERLIN: 50cr.
BRIDGEMAN ART LIBRARY: Nationalgalerie, Berlin, *Portrait of Georg Wilhelm Friedrich Hegel* (1770–1831) by Jacob Schlesinger (1792–1855) 50tl.
BROEHAN MUSEUM: 49c.

DEUTSCHE PRESSEAGENTUR: 9b, 42tr, 50tc, 50tr, 50bl, 51tl, 51b, 62tc, 62tr, 62c, 63tl, 63tr, 63cr.
DEUTSCHES HISTORISCHES MUSEUM: 15t, 18cl, 42cr, 51c; *Gloria Victis* by Antonin Mercie 14c; *Martin Luther* by Lucas Cranach the Elder (1529) 14b; *Opening of the German Reichstag* (1871) 15b. DEUTSCHES TECHNIKMUSEUM: 103bl.

HENRY MOORE FOUNDATION: *Three Way Piece Nr. 2. (The) Archer* (1964–5) 35t.
HOTEL VILLA KASTANIA: 178tl.

KÄTHE-KOLLWITZ-MUSEUM: *Mother and Child* by Käthe Kollwitz 83bl.
KOMISCHE OPER BERLIN: Arwid Lagenpusch 112tr.

MUSEUM FÜR NATURKUNDE: 47tr.

STIFTUNG STADTMUSEUM BERLIN: 14t; Peter Straube 130tr. STIFTUNG PREUSSISCHE SCHLÖSSER UND GÄRTEN BERLIN-BRANDENBURG: 152tr, 153br, *Frederick's Watteau Paintings* by Antoine Watteau (1720) 30tc; *Frederick the Great* by Antoine Posne 31tl, *Frederick Playing the Flute* by Adolf von Menzel 42b, 152cl.

WERNER OTTO BILDARCHIV, OBERHAUSEN: 76–7.

JACKET: All special photography except Corbis: Hugh Rooney: Eye Ubiquitous F/C bottom; Gregor Schmid F/C main image; Telegraph Colour Library/Getty Images: Messerschmidt F/C centre above.

All other images © Dorling Kindersley London. For further information see:
www.dkimages.com

Phrase Book

In an Emergency

Where is the telephone?	Wo ist das Telefon?	voh ist duss tel-e-fone?
Help!	Hilfe!	**hilf**-uh
Please call a doctor	Bitte rufen Sie einen Arzt	**bitt**-uh **roof**'n zee ine-en artst
Please call the police	Bitte rufen Sie die Polizei	**bitt**-uh **roof**'n zee dee poli-**tsy**
Please call the fire brigade	Bitte rufen Sie die Feuerwehr	**bitt**-uh roof'n zee dee **foyer**-vayr
Stop!	Halt!	**hult**

Communication Essentials

Yes	Ja	**yah**
No	Nein	**nine**
Please	Bitte	**bitt**-uh
Thank you	Danke	dunk-uh
Excuse me	Verzeihung	fair-**tsy**-hoong
Hello (good day)	Guten Tag	**goot**-en tahk
Goodbye	Auf Wiedersehen	owf-**veed**-er-zay-ern
Good evening	Guten Abend	goot'n **ahb**'nt
Good night	Gute Nacht	goot-uh **nukht**
Until tomorrow	Bis morgen	biss **morg**'n
See you	Tschüss	**chooss**
What is that?	Was ist das?	voss ist duss
Why?	Warum?	var-**room**
Where?	Wo?	**voh**
When?	Wann?	**vunn**
today	heute	**hoyt**-uh
tomorrow	morgen	**morg**'n
month	Monat	**mohn**-aht
night	Nacht	**nukht**
afternoon	Nachmittag	**nahkh**-mit-tahk
morning	Morgen	**morg**'n
year	Jahr	**yar**
there	dort	**dort**
here	hier	**hear**
week	Woche	**vokh**-uh
yesterday	gestern	**gest**'n
evening	Abend	**ahb**'nt

Useful Phrases

How are you? (informal)	Wie geht's?	vee gayts
Fine, thanks	Danke, es geht mir gut	dunk-uh, es gayt meer goot
Where is/are?	Wo ist/sind...?	voh ist/sind
How far is it to...?	Wie weit ist es...?	vee **vite** ist ess
Do you speak English?	Sprechen Sie Englisch?	shpresh'n zee **eng**-glish
I don't understand	Ich verstehe nicht	ish fair-**shtay**-uh nisht
Could you speak more slowly?	Könnten Sie langsamer sprechen?	**kurnt**-en zee **lung**-zam-er **shpresh**'n

Useful Words

large	gross	**grohss**
small	klein	**kline**
hot	heiss	**hyce**
cold	kalt	**kult**
good	gut	**goot**
bad	böse/schlecht	**burss**-uh/**shlesht**
open	geöffnet	g'**urff**-nett
closed	geschlossen	g'**shloss**'n
left	links	**links**
right	rechts	**reshts**
straight ahead	geradeaus	g'**rah**-der-**owss**

Making a Telephone Call

I would like to make a phone call	Ich möchte telefonieren	ish mer-shtuh tel-e-fon-**eer**'n
I'll try again later	Ich versuche noch ein mal später	ish fair-zookh-uh nokh ine-mull **shpay**-ter
Can I leave a message?	Kann ich eine Nachricht hinterlassen?	kan ish **ine**-uh nakh-risht hint-er-**lahss**-en
answer phone	Anrufbeantworter	an-roof-be-**ahnt**-vort-er
telephone card	Telefonkarte	tel-e-**fohn**-kart-uh
receiver	Hörer	**hur**-er
mobile	Handi	han-dee
engaged (busy)	besetzt	b'zetst
wrong number	Falsche Verbindung	falsh-uh fair-**bin**-doong

Sight-Seeing

library	Bibliothek	bib-leo-**tek**
entrance ticket	Eintrittskarte	ine-tritz-**kart**-uh
cemetery	Friedhof	**freed**-hofe
train station	Bahnhof	**barn**-hofe
gallery	Galerie	**gall**-er-ree
information	Auskunft	**owss**-koonft
church	Kirche	**keersh**-uh
garden	Garten	**gart**'n
palace/castle	Palast/Schloss	pallast/shloss
place (square)	Platz	**plats**
bus stop	Haltestelle	**hal**-te-shtel-uh
national holiday	Nationalfeiertag	nats-yon-**ahl**-fire-tahk
theatre	Theater	tay-**aht**-er
free admission	Eintritt frei	ine-tritt fry

Shopping

Do you have/Is there...?	Gibt es...?	geept ess
How much does it cost?	Was kostet das?	voss **kost**'t duss?
When do you open/close?	Wann öffnen Sie? schliessen Sie?	vunn **off**'n zee **shlees**'n zee
this	das	duss
expensive	teuer	**toy**-er
cheap	preiswert	**price**-vurt
size	Grösse	**gruhs**-uh
number	Nummer	**noom**-er
colour	Farbe	**farb**-uh
brown	braun	brown
black	schwarz	**shvarts**
red	rot	**roht**
blue	blau	**blau**
green	grün	**groon**
yellow	gelb	**gelp**

Types of Shop

antique shop	Antiquariat	antik-**var**-yat
chemist (pharmacy)	Apotheke	appo-**tay**-kuh
bank	Bank	**bunk**
market	Markt	**markt**
travel agency	Reisebüro	**rye**-zer-boo-roe
department store	Warenhaus	**vahr**'n-hows
chemist's, drugstore	Drogerie	droog-er-**ree**
hairdresser	Friseur	freezz-**er**
newspaper kiosk	Zeitungskiosk	tsytoongs-kee-osk

bookshop	Buchhandlung	**bookh**-hant-loong
bakery	Bäckerei	beck-er-**eye**
post office	Post	posst
shop/store	Geschäft/Laden	gush-**eft/lard**'n
film processing shop	Photogeschäft	**fo**-to-gush-**eft**
self-service shop	Selbstbedienungs-laden	selpst-bed-**ee**-nungs-lard'n
shoe shop	Schuhladen	shoo-**teek**-uh
clothes shop	Kleiderladen, Boutique	klyder-lard'n boo-**teek**-uh
food shop	Lebensmittel-geschäft	**lay**-bens-mittel-gush-eft
glass, porcelain	Glas, Porzellan	**glars**, Port-sellahn

Staying in a Hotel

Do you have any vacancies?	Haben Sie noch Zimmer frei?	harb'n zee nokh **tsimm**-er-fry
with twin beds?	mit zwei Betten?	mitt tsvy bett'n
with a double bed?	mit einem Doppelbett?	mitt ine'm **dopp**'l-bet
with a bath?	mit Bad?	mitt **bart**
with a shower?	mit Dusche?	mitt **doosh**-uh
I have a reservation	Ich habe eine Reservierung	ish **harb**-uh ine-uh rez-er-**veer**-oong
key	Schlüssel	**shlooss**'l
porter	Pförtner	**pfert**-ner

Eating Out

Do you have a table for...?	Haben Sie einen Tisch für...?	harb'n zee **ine**-uhn tish foor
I would like to reserve a table	Ich möchte eine Reservierung machen	ish **mer**-shtuh ine-uh rezer-**veer**-oong makh'n
I'm a vegetarian	Ich bin Vegetarier	ish bin vegg-er-**tah**-ree-er
Waiter!	Herr Ober!	hair **oh**-bare!
The bill (check), please	Die Rechnung, bitte	dee **resh**-noong bitt-uh
breakfast	Frühstück	**froo**-shtock
lunch	Mittagessen	**mit**-targ-ess'n
dinner	Abendessen	**arb**'nt-ess'n
bottle	Flasche	**flush**-uh
dish of the day	Tagesgericht	**tahg**-es-gur-isht
main dish	Hauptgericht	**howpt**-gur-isht
dessert	Nachtisch	**nahkh**-tish
cup	Tasse	**tass** uh
wine list	Weinkarte	vine-kart-uh
tankard	Krug	khroog
glass	Glas	**glars**
spoon	Löffel	**lerff**'l
teaspoon	Teelöffel	tayler-ff'l
tip	Trinkgeld	**trink** gelt
knife	Messer	**mess**-er
starter (appetizer)	Vorspeise	**for**-shpize-uh
the bill	Rechnung	**resh**-noong
plate	Teller	**tell**-er
fork	Gabel	**gahb**'l

Menu Decoder

Aal	arl	eel
Apfel	**upf**'l	apple
Apfelschorle	**upf**'l-shoorl-uh	apple juice with sparkling mineral water
Apfelsine	**upf**'l-seen-uh	orange
Aprikose	upri-**kawz**-uh	apricot

Artischocke	arti-**shokh**-uh- or-ber-jeen-uh	artichoke
Aubergine		aubergine (eggplant)
Banane	bar-**narn**-uh	banana
Beefsteack	**beef**-stayk	steak
Bier	beer	beer
Bockwurst	**bokh**-voorst	a type of sausage
Bohnensuppe	burn-en-zoop-uh	bean soup
Branntwein	brant-vine	spirits
Bratkartoffeln	brat-kar-toff'ln	fried potatoes
Bratwurst	brat-voorst	fried sausage
Brötchen	bret-tchen	bread roll
Brot	brot	bread
Brühe	bruh-uh	broth
Butter	**boot**-ter	butter
Champignon	**shum**-pin-yong	mushroom
Currywurst	**kha**-ree-voorst	sausage with curry sauce
Dill	**dill**	dill
Ei	**eye**	egg
Eis	**ice**	ice/ ice cream
Ente	**ent**-uh	duck
Erdbeeren	ayrt-**beer**'n	strawberries
Fisch	**fish**	fish
Forelle	for-**ell**-uh	trout
Frikadelle	Frika-dayl-uh	rissole/ hamburger
Gans	ganns	goose
Garnele	**gar**-nayl-uh	prawn/shrimp
gebraten	g'**braat**'n	fried
gegrillt	g'**grillt**	grilled
gekocht	g'**kokh**t	boiled
geräuchert	g'**rowk**-ert	smoked
Geflügel	g'**floog**'l	poultry
Gemüse	g'**mooz**-uh	vegetables
Grütze	**grurt**-ser	groats, gruel
Gulasch	**goo**-lush	goulash
Gurke	**goork**-uh	gherkin
Hammelbraten	hamm'l-**braat**'n	roast mutton
Hähnchen	**haynsh**'n	chicken
Hering	**hair**-ing	herring
Himbeeren	him-beer'n	raspberries
Honig	**hoe**-nikh	honey
Kaffee	kaf-**fay**	coffee
Kalbfleisch	kalp-flysh	veal
Kaninchen	ka-**neensh**'n	rabbit
Karpfen	**karpf**'n	carp
Kartoffelpüree	kar-toff'l-poor-ay	mashed potatoes
Käse	**kayz**-uh	cheese
Kaviar	**kar**-vee-ar	caviar
Knoblauch	**k'nob**-lowkh	garlic
Knödel	**k'nerd**'l	noodle
Kohl	**koal**	cabbage
Kopfsalat	**kopf**-zal-aat	lettuce
Krebs	**krayps**	crab
Kuchen	**kookh**'n	cake
Lachs	**lahkhs**	salmon
Leber	**lay**-ber	liver
mariniert	mari-neert	marinated
Marmelade	marmer-**lard**-uh	marmalade, jam
Meerrettich	may-re-tish	horseradish
Milch	**milsh**	milk
Mineralwasser	minn-er-**arl**-vuss-er	mineral water
Möhre	**mer**-uh	carrot
Nuss	**nooss**	nut
Öl	**erl**	oil
Olive	o-**leev**-uh	olive

Petersilie	payt-er-**zee**-li-uh	parsley
Pfeffer	**pfeff**-er	pepper
Pfirsich	**pfir**-zish	peach
Pflaumen	**pflow**-men	plum
Pommes frites	pomm-**fritt**	chips/ French fries
Quark	kvark	soft cheese
Radieschen	ra-**deesh**'n	radish
Rinderbraten	**rind**-er-brat'n	joint of beef
Rinderroulade	**rind**-er-roo-lard-uh	beef olive
Rindfleisch	**rint**-flysh	beef
Rippchen	**rip**-sh'n	cured pork rib
Rotkohl	roht-koal	red cabbage
Rüben	rhoob'n	turnip
Rührei	**rhoo**-er-eye	scrambled eggs
Saft	**zuft**	juice
Salat	zal-aat	salad
Salz	**zults**	salt
Salzkartoffeln	zults-kar-toff'l	boiled potatoes
Sauerkirschen	zow-er-**keersh**'n	cherries
Sauerkraut	zow-er-krowt	sauerkraut
Sekt	**zekt**	sparkling wine
Senf	**zenf**	mustard
scharf	sharf	spicy
Schaschlik	shash-lik	kebab
Schlagsahne	shlahgg-zarn-uh	whipped cream
Schnittlauch	shnit-lowhkh	chives
Schnitzel	**shnitz**'l	veal or pork cutlet
Schweinefleisch	**shvine**-flysh	pork
Spargel	**shparg**'l	asparagus
Spiegelei	shpeeg'l-eye	fried egg
Spinat	shpin-art	spinach
Tee	**tay**	tea
Tomate	tom-art-uh	tomato
Wassermelone	vuss-er-me-lohn-uh	watermelon
Wein	vine	wine
Weintrauben	**vine**-trowb'n	grapes
Wiener Würstchen	**veen**-er voorst-sh'n	frankfurter
Zander	**tsan**-der	pike-perch
Zitrone	tsi-trohn-uh	lemon
Zucker	**tsook**-er	sugar
Zwieback	tsvee-bak	rusk
Zwiebel	**tsvee**b'l	onion

Numbers

0	null	**nool**
1	eins	**eye**'ns
2	zwei	**tsvy**
3	drei	**dry**
4	vier	**feer**
5	fünf	**foonf**
6	sechs	**zex**
7	sieben	**zeeb**'n
8	acht	**uhkht**
9	neun	**noyn**
10	zehn	**tsayn**
11	elf	**elf**
12	zwölf	**tserlf**
13	dreizehn	**dry**-tsayn
14	vierzehn	**feer**-tsayn
15	fünfzehn	**foonf**-tsayn
16	sechzehn	**zex**-tsayn
17	siebzehn	**zeep**-tsayn
18	achtzehn	**uhkht**-tsayn
19	neunzehn	**noyn**-tsayn
20	zwanzig	**tsvunn**-tsig
21	einundzwanzig	**ine**-oont-tsvunn-tsig
30	dreissig	**dry**-sig
40	vierzig	**feer**-sig
50	fünfzig	**foonf**-tsig
60	sechzig	**zex**-tsig
70	siebzig	**zeep**-tsig
80	achtzig	**uhkht**-tsig
90	neunzig	**noyn**-tsig
100	hundert	**hoond**'t
1000	tausend	**towz**'nt
1,000,000	eine Million	**ine**-uh **mill**-yon

Time

one minute	eine Minute	**ine**-uh min-**oot**-uh
one hour	eine Stunde	**ine**-uh **shtoond**-uh
half an hour	eine halbe Stunde	**ine**-uh hullb-uh **shtoond**-uh
Monday	Montag	**mohn**-targ
Tuesday	Dienstag	**deens**-targ
Wednesday	Mittwoch	**mitt**-vokh
Thursday	Donnerstag	**donn**-ers-targ
Friday	Freitag	**fry**-targ
Saturday	Samstag/ Sonnabend	**zums**-targ zonn-ah-bent
Sunday	Sonntag	**zon**-targ
January	Januar	**yan**-ooar
February	Februar	**fay**-brooar
March	März	**mairts**
April	April	april
May	Mai	my
June	Juni	**yoo**-ni
July	Juli	**yoo**-lee
August	August	ow-**goost**
September	September	zep-**tem**-ber
October	Oktober	ok-toh-ber
November	November	no-**vem**-ber
December	Dezember	day-**tsem**-ber
spring	Frühling	**froo**-ling
summer	Sommer	**zomm**-er
autumn (fall)	Herbst	**hairpst**
winter	Winter	**vint**-er